IMPROPER ADVANCES

The Chicago Series on Sexuality, History, and Society
Edited by John C. Fout

IMPROPER ADVANCES

Rape and Heterosexual Conflict
in Ontario, 1880–1929

KAREN DUBINSKY

The University of Chicago Press

Chicago and London

Karen Dubinsky is assistant professor of history at Brock University in St. Catharines, Ontario.

The University of Chicago Press, Chicago 60637
The University of Chicago Press, Ltd., London
© 1993 by The University of Chicago
All rights reserved. Published 1993
Printed in the United States of America

02 01 00 90 98 97 96 95 94 93   5 4 3 2 1

ISBN (cloth): 0-226-16753-4
ISBN (paper): 0-226-16754-2

Library of Congress Cataloging-in-Publication Data

Dubinsky, Karen.
    Improper advances : rape and heterosexual conflict in Ontario,
  1880–1929 / Karen Dubinsky.
        p.   cm. — (Chicago series on sexuality, history, and
  society)
    Includes bibliographical references (p. 209) and index.
    ISBN 0-226-16753-4 (cloth). — ISBN 0-226-16754-2 (pbk.).
    1. Rape—Ontario—History.   2. Women—Ontario—Crimes
  against—History.   3. Ontario—Social conditions.   I. Title.
  II. Series.
  HV6569.C32O583   1993
  364.1′532′09713—dc20   92-44673
                                                            CIP

⊗The paper used in this publication meets the
minimum requirements of the American National Standard
for Information Sciences—Permanence of Paper for
Printed Library Materials, ANSI Z39.48-1984.

This book is printed on acid-free paper.

About the frontispiece (p.12): Free trade with the United States was a major issue in this election. In the upper image, the men pursuing Miss Canada under the approving and lustful gaze of "Uncle Sam" are identifiable Liberal politicians, including Wilfrid Laurier and Richard Cartwright. Miss Canada is being forced out of the fenced area—a symbolic way of expressing the Liberal platform which advocated free trade. Below, Conservative leader Sir John A. Macdonald saves the day. A symbolic representation of a newly independent country, "Miss Canada" was a popular figure in editorial cartoons of the nineteenth and early twentieth centuries. This cartoon also illustrates the way ideas about gender, sexuality, and nation could combine to provoke powerful reactions to political and economic questions.

CONTENTS

Contents

ACKNOWLEDGMENTS

T HE MANUSCRIPT OF THIS VOLUME WAS, for many years, my long-time companion. As demanding as an infant and as all consuming as a lover, it was only rarely as much fun as either. That it is now the volume you hold in your hand is due in part to the support of my family, friends, and colleagues.

I completed most of my work on this volume in the company of other feminist historians in and around Toronto. The collective knowledge and support of a number of colleagues and friends, in three challenging study groups and informally, have been most helpful. I thank those who read parts of my manuscript and shared their books, brains, and reflections on women's history with me: Mary-Louise Adams, Debi Brock, Lykke de la Cour, Nancy Forestell, Ruth Frager, Julie Guard, Margaret Hobbs, Franca Iacovetta, Margaret Little, Lynne Marks, Kate McPherson, Cecilia Morgan, Suzanne Morton, Janice Newton, Susan Prentice, Becki Ross, Tori Smith, Carolyn Strange, Shirley Tillotson, Mariana Valverde and Cynthia Wright. Adam Givertz, Annalee Golz and Angus McLaren have also supported my work. Thanks also to Steven Maynard, with whom I shared a mutual discovery of the history of sexuality and who helped me conceptualize this topic in the early stages. My thesis examining committee, Jane Errington, Mary Morton, Ian McKay, Robert Malcolmson and especially Kathy Peiss, made many helpful comments on my work. Jane Abray's generous and good-humored assistance in reviewing the final draft eased my prepublication anxieties and made this a better book, and Annalee Golz,

Gregor McNish, Tom Patterson and Carol Whitehead also helped me, and this book, go public.

For insisting that I spend some time in the present, for lifting my spirits, and especially for learning when and when not to ask me about my progress, I thank Peter Birt, Miriam Edelson, Lynne Grimes, Roberta Hamilton and Geoff Smith, Ted Ho, Margaret Hobbs, Joy McBride, Tracy Read, Ruth and Rebekah Warner, Carol Whitehead and Gerard Coffey, and my friends at the Canadian Women's Movement Archives. As I was writing, I enjoyed a unique neighborliness with three friends engaged in similar pursuits. Jan Borowy, Margaret Little, and Eleanor MacDonald helped me to see the way through difficult times, time after time. My family, all of whom kept jokes to a minimum about the eldest being the last to finish school, has always been a tremendous source of love and support. For providing variety, eternal gratitude to the Toronto Downtown and West End Ys, CODCO, and the Kids in the Hall.

Deborah Gorham introduced me to the pleasures of women's history as an undergraduate and remains a source of inspiration. As I learn how to convey history myself, I appreciate her skills and enthusiasm for teaching even more. I am happy to say in print that Varda Burstyn is the smartest person I know. In writing she has always made me think, in person she made me laugh, kept me on this side of sanity while writing, and helped me regain my voice. Roberta Hamilton has juggled with grace and humor the many roles I have (arbitrarily) assigned to her. As teacher, editor, sister and friend, she has taught me more than she realizes about how to write and how to live.

Bryan Palmer did not, I think, expect to be supervising a dissertation on the history of sexuality when he took me on as a student. But we came, as he once put it, "not to agree but to respect each other." We have also become friends, and I can't think of anyone else with whom I have enjoyed disagreeing so much. I benefited enormously from his range of historical knowledge, his incisive and always prompt comments on the many drafts of this work, and especially his confidence in pushing me to go further and ask bigger questions than I often thought I could.

Susan Belyea came into my life as this work was in transition from thesis to book. She is fortunate she missed the first part; I am lucky (and grateful) that she is around for the rest. These are better days.

I also thank the archivists at the Provincial Archives of Ontario (particularly Catherine Shepard) and the National Archives of Canada and, for funding, the Social Sciences and Humanities Research Council and the Queen Elizabeth II Fellowship. A popular plot of early twentieth century 'white slave' stories was the tale of the Canadian girl lured from southern Ontario to her ruin in Chicago. I am happy to report that, aside from insist-

Acknowledgments

ing on the Americanization of my Canadian spelling, my Chicago col-
leagues were most co-operative. At the University of Chicago Press, John
Fout's enthusiasm for this book was very gratifying, and the labors of
Kathryn Gohl and Douglas Mitchell were much appreciated.

This book is dedicated, with love, to the eldest and youngest Dubinskys.
My baba, Ksenia Dubinsky, tells me that my education makes her proud.
Her life and her convictions have made it possible. And for my nephew
Sam, in hopes that his world is better than the one this book docu-
ments.

INTRODUCTION

Historians live in the present. As I buried myself in tales of nineteenth-century sexuality, power and domination, the world continued to spin and offer up similar stories in which I often heard an eerie historical echo. So while this volume is a work of history, it is most definitely informed by contemporary sexual politics. During my work on this book, a Canadian judge accused a three-year-old girl of acting in a "sexually aggressive" manner toward the man who molested her; another, in a rape trial, invoked a nineteenth-century precedent concerning a woman's "immorality". In the Ontario resort region of Muskoka, ironically the site of a panic over morality and regional reputation in 1916, a community rose up angry against a planned retreat for persons with AIDS, worrying that the hospice would sully the good name of the area.[1] In the United States, several high-profile stories of rape and sexual harassment brought complicated questions of sexual conflict, power and race into the living rooms of the nation. In Canada, changes in federal sexual-assault legislation also provoked intense public debate about sexual conflicts and boundaries, including the often-repeated claim that male sexual aggression is a biological and historical imperative. The most chilling contemporary story remains the tragedy of December 1989: in Montreal a man proclaimed his hatred of feminists by killing fourteen young women, victims of their audacity to enter privileged male professional territory. Do we need any more evidence of the power of sexual politics?

Of the innumerable stories of sexual violence which surface daily, one caught my attention early in my research and has stayed with me through this project. The rape and murder of Heather Fraser in 1985 defied several of the stereotypes of sexual crime. She lived in a small town, Smith Falls, a pleasant-looking community I drove through regularly. She was killed not by a mysterious stranger, a wandering tramp or an evil outsider, but by another teenager in the community, James Giff, who had spent the evening embroiled in a battle with another young woman, his girlfriend. Why he chose Heather Fraser as his victim was unclear, but when Giff confessed to the crime, he used the candid language of gender and power to explain his act. "I'm a man," he stated, "I had to kill her."[2] What, I wondered as I began this research, had James Giff learned in his eighteen years of being a 'man' which would bring this discourse so easily into his mind and out of his mouth? If there is a sole guiding purpose to my enterprise, it is to discover the historical roots of the association of gender, sexuality, and conquest. There is no single answer to my own question, but I have discovered much about the family forms, gender, race and class relations, and styles of sexual politics which shape sexual conflicts.

Some feminists might feel a certain horrified vindication at the actions of the Montreal assassin, Marc Lepine, or the explanation of James Giff. Perhaps Giff has revealed what 'we' knew all along: that male sexuality has become so completely infused with violence and domination that we need explain sexual crime only by reference to the male sex. Men rape. Sometimes they also kill. As Andrea Dworkin's often-quoted remark, "sexuality is the stuff of death, not love," reveals, many feminists have abandoned the task, so vital to the early promise of women's liberation, of sexual exploration.[3] In place of an enthusiastic defiance of the patriarchal double standard, some feminists have opted instead for a pessimistic retreat from sexuality all together. "If it doesn't subordinate women, it's not sex," charges the United States radical feminist group, Women Against Sex. Others claim that heterosexuality, not sex itself, is the problem. British feminist Sheila Jeffreys' remarkable assertion that "it is difficult to imagine how heterosexual desire—considering the role playing in just about every relationship—could possibly be egalitarian," reminds us of the resiliance of 1970s-style political lesbianism, in which questions of desire and fantasy are subsumed under the strait jacket of 'correct' sexual sensibilities.[4] Feminists have indeed succeeded in exposing the underside of heterosexuality and in documenting how male power is exercised daily on the bodies and psyches of women. But, as Ann Snitow has suggested in her accounting of the shifts in feminist sexual politics, "it was almost as if, by naming the sexual crimes, by ending female denial, we frightened ourselves more than anyone else."[5]

Sexual violence is indeed frightening. This book ranges through treacherous territory. I have examined the stories of four hundred Ontario women who, between the years 1880 and 1929, brought their complaints of unwanted, physically coerced sex to the police. Many found that abuse at the hands of one man was later replicated by many. Over half of these women left the courtroom empty-handed, their stories disbelieved, their intimate lives subject to the hostile gaze of the all-male cast of police, jury, judge, and court reporters. If these survivors of sexual assault had found more support, one wonders how many more women would have made their stories public.

I have studied the history of sexual crime in order to understand more fully the forces that have shaped sexual danger. I am particularly interested in the links, which seem so tenacious, between masculinity, sexuality and domination. Yet this formula does not, I believe, tell the full story of gender, power and sexuality. I am reluctant to retreat from sexuality as a place of strength, liberation and pleasure for women and to view it exclusively, as Carol Vance has warned against, "through the lens of the oppressors."[6] A patriarchal culture such as our own sets the context for sexuality. The woman in the 1890s who strained against the ties of domineering parents might have had her evening out, but she also might have been assaulted by her boyfriend as they strolled down darkened country roads. A young domestic servant might have used the opportunity afforded by outside work to flirt with the hired man, only to be abandoned by him when she discovered her pregnancy. Another girl, recently arrived in town from her home on the farm, might have daringly accepted a stranger's offer of a car ride, which could have resulted in an exciting evening or a brutal rape. These are not happy stories, and my principal source, criminal case files, obviously skews my research toward worst-case scenarios. Yet the fact that heterosexual social relations were (and are) played out in the shadow of possible male violence or exploitation does not make the two synonymous, nor does it make dupes or stooges of women who try to claim their share of pleasure in a dangerous world. The question we should ask is not why women persist in seeking heterosexual adventure and companionship, but rather why male rage is turned so often on women.[7]

Sexuality is not reducible to gender, but it is gendered, and women experience it in more troubled ways than do most men. In the face of massive evidence—historical and contemporary—of the magnitude of sexual abuse in the lives of women and children, we can begin to understand why so many feminists believe that sex holds only danger for women and that the secret of patriarchy is sexual coercion. Without wishing to minimize the effects, and effectiveness, of sexual violence, I believe that such conclusions deny the various ways women have resisted patriarchal norms of sexual behavior and attempted to carve out sexual territory. This has been the position of socialist and libertarian feminists: that 'sexual courage,' a concept developed by historian Joan Nestle to illustrate the complexities of lesbian sexuality in the 1950s, has a wider historical application.[8] The history of

sexual antagonism that this book documents is also a history of courage, resistance, and even occasional victory.

Sexuality does not reside in the hormones of biological men and women;
it is constructed socially and historically. People, we might paraphrase,
make love, but not under conditions of their own choosing. For women, sexuality is built around the twin poles of pleasure and danger, autonomy and
victimization. From this perspective—which I have adopted as my own—
the historical records of sexual crime reveal more than they were ever intended to. The records of prosecutions for sexual offenses allow historians
to study a rarely seen aspect of social life in the past: heterosexual
intimacy—sometimes at its ugliest, other times at its most tender. At their
richest, court records provide a window into instances of personal life;
through these documents we can learn about romantic and sexual expectations (and how these differed between women and men), we can hear people
talking about love, emotional and sexual intimacy, power, betrayal and broken promises. Thus this book is about the history of sexual pleasure and
courtship as well as the history of sexual violence. It is also about the creation and regulation of gendered sexual/moral standards, the attempts by
the state during 1880 to 1930 to assert legal hegemony over 'private' matters,
and the incorporation of a discourse of sexuality into the project of nation
building, civic pride and economic renewal.

The years 1880 through the 1920s are perhaps the fifty most-studied
years in Canadian history, particularly among women's, labor and other social historians. During these years, both industrial capitalism and a Canadian working class were 'made.' This period also encompasses the industrial
revolution of the mid-nineteenth century and the triumph, by the end of the
1920s, of monopoly capitalism—two distinct chapters in Canadian economic life. Accompanying these massive economic shifts, working class
self-organization and often upheaval, and changing racial/ethnic and
rural/urban ratios of the population, produced dramatic social tensions. Social historians have explored this period in Canada's past in order to understand the impact of vast and, relative to other Western nations, fast
economic change on the social, political and cultural life of women and
men. What nineteenth-century statisticians coldly referred to as the growing number of "hands" employed by new factories points toward fundamental and irrevocable changes in the way people lived in relation to each
other: as families, neighbors, regions, classes, and as men and women.

The past, particularly times as momentous as these, also alerts us to the
complicated questions of change and choice in human affairs. Over a decade
of 'new' labor history has taught us that the 'transition' to industrial capitalism was not a self-propelled and seamless economic advance, but rather a
highly contested process which affected people differently according to

where they lived and especially to what they owned. Explorations in women's history have also helped overturn consensus-oriented accounts of Canadian social development and allowed us to see the centrality of gender as a force of historical change.

Feminist historians have documented how the social relations of industrial capitalism traded heavily on gender identities, both changing women's traditional labor at home and creating specific markets for them in the work force. Working women, like their male counterparts, also resisted industrial capitalist encroachments, sometimes subtly, often dramatically. Perhaps the dominant focus of Canadian women's history has been the social reform activities of Anglo-Saxon, middle-class women, culminating in the campaign for suffrage in the early twentieth century. Isolated by industrial capitalism in the 'private' domestic realm, appalled by a changing world over which they had little control, and fueled, as Anne Phillips has nicely put it, by the dual problem of "too little work" (for one strata of women) and "too much work" (for another), nineteenth-century middle-class women's social reform efforts set the tone for the racial, sexual, and class politics of the women's movement for decades to come.[9] The working class was not the only class which 'made itself,' economically, socially and culturally, in this period. The early twentieth century also witnessed a widespread campaign, organized primarily but not solely by middle-class women and men, to 'raise the moral tone' of Canadian life through regulation of prostitution, liquor, and the social and recreational lives of immigrants and the working class. Most of the people whose sexual misfortunes I examine in this volume were the intended constituency of the Canadian social purity movement.[10]

What does any of this have to do with sex? If recent social history teaches anything, it is that we must change and expand our conceptualizations of power, especially how and by whom it is held and exercised. Labor history has taught us valuable lessons about how the simple power of ownership of productive forces changed the daily lives of those who owned only their labor. "All that is solid melts into air," as one student of these times remarked; capitalist social relations changed not just where and how persons spent their hours of labor, but where they lived, how they amused themselves, even their sense of time and discipline.[11]

Women's history doubles the vision, revealing both women's particular oppression under capitalist productive relations and the features of domination and subordination in marriage, families and households.[12] A careful analysis of the sexual relations between women and men, rooted in particular historical contexts, lets us see yet another place where power was sought, wielded, and often resisted. As Gayle Rubin reminds us, because relationships, even nonsexual relationships, between women and men take place against a backdrop of conflicted sexuality, "much of the oppression of women is borne by, mediated through, and constituted within sexuality."[13]

Canadian social theorists have made valuable contributions to contemporary 'sex debates.'[14] But despite a growing international interest in the history of sexuality, Canadian historians are still silent on the topic. Michael Bliss's brief study of sexual attitudes, written twenty years ago, remains one of the few Canadian contributions to this field.[15] Established historians such as Kenneth McNaught, Desmond Morton and Michael Cross have explored the role of violence in Canadian history, but none thought to consider sexual violence as part of the range of coercive forces.[16] More recent literature has not always been any more sensitive to sexuality as a realm of power between men and women. Peter Ward's history of nineteenth-century courtship, for example—a remarkably under-studied topic in Canada—presents a classless, genderless and raceless portrait of heterosexuality, devoid of power and conflict (or, for that matter, sex).[17]

With this volume I hope to help remedy this silence about our national past. My interest in the history of sexuality—initially the history of seduction in particular—drew me to the records of sexual crime. I soon realized these records could be read to uncover both danger and pleasure, but this source allows little room for sentimentality about heterosexuality (even if one were so disposed). Studying sexual crime rather than, for example, a community's sexual politics, mores and experience dictates a broader geographic focus, and has allowed me to make significant discoveries about how region has historically influenced social definitions of sexuality, morality and crime.

This book looks at one relatively small slice of sexual relations: those which, between 1880 and 1929, in twenty-five rural southern and northern Ontario counties, caught (or were brought to) the attention of the legal system. I have defined 'sexual crime' broadly to include all criminal offenses which involved relations of power between women and men. Thus, I have studied rape, attempted rape, carnal knowledge, and indecent assault, as well as crimes of consensual sexual relations—charges such as seduction and abduction—and relevant abortion, incest, infanticide, libel, and sex-related murder charges. (See the appendix, tables 1 and 2, for details of the communities and crimes surveyed.) Criminal case files and newspaper commentary are surprisingly rich, revealing heart-rending details of the many ways sex became a matter of power and conflict between men and women, parents and children, communities and regions. At the same time, these sources can be resolutely silent and hopelessly biased. The police officer or justice of the peace to whom the story was originally told and the judge in whose courtroom it was evaluated were not dispassionate observers. Often the stern questioning of a defense lawyer serves to cloud the story by introducing doubts about a woman's previous sexual history (to use a popular example). But these inquisitions, humiliating for women through the ages, can be interrogated by the historian to reveal the strength of prevailing moral codes. It is impossible to fully deconstruct these stories, to arrive at an eventual truth of individual sexual conflicts. Rather, I attempted to use the layers of authority, local gossip, anger and self-interest in which these stories are shrouded in order to unpack the multiplicity of meanings assigned to sexual behavior and sexual power in the past.

The historical class bias of the legal system has become, ironically, fruitful for contemporary historians, particularly those interested in the intimate lives of the socially marginal. Working-class people, immigrants and farmers did not often put pen to paper to record their most personal lives, but this scarcely means they did not experience the full range of emotions—pain, pleasure, anger and jealousy—which sexual conflicts summon up. If we are curious about the lives of those who historically have been less powerful, we can find them in the records of state and quasi-state agencies: prisons, courtrooms, asylums and hospitals. Here we rarely find people speaking in their own voice, but we can read against the grain to discover the sexual and social world of domestic servants, hired men, factory workers, miners and loggers.

This book is structured from small to large. It begins with individual experience, moves on to community social life and regulation, and ends with questions of regional development and nation building. This complex mix requires some explanation.

I decided against organizing my study as court records are structured, by legal categories. Because I was more interested in the social/sexual experiences of people than in the development or interpretation of the law, it made more sense to me to try to study those experiences 'from the bottom up.' In the hands of the law, one's story might be processed as any number of crimes: rape, indecent assault, or abortion. But the basic story—for example, being assaulted and made pregnant by the hired hand—was what I was after. Since I was interested in the social circumstances which lead to criminal prosecution, it made sense to group together cases that shared certain defining features—the threat of violence, for example, or the relationship between victim and accused. Therefore, I took the more controversial approach of separating tales of sexual violence from crimes which took place between two more-or-less consenting parties, fully aware of the power disparities between women and men in this period. Using this approach, I was able to determine and comment on the social situations and relationships which seemed to result in sexual conflict and analyze which social situations were believed more readily by the court system. This approach definitely plays with legal categories, but it yields substantial results in examining the social and self-definition of sexual conflict.

I start by uncovering in chapter 1 the subjective experience of sexual violence. Rape is our beginning point not because it is the logical conclusion of how men relate to women in a patriarchal world, but rather because historically it illuminates gendered relations of power in their rawest, most brutal forms. In attempting to understand the social and historical meaning of rape, I situate myself vis-à-vis others who have studied the question, in the past and present, and pay particular attention to how women in the past experienced the crime. I contend that attempts by women to pursue punishment of their assailant, sometimes through extralegal measures, but most often, in this study, through bringing criminal charges, show us that historically sexual assault was recognized and resisted as a serious wrong by women. Fighting sexual grievances in the courtroom was not, as it turned out, a successful strategy for the majority of women seeking redress. How rape was handled by the legal system, however, comments on relations between the sexes and speaks volumes on the reigning consensus about male and female sexuality.

Chapter 2 also examines sexual violence, placing assault cases in the context of the work, social and family relationships in which they occurred. I found that when I examined the actual situations of reported sexual violence, those institutions most revered as centers of safety and moral authority—the family, the rural household, church picnics and 'respectable' employments such as domestic service—were in fact the sites of the most pervasive instances of sexual abuse. I contrast this discovery with the 'discourses of danger' about other bogeymen of the period: the wandering tramp, the dangerous foreigner, the scheming taxi driver, and the nefarious "Jack-the-Hugger." All of these cultural stereotypes contain tiny grains of reality, but they functioned, I argue, to displace culpability for sexual exploitation away from those who did far more serious harm: boyfriends, neighbors and fathers.

Patriarchal power was not unleashed by sexual brutality alone. Suppression of women's sexual autonomy was another component of the politics of sexuality. In chapter 3 I examine prosecutions for voluntary sexual activity, crimes called seduction and abduction. These were the 'good cops' of patriarchal sexual domination—laws designed to protect women from scheming sexual predators who came bearing gifts rather than guns. These offenses, however, traded heavily on the distinction between 'good girls' and 'bad girls' or to use the language of the times, maidenly girls and designing women (perhaps one of the most profound binary oppositions in history). They served as much to cement a parent's hold over a delinquent daughter as to punish an errant young man. I argue that, in both coercive and consensual sexual relations, the sexual politics of the period—especially the absence of a feminist movement that might have offered a competing politic to the 'good girl/bad girl' distinction—were crucial in determining social and self-definitions of right and wrong.

Chapter 4 continues to explore how the legal system handled sexual crime. Through examining popular sexual scandals we can see how the law and the community acted, sometimes in concert, sometimes at cross-purposes, to regulate sexual behavior. In this period and in these regions, the courts were not only legal forums, but theater, popular circuses which entertained an appreciative crowd. My purpose here is to reveal the ongoing struggle for legal hegemony, fought in these times between an emerging but as yet incomplete legal system and communities that had developed time-honored traditions of dealing with sexual misbehavior. This battle was waged for many years over all manner of criminal offenses. When we look at the entrenchment of legal discourses for sexual offenses, however, we see the class- and gender-based privileges of privacy.

Chapters 5 and 6 take us farther afield. Chapter 5 documents the construction of sexual norms and standards, which I demonstrate to be products of race, gender and class. It was these social prejudices which judges and juries applied when weighing instances of sexual conflict, but women and men also learned to apply the sexual rules when courting. In addition I examine three of the main agents of these rules during the period—the family, the community and the state.

In chapter 6 I look at the geographic dimensions of sexual violence and sexual morality. Like classes, races and genders, regions can bear distinct sexual reputations. Social divisions can acquire a spatial footing, and places often become associated with particular values or feelings. The turn-of-the-century "rural problem," largely one of declining population and economic activity, and the attempt to promote northern Ontario as a new industrial frontier were about political and economic changes. But the two were often expressed in the language and politics of sexuality, which sometimes served to displace what were often other concerns. In the north, for example, a moral panic about declining church attendance was also a thinly veiled response to the large number of foreign-born politically radical men in the area. There was, however, a reciprocal relationship between regional moral reputation and economic growth. Spatial expressions of race, gender and class divisions helped define sexual crime and could be incorporated into attempts to boost social and economic development and, indeed, build nations.

Thus we end at the largest and most abstract. But before I begin to document these various claims, I must address the troubling question of historical change.

I began this study armed with socialist feminism's strongest dictums, that patriarchy is materially based and thus liable to change. My most vexing discovery has been how familiar some of these stories are. Virtually all of the characteristics and myths that feminists today have identified about sexual violence were also at work in the nineteenth century: the myth of the rapist as stranger or 'dangerous foreigner,' the punishment of women for 'provocative' behavior, the suspicion of a woman's sexual past—all led to public humiliation of women on the witness stand and generally to low rates of conviction in the courts. There were, as we shall see, significant differences in a woman's credibility according to the situation in which she found herself. There were also important quantitative changes in conviction rates for cases of sexual violence, corresponding, I suggest, to the sexual politics of the period. Qualitative changes, however, in the experience of sexual danger and in the treatment a woman received in the legal arena are much more elusive. How can we explain the apparent timelessness of sexual violence, not only within the fifty years of this study but also compared to our own time?

One part of the answer lies in the focus of this study. While I have examined the way sexual danger and sexual pleasure were experienced by women and men in the past, I have paid less attention to the construction of the law and social policy, or to the terrain of moral or social reform. This study does recount the impact of social changes on 'personal' life, as, for example, increasing numbers of working women found in the workplace new opportunities for autonomy, pleasure and danger. The establishment of commercial amusements for young courting couples also gave rise to a new territory of danger, what we would today call date rape. The most significant change this book documents, the settlement of northern Ontario and the economic and social decline of the rural south, led to vast changes in the social and sexual mores in each area, though sometimes these changes were in perception, not substance.

Yet it would be erroneous to conclude that new opportunities for female autonomy led to new forms of sexual peril. We see that families, communities and the state all played a role in regulating personal morality in this period; there was no Whiggish drive away from the bondage of community toward individual liberty. Furthermore, we face the immutable fact that sexual exploitation was experienced not only by the sassy city girl on her own, but also by the demure farm girl, prudently staying at home obeying her elders.

In the end, I'm not sure anyone has adequately explained why men so often hurt women. What has changed, fortunately so, between this period and our own is the direction and growth of the women's movement. The contemporary women's movement has made sexual violence a major priority. Rather than blaming promiscuous women, working-class depravity or animalistic foreigners, all popular explanations in the nineteenth century, feminists today understand sexual assault in the context of the relations of power between the sexes. This insight does not yet constitute a new social consensus about sexual violence. Even though there is a high public awareness about sexual conflict in our times, myths about women, men and rape still flourish. Nor is there agreement among feminists about the origins and effects of male violence. But the women's movement has succeeded in creating an alternative discourse of sexuality which respects women's bodily integrity and insists that women tell the truth when it has been violated. As Linda Gordon discovered in her study of the history of male violence in the family, the sexual politics of the period are, in the end, the most significant determinant of how violence is understood, individually and socially.[18]

The records of sexual crime are a good read, particularly for the prying eyes of a feminist historian in the 1990s who is safely distanced by the passage of time and the confidence gained by a different climate of feminist sexual politics. This distance does not prevent me, nor, I hope, my readers, from being powerfully and often personally engaged with these stories.

Conservative party campaign poster, election of 1891. Reprinted courtesy of the National Archives of Canada.

CHAPTER ONE

Sex, Shame, and Resistance: The Social and Historical Meaning of Rape

WHY MEN RAPE WOMEN IS A QUESTION many people have asked and for which there are numerous political, socio-logical and psychological answers. It is not a question, however, for which there are many historical answers, since sexual violence has been the subject of surprisingly little historical inquiry. Yet without a firm understanding of the history of sexual violence, answers to this basic question rest on shaky assumptions about gender, sexuality and violence. My aim in chapters 1 and 2, at least in part, is to chart the history of sexual violence in Ontario so that we can begin to understand the meaning rape held for residents of the province during the late nineteenth and early twentieth century.

The histories of sexual violence which do exist tend to conceptualize the experience of rape in the past in much the same way as some feminists an-alyze sexual violence today. Guido Ruggiero, for example, in his fascinating study of sexual crime in Rennaisance Italy, is one of several historians who advances what might be termed a 'rape-as-life' thesis. He suggests that his-torically, the fusion of violence and sexuality was so complete that, partic-ularly among the "lower social levels," rape and 'normal' sexuality were almost indistinct.[1] Ellen DuBois and Linda Gordon, in their pioneering analysis of the sexual politics of nineteenth-century feminists, have sug-gested that their relative silence on the topic of rape was due to its proximity to heterosexuality in general: "It is as if the norms of legal sexual intercourse were in themselves so objectionable that rape did not seem that much worse!"[2] Such conclusions about the meaning of rape historically echo some feminist arguments of the 1980s and 1990s, which simply conflate sexual violence and heterosexuality.[3]

It is not my intention to deny the enormous power of male violence—sexual and physical. Patriarchy indeed has its coercive apparatus, and women ignore it at their peril. But just as contemporary analyses which place sexual violence at the apex of male domination tend to simplify the complexity (and persistence) of patriarchal hegemony, so too historical studies that equate rape with 'normal' heterosexuality overlook the specificity of sexual violence. This way of thinking minimizes the trauma and the resistance of women who have experienced sexual assault. Furthermore, to suggest that rape is the logical conclusion of the way men relate to women in this culture patronizes women who are attempting to negotiate autonomous, pleasurable space within bisexuality or heterosexuality, resulting in a feminist version of a Leninist "false consciousness" argument.

Rape is qualitatively different that other acts of physical harm men inflict upon women. Touching, as it does, one of the most intimate aspects of relations between women and men—sex—it unleashes a storm of anxieties about physical safety, bodies, desire and moral reputation. Rape is also an act which contains a different meaning at different moments in history, shifting according to prevailing standards of sexual conduct, gender relations, and class and race contexts. To truly appreciate the history of sexual violence requires that we make some attempt to understand the historical meaning of assault from the perspective of those involved. If we understand how sexual violence was recognized and resisted by women in the past, our sense of both its history and its place in the oppression of women will be enriched.

A recent Gallup poll in Canada indicates that 56 percent of Canadian women are fearful of venturing out-of-doors in the evening, compared to 18 percent of men.[4] Whether women have historically feared rape to the same extent that they do today is a question at least one historian has answered in the negative. Roy Porter contrasts current feminist writing about the controlling power of rape fear in women's lives with the near total silence on the topic in the writings of nineteenth-century women, feminists and nonfeminists. On this basis, he claims that sexual violence as an instrument of patriarchal domination is of fairly recent origin, that rape has become invested with political significance only as traditional gender arrangements have become destabilized. As the coercive arm of patriarchy, sexual violence becomes more pronounced only when traditional forms of legitimation and control cease to function effectively.[5]

While Porter's is a creative attempt to truly historicize sexual assault, he has, I believe, misread the place of sexual fear in the lives of women historically. Sexual fear took a different form for these women, but it was never absent.

In the past, other acts of physical violence seem to have rarely accompanied sexual assault. Fewer than ten women in this study reported additional physical abuse as well as sexual assault, and fewer than ten men used a weapon to threaten their victims. While many more men verbally threatened women, either to frighten them into submission or to silence them after the fact, extreme physical coercion (in addition to the physically painful experience of sexual assault) does not seem to have been a significant component of rape.

Women were afraid of sexual assault, but in the time and place of this study that fear seemed to revolve around public disgrace and community disapproval. Fears about moral standing eclipsed concerns about physical safety. Fear of disgrace helped determine when and to whom women might speak about their experiences, and whether or not they saw the legal system as an appropriate place to seek redress. Sexual shame might prove as effective a weapon as a gun or a knife in silencing or otherwise preventing women from confronting their experience. Thus sexual danger for women operated historically on several levels. As well as the very real pain of sexual assault, tightly drawn boundaries of permissible female sexuality determined that getting 'caught,' by parents, neighbors or police, could prove almost as threatening or humiliating as sex itself, desired or coerced.

Females who had stayed out late, had accepted rides from men, had been drinking, or had had previous romantic involvements (whether sexual or not) were often reluctant to report their assault. Verna J. spent many evenings strolling downtown Oshawa with boys, despite repeated "thrashings" by her father for doing this. The night in 1919 she was assaulted, she had avoided the main streets of Oshawa because she was afraid her father might see her. Her story only became known when a policeman saw her pinned down behind town hall. Like many other young women, Verna was blamed for being assaulted, and her father beat her severely that evening.[6] Girls who got pregnant as a result of illicit or unwanted sexual relations were the most shamed; they almost never told anyone until their pregnancy was discovered. When even an innocent action resulted in sexual assault, women were forced to reexamine their behavior in a different light. After Sarah H. was attacked by a man she let into her home because he said he wanted a light for his cigarette, she agreed with her sister who told her, "I ought to be ashamed of myself for my actions were disgraceful."[7]

Shame could also immobilize 'good girls.' Barbara H. should have been the perfect victim. According to a police investigation of her background (a common occurrence in rape cases), she came from a good family, had a "responsible position" as a stenographer, and lived with her mother in "one of the finest residential areas of Detroit." Yet after Allan M., a doctor she had been dating for a couple of summers at the resort town of Port Stanley, assaulted her one night on the beach, she was so mortified by the resulting publicity she refused to testify at his trial.[8]

Here we have one of the historical contradictions of sexual assault: 'bad girls' could not be believed, and 'good girls' avoided the embarrassment of publicity. Most girls, of course, were neither wholly good nor thoroughly bad. But regardless of each one's place on the moral hierarchy, all could be frightened into submission or silence by the threat of a tarnished reputation. More than one man used this to his advantage, such as Alfred S., who threatened his neighbor Lily S. that "he would tell everyone in the Soo that I was a bad woman" if she did not consent to sex with him.[9] The more socially or economically vulnerable women were, the more powerful this threat might seem. When German immigrant Augustine H. threatened to report her lawyer, Marshall J., he had the combined forces of class, ethnicity and gender on his side. "He said [if I told my husband] he would give me the worst name any woman ever had in Goderich and that I could not even talk English right and that all the men around here would be friends of his."[10]

Disgrace was a consequence of having one's name linked with public sexual scandal. The experience of sexual assault tainted women, and this held whether a woman was 'good' or 'bad,' and whether her assailant was found guilty or not. One judge, presiding over a gang rape case, commended the accused men for pleading guilty, thereby saving the woman involved from "disgrace," but a more common stance was adopted by the judge who proclaimed a man not guilty despite acknowledging the disgrace his actions brought on the woman.[11] Some women told the court that they brought charges in order to protect their character, to stop rumors or innuendo about their behavior, or to redress a perceived wrong. Others, however, admitted that they had initially avoided pressing charges and did so only to placate parents or husband. In light of the amount of publicity afforded sexual crimes as well as the treatment of women by the judicial system, this caution was certainly warranted.

RAPE AND RESISTANCE

Though women might have been ambivalent about using the legal system for redress, they did not necessarily accept male violence meekly. When women spoke about sexual assault, their language made it clear that they had experienced a wrong. Still we must be cautious, for it is not always possible to discern in the case files when women and men are speaking in their own voices and when the voice of the legal system (the police or justices of the peace who swore out the initial complaint) has taken over. All of these stories are filtered, of course, through the often hostile and intimidating legal gaze. But in some cases it seems that legal authorities literally rendered complainants voiceless, since the language used to describe sexual assault often mimicked the formalistic and awkward terms of the legal system, as in "he had criminal connection with me." That most women did not speak this way is obvious, particularly when we contrast this language with the idiomatic forms of expression other women used in their complaints.

To be 'insulted,' 'interfered with' and 'used roughly' were among the phrases repeated by women to describe sexual assault. Such language clearly conveys a sense of grievance. But the language of assault also arose from dominant notions of female sexuality. Historically, chastity was treated as a woman's most important possession, but always one in which men's rules figured forcefully; women were not completely free to 'trade' or 'sell' it as they wished. This applied not only to chastity, but to sex itself. Sex was something women had and men wanted. Sexual assault was a contest in which men took, forcibly, from women. Men demanded that women 'give them a fuck,' men 'took liberties,' 'took advantage,' 'took his will,' 'got what he wanted,' 'satisfied himself,' made 'improper advances.' The structured assymetry of heterosexual desire was conveyed clearly: men had it and took it; women were taken. Only male pleasure was addressed: men bragged about the size of their penis and how 'hard' women would make them. It was a discourse which rendered women objects and men subjects, which helps explain the condemnation of women who attempted to act as sexual agents. To transgress the boundaries of propriety was to upset a carefully constructed balance of sexual power.[12]

But perhaps the most convincing argument that sexual assault was experienced by women as an injustice was that it was resisted. The concept of resistance has become popular with historians of late. A generation of social historians has invoked a new and subtly crafted theory of resistance which seeks to understand the experience and response of the dispossessed in their own terms. Historically, subordinate groups often made sense of their experience in ways we do not immediately recognize as political. Yet this does not at all imply that previous generations were complicit in their own oppression, nor does it necessarily signify a lack of awareness or recognition of domination on the part of historical actors. They, as E. P. Thompson reminds us, "lived through these times of acute social disturbance, and we did not."[13]

This appreciation can be fruitfully applied to the history of women's responses to sexual violence. In the nineteenth and early twentieth century the response by organized feminism to male violence against women was ambiguous, and little is known about this specific question in Canadian history. American historians argue that first-wave feminists in the United States often shared middle-class prejudices about the 'brutishness' of working-class and immigrant men.[14] It was prostitution, rather than sexual assault, which seems to have caught the attention of an earlier generation of feminist social reformers. DuBois and Gordon see a parallel between the nineteenth-century focus on prostitution and the modern emphasis on rape as the "quintessential sexual terror."[15] Feminist considerations of male sexual abuse were contained within the movement for social purity, a motley crew of social reformers with a curious assortment of politics, sexual and otherwise. As Valverde has argued, feminists in the Canadian social purity movement indeed put forward a critique of male sexuality, but they framed their discussions in such a way as to entrench hierarchies of class, race and ethnicity.[16]

There is much more to uncover in Canadian history about the sexual politics of first-wave feminists. In Canada, as in the United States, early feminists were more concerned about the 'social evil'—prostitution—than garden-variety sexual assault. There are several issues to consider here. Given the class and race of most first-wave feminists, it is not surprising that these middle-class Anglo-Saxon women would replicate some of the cultural stereotypes about the presumed sexual depravity of the 'lower orders' and foreigners, thereby displacing questions of gender relations onto those of class and race.[17] The prevailing political ideology which informed Canadian feminist activism, maternal feminism, was not conducive to developing an ideology of women's sexual self-determination or a sustained critique of personal relations between the sexes. Maternalism highlighted the 'good' which women's role in the family promoted and attempted to extend this farther afield.[18] Most telling of all, in this period there was little cultural or economic space for women to live apart from men or families, and thus few could develop the distance necessary to engage in serious critique or experimentation. It is no coincidence that second-wave feminists, the first generation of women to experience the possibility of living relatively independent lives, were the first to develop a critical analysis of the family and male sexual violence.

First-wave feminists failed to engage politically with issues of sexuality in a way that challenged fundamental distinctions between 'good' and 'bad' female behavior. That there was little material support for victims of sexual violence—no assistance in handling police and medical examinations, or in coping with the attendant emotional traumas—no doubt made the experience of assault in this period extremely lonely. That feminists, or any others interested in ameliorating social pain, for that matter, did not challenge the sexual culture which made 'irresponsible' girls culpable for their own misfortune also made sexual assault a worse experience. In the absence of a feminist political movement that articulated all women's right to refuse unwanted sexual attention, standards of bodily inviolability among women varied. For some women, disadvantages of class or race often eclipsed their rights as women. In such an atmosphere, individual acts of resistance were plentiful but did not substantially change the social context in which sexual antagonisms took place.

When faced with unwanted sexual advances, women had various options. On rare occasions, women resisted physically.[19] A few women used various objects at hand—the parasol, a broom, once a pillow—to attempt to beat off their assailant, usually unsuccessfully. One particularly feisty young orphaned woman, home alone while her brother was in town, had a "scuffle" with a friend of her brother's who had dropped by for a visit. The next day she sent her brother to town to purchase a revolver for her, and while he was gone her assailant returned to attack her again. This time she chose legal prosecution rather than self-defense. The jury ruled not guilty.[20] Had she used her revolver, she may have been better off. Under some circumstances, women who murdered in defense of their 'honor' were treated with extreme leniency. In 1910 a young Ukrainian immigrant in Fort William, Mary M., took a gun to her neighbor Paul L., who had been "annoying her and making indecent proposals" for some time. During the trial it was revealed that Mary had been raped twice by the man. She was several months pregnant (by her husband) at the time of the shooting. In the court room the story took on racist dimensions: the coroner's jury lamented the fact that the "riff raff of the world were being herded here like sheep," and the judge at the trial deplored the habit of foreigners owning guns, remarking that he "never found he needed one" in Canada. Yet in this case racism combined with chivalry to let Mary off the hook. The coroner recommended that criminal charges not be laid, since "home is the most sacred word in any civilization . . . home is the Briton's castle," and as Mary acted to save the life of her unborn child, her crime was "commendable."[21] Outside Ottawa in 1882, a woman who was seduced and abandoned, pregnant by her lover, and who avenged herself by shooting him, was also found not guilty, much to the delight of the crowd in the courtroom.[22] An even more sensational story unfolded in Stratford in 1921, when Margaret S. went on trial for the murder of her husband, who, it had recently been discovered, had impregnated their teenage daughter. Despite strong evidence that Margaret had in fact slipped strychnine in his tea upon hearing of his relationship with their daughter Pearl, the jury chose to believe her clumsily constructed suicide theory. Again, a crowd of supportive spectators heartily approved the verdict.[23]

Being a woman might save one from hanging, but judicial chivalry operated only under very specific circumstances. Women who took 'too much' control could expect some punishment. As Carolyn Strange has argued in her analysis of the trials of two female murderers which took place in Toronto during this period, chivalric justice might save a woman's life, but the process unfolded in such a way as to mute her voice, to render her a backdrop to the all-male drama of the courtroom.[24] Yet at the level of popular support for her actions as well as the attainment of a certain measure of justice, it is certainly arguable that a woman who killed her assailant was somewhat further ahead than a woman who merely called the police.

The surest way to protect one's reputation was, sadly, to die. A woman killed in the course of a sexual assault was instantly heralded as a martyr, even when her actions preceding the attack were those—such as allowing herself to be picked up by a boy at a community fair—which would have tarnished her character severely had she 'merely' been raped. As historian Terry Chapman also found in her study of sexual crime in western Canada, death seemed to be "the only sure way to quell any conscious or subconscious doubts about lack of consent."[25]

When unwanted or illicit sexual encounters resulted in pregnancy, abortion or infanticide could provide necessary (but extremely dangerous) relief from the stigma of unwed motherhood. Most of the women prosecuted for infanticide (or the more common charge, concealment of birth) were young single women living on their own, often working as domestic servants or waitresses. But whether women lived on their own or with their family, what is remarkable about many infanticide cases was how quiet women remained about their pregnancy. The bodies of most of these babies were found accidentally, though many women made a half-hearted attempt to hide them. On rare occasions women might enlist the help of a woman friend or a sister to help them dispose of the body. But most women endured nine no doubt anguished months of pregnancy, then carried out the murder of the child, completely on their own. Except in cases of incest, it was rare that the father's identity was ever revealed. Juries it seemed were reluctant to convict these women. Legal historian Constance Backhouse's study of Canadian prosecutions between 1840 and 1900 reveals a conviction rate of 7 percent when the charge was murder, 33 percent for manslaughter, and 43 percent for the lesser charge of concealment of birth.[26]

Abortion was an alternative for married women who had decided, for economic reasons, that they could not have another child, and for young single women 'seduced' by men who then refused to marry them when pregnant. Getting an abortion was tricky business in this period, however. Usually women relied on the assistance of woman friends, husbands or errant boyfriends to make arrangements for them. Abortions were performed either by doctors or laywomen and men, or were self-induced by popular abortifacients. The amount of planning required made this option available only in limited numbers of cases; no women pregnant as a result of incest or rape were found in abortion case files. And while abortion may have helped women avoid the economic or social costs of an unwanted pregnancy, it was extremely dangerous. In approximately one-third of these cases, the abortion came to light because it proved fatal.[27]

Females also coped with sexual domination through the exchange of money. Children in particular were often bribed into having sex. So too many women accepted money or goods as part of the sexual bargain struck with their boyfriends. Other women accepted money as the price of their silence, and still other women (often with the help of their families) tried to negotiate a financial settlement with men after the event, sometimes, but not always, when they discovered they were pregnant. Sometimes negotiations were initiated by accused men fearful of a prison sentence. Dana M. wrote his father while in prison awaiting trial for the assault of his neighbor, asking that he offer the woman and her family ten dollars to "persuade them not to appear against me."[28] (The letter, which included an ironic postscript urging his father not to reply because the "head man of the jail" reads all the letters which are sent to prisoners, was used against him in court.) At other times women, or, more likely, a woman's parents, approached the man involved and demanded a settlement. Upon learning of her daughter's harassment by her employer, Ann P. immediately confronted Enoch P. and his wife, claiming she had a right to damages and demanding two hundred dollars.[29]

Interpreting the place of financial transactions in sexual assault cases is difficult. A common legal defense was to insinuate prostitution. In many cases women flatly denied that they had accepted money, and one must judge whether men constructed the story after the fact or if women lied because of the moral condemnation such an act would bring upon them. Negotiating with one's assailant certainly imperiled a woman's chances of success in the courts. When legal authorities discovered any evidence that the woman (or her family) had tried to bargain before bringing charges, her morality, and thus her version of the sexual assault story, immediately became suspect. As soon as the judge heard that Betsy P. and her husband had approached Fred L. to settle for fifteen dollars, for example, he dismissed the case.[30] Conversely, the judge in the case of Ada Q., a young woman assaulted by her teacher at school, complimented the girl's father profusely and recommended the jury bring in a guilty verdict because he had gone to the police rather than "taking the matter in his own hands." "This was not," the judge declared, "a case of a designing woman against an unprotected man."[31]

The practice of negotiating, for money or sometimes for goods such as livestock or even farmland, was widespread and occurred in cases of voluntary and involuntary sexual crime. I return to this issue when I examine prosecutions for voluntary sexual relations, in order to more fully understand the informal routes women and men chose to redress sexual grievances.

SEX CRIME IN THE CRIMINAL COURTS

The procedure for pursuing a criminal case was relatively simple. The initial complaint was heard by the local police or justice of the peace. The complainant was asked to swear an information, essentially a written allegation in which she told her version of the incident. Informations were sworn by the complainant herself, a parent (usually her father) or other family member, or less often, the police. The police then investigated to determine whether an arrest was warranted. If the accused was arrested, a preliminary hearing was held, heard by a justice of the peace or a police court magistrate. (Police court was the lowest level in the court system.) If the accused was committed for trial, he had a choice between the county (or district) court judges' criminal court, which was a nonjury court, or the highest level of the criminal court system, the criminal assize court. Most sexual crimes were heard by the criminal assize court, which was presided over twice yearly in county towns by traveling judges. A grand jury, impaneled to hear all the criminal cases in a session, heard the initial evidence and decided whether or not a trial would be held. If a 'true bill' was returned by the grand jury, a trial lasting between a couple hours to several days was heard and a verdict rendered. By our standards the entire process was speedy. The matter could be disposed of within a few months, depending on when the crime was committed in relation to the scheduled visits of criminal assize judges.[32]

The laws with respect to sexual assault underwent many changes during this period, the details of which have been summarized by a number of historians.[33] Beginning in the mid-1880s, various new and more restrictive categories of sexual relations were criminalized. Legal historian Graham Parker claims that, with the codification of the criminal law in 1892, Canada had the most comprehensive framework for protecting women and girls from what he terms "sexual predators."[34] The major trend in sexual assault legislation throughout the nineteenth and early twentieth century was a movement away from considering rape a crime against a woman's husband or father, toward the notion that it was a crime against a woman herself. In keeping with this trend, rigid requirements for conviction, such as proof of penetration and "the emission of seed," were relaxed toward the end of the century.

The written particulars of the law were applied and interpreted by an all-male cast of police, lawyers, judge and jury. It is a truism of feminist analysis today that the treatment of rape victims by the legal system constitutes a second rape. Women's experience in the courts in the nineteenth and early twentieth century also deserves this cliché. Prejudice, mistrust and outright misogyny were the order of the day for women who brought their stories to the criminal courts.

General suspicion of sexual assault victims touched all aspects of their experience, including their story and the manner in which they brought it forward. Evidence of a woman's negotiations to reach a financial settlement with the accused was considered by the court to diminish the seriousness of her claim. 'Designing women,' by this logic, forfeited their right to legal redress. If women did not report the assault immediately, this too suggested the complaint was frivolous or made up. A judge in Goderich explained to a jury in 1881 that "if the woman does not at once lodge an information, but leaves it off for a time, doubts are liable to be thrown upon her testimony."[35]

Other historical studies of sexual assault convictions identify two sets of factors which determined whether women's stories were believed. Terry Chapman's study of western Canada and Barbara Lindemann's analysis of Massachusetts both suggest that the degree of physical resistance women could prove greatly helped their case before a jury. Overheard screams, a disheveled appearance, torn clothing, or better still, marks of physical conflict such as bruises or inflamed genitals (sworn to by a doctor) did not of themselves guarantee a guilty verdict, but without them a case was on extremely shaky ground.[36]

Another set of factors which determined the outcome of sexual assault trials was the status of the victim and/or the assailant. Guido Ruggiero and Nazife Bashar, studying sexual crimes in Renaissance Venice and sixteenth-century England respectively, conclude that the age of the victim was the most important determining feature. Assaults against children were treated far more seriously than assaults against adult women. Similarly, both Ruggiero and Lindemann point out that the class of the assailant was also significant; men at the lower end of the social and economic hierarchy were punished more often than upper-class men.[37]

All of these general trends are pertinent to this study, yet I have found that the relationship between victim and accused, and the scenario of the assault, also played a significant role in determining conviction rates (see the appendix, table 3). Assaults between strangers were the most likely to result in a guilty verdict (68 percent). Gang rapes and assaults against children and among family or household members had a relatively equal conviction rate, ranging from 50 percent to 59 percent. Most often disbelieved were assaults by neighbors (45 percent), dates (42 percent), work-related assaults (33 percent), assaults by family friends (30 percent), and those committed by men who 'picked up' women as first-time dates (28 percent). The fact that assaults by strangers constitute by far the most believed category of sexual assault is itself a telling indicator of prevailing sexual standards. It would seem that any degree of familiarity between a man and woman raised the possibility of consent. Only when a woman was chosen at random might her sexual integrity remain unblemished.

The conviction rates in this sample changed over time. As table 4 in the appendix indicates, women who had been assaulted in the later decades of this fifty-year study had an easier time convincing the courts of the crime. In the 1880s, 38 percent of cases of sexual violence resulted in a guilty verdict, while 51 percent were found not guilty (in 11 percent of cases the verdict could not be determined from the records). By the 1910s, 56 percent of such cases resulted in a guilty verdict, while 35 percent were found not guilty (10 percent were indeterminable). It is likely that these changes reflect changes in both evidence required for conviction as well as the sexual climate of the early twentieth century. As the social purity movement spread its tales of white slavery and female victimization, judges and jurors seemed more disposed to believe women's versions of assault stories. Historians have highlighted the harmful legacy of the social purity movement, especially its use of sexual and moral virtue to intensify racial, ethnic and class conflicts. Nor was the movement especially beneficial to most women. Citing the large increase in arrests of young women for prostitution and vagrancy in Toronto at this time, Carolyn Strange argues that "young women ultimately bore the brunt of the campaigns to rid the city of immorality."[38] The social purity movement helped create a climate of sexual fear in early twentieth-century Ontario, and social perceptions of female vulnerability soared. It makes sense, then, that women who brought their stories of victimization forward at this time faced less disbelief than an earlier generation of women did.

Yet even more than age, status, relationship or scenario, the single most important factor in determining the outcome of a sexual assault trial was character. Such concerns were in fact incorporated into the bureaucracy of the legal system. It was not unusual for police to launch an investigation into a woman's character before proceeding with criminal charges, or for a judge to order an investigation into an accused man's background before sentencing.

Character was, of course, a malleable concept which derived meaning from such forms of power as gender, race and class. Yet respectability was not a mere reflection of class, race or gender; it wasn't as though men were automatically more reputable than women or that working-class people were necessarily always morally suspect.[39] Standards of appropriate behavior and reputation were applied to men as well as women. But moral scrutiny was applied more often and more harshly to women. The gender difference in the application of sexual standards was this: men could make mistakes in the pursuit of sex, mistakes involving the choice of partner, location, or perhaps their behavior after the incident. Sometimes such mistakes were thought to warrant punishment through the criminal justice system, sometimes they were not. Some lamented the fact that certain mistakes or indiscretions on the part of men were not subject to legal redress. During infanticide trials for the death of illegitimate infants, for example, women's groups, labor groups and judges expressed profound regret that the man 'responsible' for the pregnancy was not also prosecuted. For women, however, it was not an occasional error in judgment which might result in a lost criminal case, but rather any activity, sexual or otherwise, which departed from rigidly circumscribed norms.

Sex was the central but not sole determinant of character. Contemporary feminists have been justly critical of the way a woman's sexual reputation can be used as evidence in a rape trial, as though if one has had sex willingly once, all sexual acts must therefore be voluntary. Use of a person's sexual reputation in rape trials remains a contested political issue. The latitude allowed judges and defense lawyers in this earlier period was overwhelming. Nineteenth-century judges and juries drew from a vast pool of social assumptions about what constituted proper deportment. Questions about a woman's employment history, school attendance and performance, and church attendance were routine. Women who were assaulted in men's homes (while visiting friends and neighbors, for example) or outside in the evening were subject to a barrage of questions concerning their motives and purpose in leaving their home.

For men, attempts to establish good character drew even more heavily on nonsexual issues, not surprisingly, given that sex was not as forbidden for men. Men were questioned about whether they were cigarette smokers, attended picture shows, or drank liquor. It was common for the families, friends and employers of accused men to circulate petitions, often signed by entire communities, testifying to the men's good moral character. Such petitions usually discussed the man's family background, his skills or obedience as a worker, and his value to his family as a breadwinner (even when the charge was incest). The employer of Percy B., charged, along with another man, of rape, went out of his way to intervene on Percy's behalf. After Percy was released on bail, pending trial, his employer in Whitby rehired him, though as he explained to a local legal authority, "since his position brought him into close connection with the factory girls, . . . for obvious reasons we gave him a place that would avoid any difficulty." Percy, he continued, was a man whose "manners and ability were above average," and he implored the official to "overlook" his "mistakes."[40]

It is important to keep in mind the extent to which, in the nineteenth century, the quest for a 'respectable character' informed people's lives and live-

lihoods. Women, as British historian Ellen Ross has argued, embodied respectability in everything from housekeeping and child-rearing practices to sexual behavior.[41] Women were especially vulnerable to charges of immorality. The accusation of prostitution could not only wreck a woman's chances of securing a conviction in a sexual assault trial. A woman's sexual reputation influenced her freedom of movement—her ability, for example, to travel in particular neighborhoods at particular times—as well as more tangible questions of employment.[42] 'Respectability' was a requirement for most women's jobs, especially teaching and domestic service, and some men's jobs such as law, throughout the nineteenth century. And of course breaches of social respectability in the workplace also had a more serious impact on women. For example, female teachers charged with moral infractions were dealt with far more severely than male teachers charged with the same or more serious violations.[43] The Victorian doctrine of female passionlessness and purity increased the stakes for women; it meant they had further to fall.[44]

Nineteenth-century notions of respectability were so broadly conceived as to include most areas of life, but in the courtroom, sex was at the center. How a woman behaved in the company of men was at the heart of whether her story of sexual assault was believed by a jury. Certain rules were obvious. Women who admitted to having consumed alcohol, either before the incident or even as a general rule, were automatically suspect. Matilda O., an elderly widow, was attacked by two men in an outhouse behind her residence in Kingston in 1880. When the police learned that the three had been drinking together earlier that day, they arrested all of them, which in itself speaks volumes about the degree of protection afforded women who transgressed certain boundaries. Matilda was put in the same cell as her assailants, and several hours later the police noticed that the three of them were sharing a drink again, a fact which no doubt contributed to an immediate acquittal.[45]

Women who became pregnant as a result of 'illicit' sexual relations also decreased their chances of successful criminal prosecution. Most pregnant women pursued seduction charges against errant boyfriends who, they claimed, reneged on a commitment to marriage. But several women, pregnant as a result of incest or sexual assault, laid rape charges. The difficulty facing women who became pregnant, of course, was in convincing authorities that forced sex had occurred a limited number of times or that the accused man was in fact the father of the child. As a doctor who testified at the trial of Nelson H., a Lambton County farmer accused of sexually assaulting his young neighbor, explained, "I have always had the opinion that a woman was not likely to become pregnant under such circumstances." But, he conceded, "medical men differ on this question."[46]

Previous sexual history was the most common route defense lawyers chose to probe a woman's character. Some women were easy targets. Annie S. pressed a rape charge against her neighbor Daniel M., who succeeded in "getting her down" after harassing her previously on several occasions. Naively, as it turned out, Annie thought that the harassment had come to an end because of the newly respectable status her recent marriage had conferred upon her. The problem was that Annie had an illegitimate son. This unforgivable fact eclipsed any virtue marriage bestowed on her, both in the eyes of her assailant and also in the opinion of the criminal court. In every case in which the woman was discovered to have had illegitimate children, sexual assault charges were dismissed.[47]

The most common line of questioning designed to cast doubt on a woman's character involved previous relationships with men, either the accused or anyone else. The stipulation that a victim be "of chaste character" applied only to charges of voluntary sexual relations such as abduction and seduction; it was not a legal requirement in sexual assault charges. Yet time after time women were subject to questions about their relations with the opposite sex. A common defense tactic was to toss out a number of men's names to a woman on the witness stand, forcing her to deny that she had either 'kept company' or 'had connection' with them. Even if she denied knowing these men, a cloud of suspicion was created. If a woman was candid about her sexual past, she was humiliated in court. Marian B., a young woman who was attacked by three neighborhood boys as she was walking through the bush on her way home from music lessons, signed a statement, later read into the court record, which stated the number and names of boys she had "had connection with" in the past.[48] Isaac G. was one of many men who tried to harness prejudices against 'loose' women to his advantage. While he was in jail awaiting trial for sexually assaulting his neighbor, Margaret B., he wrote a remarkable letter to his brother. He asked him for help to get out of the "scrape he'd gotten into by the doings of that Bitch" by rounding up some friends who would "all swear you all had been with her and that will make her out what she really is." Curiously, there was no mention of this incriminating letter in press accounts of the trial, and Isaac was found not guilty.[49]

Another route to pursue in uncovering women's sexual history was medical evidence. Doctors often played a crucial role in sexual assault trials, usually in the case of teenagers or young girls. While rape was generally considered a moral rather than medical issue, many parents would take their daughters to a doctor immediately upon hearing about their assault, even before reporting it to the police. In court, doctors testified as to whether physical evidence corroborated a woman's story—whether semen was found; whether a woman's genitals showed evidence of, as one gentleman discreetly put it, "tampering"; and whether any sexual disease had been transmitted.

Yet doctors were also asked to comment on the general condition of a woman's vagina, and from this evidence some rather sweeping conclusions about her social life and character could be inferred. Some doctors claimed to be able to tell whether or not a woman was "in the habit" of having sexual intercourse; others gave evidence claiming a woman had not been a virgin at the time of the rape. This, of course, was legally irrelevant and presented a physiological challenge to substantiate. One doctor suggested that masturbation rather than rape may have been the cause of a woman's ruptured hymen; another thought that bicycle riding might have been the culprit. In her study of the social opinions on rape expressed in nineteenth- and twentieth-century U.S. medical journals, Elizabeth Anne Mills argues that most doctors saw themselves as purveyors of indisputable medical truths, against "designing demi-mondaines" who continually lied about their rape stories. Some doctors believed that it was simply a physical impossibility for a woman to have sex against her will. As one medical man wrote in 1917: "Every physician knows that so long as a consciousness and consequent physical ability to resist remain, no adult female can be forcibly compelled to acquiesce, since for anatomic and physiologic reasons the male is incapable of successfully 'fighting and copulating' at the same time."[50]

Virginity was effectively part of what constituted the 'good character' of unmarried women. A successful rape prosecution also hinged on the deportment of victim and assailant before and after the assault. One of the reasons for the difficulty in securing convictions for date rapes was because courts tended to regard any degree of socializing on the part of the couple as evidence that the woman consented to sex. Flirting, which might include walking, dancing, sending letters or other communication, indicated moral weakness. To be considered truly good, women were to be oblivious to the men around them. As one young woman trying to carve out 'good girl' territory put it, she "never let on that she noticed" the family farmhand before he assaulted her.[51]

Not all judges, of course, permitted legal defenses which attempted to discredit a woman's character. During this period a discernible shift occurred in the types of evidence considered within the bounds of propriety. Through the 1880s there was less of a tendency to impute malicious motives to women pressing sexual assault charges. One particularly enlightened judge instructed a jury in 1881 that "if they believed the woman was not a consenting party even although the person laying the information was a prostitute, the testimony should not be thrown out."[52] It was also widely perceived in this period that sexual assaults were on the increase. After a highly publicized gang rape trial in Gananoque in 1882, the *Gananoque Re-*

porter condemned the community for fostering a "monstrous" set of ideas with respect to the rights of women. "Women who were known, or even suspected, to be not just what they should be in point of virtue, were regarded as having no rights that men or boys were bound to respect," a sentiment which the paper claimed was responsible for an increase in crimes of violence against women.[53]

Yet as more and newer types of sexual crimes were added to the law books, many began to balk. In 1895, for example, a judge in Cornwall complained that "since the recent changes in the law, increasing the gravity of such offenses [indecent assault, in this instance], people were becoming more prudish." He reminded the jury that they should "have a human feeling for weakness, and [take] into account the passions with which men were endowed by nature and which under certain circumstances became almost uncontrollable."[54] By 1903 a Parry Sound judge noted with regret that juries were tending to ignore evidence given by young men which implied that women were not of good character.[55]

Discrediting a woman's character was not the only way accused men explained themselves in court. Often they suggested an alternative version of events. Some men denied the story completely, claiming mistaken identification or asserting (sometimes with their wife or parents as alibis) that they were elsewhere at the time. Others, such as Marshall J., said he "considered himself just as seduced as she was" and denied that coercion had been involved. Men often presented themselves as victims of feminine enticement. David C., for example, claimed it was his cousin Elizabeth's idea to have sex and offered as proof that she was wearing no "drawers" at the time.[56] Hubert M., who 'picked up' Mary P. in downtown Peterborough, was shocked when the police appeared at his door, for, as he put it, "I thought she knew what I took her for."[57]

Some assault stories were portrayed by accused men as grudge matches. Several men suggested that they had been framed, victims of a conspiracy on the part of the woman or her family to avenge past wrongs. William W. claimed that his neighbor Adeline B.'s story—that he was the masked man who attacked her on a deserted road—was fabricated by her father to get back at William for stealing his sheep during a Halloween prank.[58] Other men who became "bad friends" with their neighbors as a result of disputes over such things as shared farm implements, or farm animals straying into another's territory, suggested that an assault charge was trumped up.[59] Family or marital feuds also provided a defense; John V., for example, denied that he assaulted his sister-in-law Mae K. and suggested instead that the charge was "all made up on me" by his wife and her sister.[60] Conspiracy defenses were successful. The vast majority of accused men who made such allegations were not convicted. Whether they were true or simply good stories likely to have legal credibility is more difficult to ascertain. These stories do indicate, however, the multiplicity of social meanings assigned to sexual conflicts historically.

Men's definitions of the boundaries between wanted and unwanted sex were indeed different from women's, but they also varied among themselves. Some who agreed with the women's rendering of the story denied they had committed a wrong, either socially or legally. Male sexual arrogance could reach mammoth proportions. Louis S., for example, was a foreman in a logging camp in northern Ontario. He kept his young cook, Tockha K., as his sexual prisoner in the camp over the winter. According to a witness who tried to intervene on behalf of Tockha, Louis resisted his attempts, telling him "he had a right to the woman."[61] Francis H. told Hazel B., a woman he assaulted in his taxi cab, that "this is what God made men and women for" and urged her not to tell her husband, reminding her that "you have your character to think of." William W., a farmhand who attempted to assault his sixty-three-year-old employer, explained to police he was "just having a bit of fun."[62] Some men simply didn't act remorseful, following women home after an assault or returning to their home later to ask for a date. After assaulting Katie G. one morning on her way to church, Charles W. stopped by the family home that afternoon to visit Katie's brother.[63]

There were of course men who knew they had crossed legal boundaries. Patrick D. approached a friend to borrow money in order to leave town to evade police.[64] A few even apologized in court. Both alcohol and male biology also provided excuses when men plead guilty, particularly during the height of the social purity movement. Another farmhand, Fredrick K., told police in 1910 that "it was only a matter of passion" which led him to assault his female employer. Similarly, John M., charged with assaulting his domestic servant, told the judge sorrowfully, "I am a passionate man and should be sent away."[65]

The hostility and suspicion displayed toward women who brought their stories of sexual assault forward for legal redress help explain why some were reluctant to press charges and must lead us to speculate about the number of unreported assaults. Despite decades of legal changes which relaxed certain rules of evidence and slowly recognized the inviolability of women's bodies, concerns about sexual and moral character dominated criminal proceedings. A vast array of misogynist cultural stereotypes, about 'designing women,' overwhelming male passion, and other components of the sexual double standard, shaped both the social and self-definition of rape.

One Kingston judge expressed the conundrum facing women who pressed sexual assault charges more precisely than he realized. Commenting on a rape case in 1881, Judge Burton told the jury that it might be shown that the rape victim was of "lewd character." "That fact" he warned them, "was no palliation of the offense, although it might shake the woman's credibility as a witness."[66] As long as the prevailing moral climate of nineteenth- and early twentieth-century Ontario held women's behavior up to closer scrutiny than men's, it is hardly surprising that the legal system was not a hospitable place for women to bring sexual grievances.

SEXUAL VIOLENCE AND FEMINIST THEORY

This excursion through the rural and Northern Ontario criminal case files for rape and related crimes yields an exhaustive, often poignant tally. Women risked sexual assault from family members, total strangers and trusted friends. Women were raped on Saturday evenings as they strolled downtown streets, Sunday mornings on their way home from church, and weekday afternoons when they returned from school or work. Sexual abuse existed in isolated northern mining camps, placid rural farmlands, and bustling county towns. Rape knew no limits of age and conformed to no standards of sexual desirability.

It is this pervasive, random and ordinary quality of male sexual violence which has led contemporary feminist theorists to posit a direct relationship between rape and maintenance of male power. Susan Brownmiller is the name most associated with this position; it was her book *Against Our Will* which helped define, and continues to exert an enormous influence on, the feminist project of transforming society's understanding of sexual violence from a question of individual pathology to a highly political social structure. Brownmiller's analysis of male sexual violence has been followed by many others in the radical feminist tradition, particularly in contemporary discussions of pornography.[67]

Published in 1975, Brownmiller's analysis has been the subject of ongoing and intense debate, and the sex debates of recent years have called into question many of Brownmiller's conclusions. Particularly in dispute is the notion of rape as, in Hester Eistenstein's phrase, the "secret of patriarchy," the coercive mechanism by which, in Brownmiller's now famous formulation, "all men keep all women in a state of fear."[68] This conceptualization of sexual violence overlooks the complex interplay of structures and ideologies which support patriarchal domination and relies on an ahistorial and essentialist conception of 'all women's' or 'all men's' experience. As an explanation for rape, Brownmiller offered little more than biology. It was men's "structural capacity to rape, and women's corresponding structural vulnerability" which explained the act of rape. Men's desire to rape became simple "anatomical fiat."[69] As feminist critic Lynne Segal inquired (only, one suspects, half in jest), "how does something so vulnerable and fragile as men's genital equipment (for it is well known that a tiny tweak of the testes or a knee to a man's groin never fails to produce shrieks of pain) transform itself into something which appears as a potential weapon, an instrument to dominate and control, the very basis of men's power?"[70]

What is the basis of men's power? This question has engaged feminist scholars of all disciplines and political persuasions for some time and has yet to result in a unified or agreed-upon synthesis. Despite the thoughtful caveats advanced by some feminists, I am not troubled by the term 'patriarchy' to describe the system in which men hold structural and individual power over women.[71] Patriarchy is a complex and multifaceted system, and one which can alternately collude and conflict with other modes of oppression based on race and class.[72] The question of when, for example, racial forms of domination take precedence over others (or when they combine) is a question of historical investigation rather than abstract pronouncement. While debates on key conceptual questions about the maintenance and nature of patriarchal power continue, there is some agreement among socialist feminists about the material basis of patriarchal control. Two fundamental mechanisms of patriarchy are male control over female labor and sexuality.

Of the two, our understanding of male control of women's labor is by far the most finely tuned. Expanding (and sometimes correcting) Engels' initial reflections on women's role in the reproduction of the species, many have examined the place of the sexual division of labor (productive and reproductive) in the oppression of women.[73] Curiously, despite a theoretical aversion to economistic explanations of women's oppression, far less empirical and theoretical attention has been paid by socialist feminists to the other axis of patriarchy—sexuality. Socialist feminists have, until recently, ceded much of the territory of sexuality, especially sexual violence, to radical feminists.[74] Yet if we are to take seriously years of feminist debate on the origin, nature, and contours of patriarchal domination, it would seem wise to do for sexuality what many have done for work: study it, contextualize it, and historicize it.

This hesitancy on the part of socialist feminists to truly take on questions of sexual violence results in more than a gap in research or theorizing. Women experience male sexual domination more personally and painfully than they do economic oppression. As Varda Burstyn has pointed out, "given the connection between sexuality and feeling, the element of control over the actual body of the labouring class in generic terms is . . . much greater than that element between members of ruling and labouring classes in economic terms."[75] Sexual danger exacts a toll on women which operates on a much different, more intense and personal level than other aspects of oppression.

One of the only studies of rape to depart from the tone set by Susan

Brownmiller remains Lorene Clark and Debra Lewis's early book, *Rape: The Price of Coercive Sexuality*, published as a response to some of Brownmiller's more problematic assertions. The central insight governing the study is that rape is a social act, produced by a certain kind of society, not "an inevitable consequence of fixed human nature."[76] Clark and Lewis link rape to two key elements of patriarchal society: its denial of sexual, social and economic autonomy for women, and its corresponding appropriation of women as male sexual property. They combine a feminist analysis of the history of rape laws, which until the nineteenth century treated rape as an offense against the victim's father or husband, with some of Engels' ideas about the origin of private property. Female sexuality is commodified, they argue, but it is a commodity women themselves never truly own. Women barter their sexuality, primarily through marriage, which in turn demands a payment from men. Sexual antagonisms arise from these underpinnings, structured into the everyday life of heterosexual relations in a patriarchal, capitalist world.

Thus Clark and Lewis are able to explain the many contradictory social meanings assigned to rape. Rape is on one level a serious crime, yet at the same time its victims' treatment by the legal system is notoriously unfair. But for Clark and Lewis the problem is not malfunction or bias in the legal system (which, Brownmiller suggested, could be rectified by hiring more policewomen). Rather, given the social context within which rape laws were developed and continue to be played out, the results are predictable. Rape laws, they argue, were never meant to provide women with sexual autonomy. Rather, "rape laws were designed to preserve valuable female sexual property for the exclusive ownership of those men who could afford to acquire and maintain it."[77]

This kind of materialist approach leads toward an investigation of the class dimensions of sexual violence, a complex issue many feminist commentators prefer to sidestep. The empirical findings of Clark and Lewis suggest that there is a huge class bias in the backgrounds of rapists: 90 percent of their sample of 129 convicted rapists in Toronto came from poor and working-class backgrounds. While they cite the traditional class bias of the legal system as a likely reason for the underrepresentation and reporting of middle- and upper-class rapists, they also conclude that working-class men "lack the purchasing power to buy the sexual property they want . . . physical force is the method used by men who lack other, subtler means of sexual coercion."[78] Lynne Segal has recently put forward a similar argument, suggesting that sexual violence is most pronounced among men who are "most removed from the confirmations of manliness derived from wealth or position."[79]

Against Our Will and *Rape: The Price of Coercive Sexuality* each represent significant milestones in the development of feminist thought and practice. Clark and Lewis help redress some of the analytical flaws in Brownmiller's important polemic. Yet there is an economism in their analysis that sexual violence arises from women's oppression as male property, and this tends to diminish the sexual specificity of rape.[80] It is by now feminist common sense to argue that rape is not an act of passion but rather an expression of violence, part of the misogyny inherent in a patriarchal culture. This is, to be sure, an advance over analyses of sexual violence which suggested instead a facile relationship to 'stronger' male hormones or frustrated sex drives.[81] But this approach does not settle the issue. Why do men *rape* women? Why don't they 'just' beat them up? What accounts for the tremendous guilt, fear and shame rape instills in women, a fear far more potent than that instilled by physical abuse alone.[82] Women physically abused by their husbands, for example, are frequently asked why they stay, but only the most misogynistic presume that the women encouraged it or liked it. An analysis that diminishes the sexual component of rape cannot help us illuminate the crucial role sexual violence plays in heightening women's sense of shame and in making the pursuit of sexual pleasure such a minefield for women.

Patriarchal norms about relations between women, men and sexuality set the context for sexual violence, creating both the assumptions and opportunities for it to occur. Contested gender relations result in many forms of coercion, of which sexual violence is one particularly brutal component. Rape alone does not cause or maintain patriarchy, but it is an effective and remarkably durable facet of women's subordination. We have seen that historically both the experience of sexual conflict and its 'handling' in the legal arena helped construct female sexuality in such a way as to highlight danger, shame, vulnerability, and humiliation and to obscure or at least make much more complicated pleasure. I continue this examination of the experience of sexual assault by contrasting the actual situations of reported sexual crimes with the discourses of danger—men, situations, and places—which predominated in turn-of-the-century Ontario.

CHAPTER TWO

Discourses of Danger: The Social and Spatial Settings of Sexual Violence

T HE SOCIAL CONTEXT IN WHICH SEXUAL
assault occurred had an important impact on how the legal system judged
these incidents. For example, women who had socialized with their assailant prior to an assault usually had their character and therefore their version of the story questioned in court. As we have seen, women had to prove
an unblemished character and reputation in order to substantiate a sexual
assault complaint. An analysis of social scenarios of sexual violence can,
however, illuminate more than the legal determination of guilt or innocence. Understanding the family, community, social, or work relationships
which resulted in sexual assault charges can also help us grasp the broader
historical meaning and place of sexual danger in women's lives.

Examining the spatial and social settings of assault helps uncover how notions of sexual peril were formed. The 1880s through the 1920s were considered by contemporaries as sexually dangerous times, a period of what
historians have called a 'moral panic.' This concept, popularized by British
historian Jeffrey Weeks, refers to moments in history during which widespread fears and anxieties crystallize; these fears are dealt with by displacing
them onto "'Folk Devils' in an identified social group (often the 'immoral' or
'degenerate')."[1] Changes such as economic upheavals or shifting patterns of
race or gender relations are thus cloaked and reinterpreted socially as crises
of sexuality.

This concept should be instantly familiar to observers of the late twentieth-
century social landscape. The contemporary AIDS panic, concerns about
pornography and prostitution, and the rise of right-wing antiabortion and

antifeminist movements all testify to the resiliance of sexuality as a site of contesting anxieties over race, class and gender relations.[2] Historians are beginning to document how the global cold war of the 1950s was also a domestic war, fought over competing definitions of family life and sexual deviance.[3] In Victorian Canada we can also see escalating battles over delineations of appropriate sexuality, which were played out in the context of shifting relations of power: between the sexes, classes, and racial and ethnic groups.

The meaning of sexual acts varies historically. Michel Foucault has noted that in certain contexts, innocent, "inconsequential bucolic pleasures" could become "the object of not only a collective intolerance but of a judicial action, a medical intervention, a careful clinical examination, and an entire theoretical elaboration."[4] It would be wrong to argue that contemporary feminists discovered the problem of rape and other forms of sexual abuse, for nineteenth-century moral reformers indeed developed a distinct elaboration of sexual dangers. Certain kinds of women, men, neighborhoods, regions, social relations and sexual acts were invested with significant moral (or immoral) power. But to fully understand the meaning of sexuality historically, we must interrogate moral silences as well as panics. As we shall see, a host of social institutions and relations were in fact sexually harmful and exploitative, chiefly of women and children, but these did not become the subject of intervention, commentary or criminalization. There were a plethora of bogeymen of the period: the dangerous foreigner, the wandering tramp, the immoral taxi driver. This focus on the evil stranger, however, left obscure the persons and places which were in fact the most dangerous to women and children. The family and household, and the rural or small-town community, were rarely subjected to moral scrutiny or condemnation. In this chapter, I demonstrate that significant sexual abuse and exploitation occurred in these places, where it was least expected and policed.

The total number of sexual violence charges (officially, the crimes of rape, attempted rape, indecent assault and some carnal knowledge charges) in this survey is 446. Of these, 348 cases contain sufficient additional information to determine something about the relationship between the parties. I have divided these cases into ten categories, reflecting both relationships and situations (see the appendix, table 3). It is important to note that rearranging legal categories into social categories groups crimes with a higher criminal penalty (such as rape) alongside crimes with a relatively lower one (such as indecent assault). Since it is arguable that juries were less likely to convict in cases that carried a more severe sentence, to group cases together in this way obscures other reasons, internal to the courtroom, for the pattern of conviction rates. Readers should bear this point in mind throughout this chapter. Yet I believe the patterns these social categories reveal are valuable indicators of perceptions of women, men and sexual danger which informed the decisions of judges and juries at this time.

STRANGERS

We've been told not to do this alone, and not to go down into the ravine by ourselves. There might be men down there, is what Carol says. These are not ordinary men but the other kind, the shadowy, nameless kind who do things to you.

Margaret Atwood, *Cat's Eye*

Of all the cultural stereotypes about sexual assault, perhaps the most enduring is the notion that real sexual danger awaits those women so imprudent as to venture out alone at night, take a walk through the 'wrong' neighborhood, or even forget, in their own homes, to lock a window or door before retiring. Whatever the imagined location, the villain in this scenario is always a stranger, lurking in the shadows, ready to pounce. In the past, as in the present, this image of sexual violence looms much larger than its actual occurrence.[5]

Compared to assaults committed between men and women acquainted with each other, attacks by strangers accounted for a minority of prosecutions in this survey. Then as now, more women experienced sexual assault from men they knew, even members of their family and household, than from mysterious strangers jumping out of bushes.

The image of the rapist as stranger is not, however, without some basis. One-third of these cases involved women and men with no prior relationship to each other. Of the 71 such cases, 38 involved attacks outside, 10 involved men breaking into women's homes, 4 involved women traveling in taxis or trains, and an additional 20 (10 each) involved gang rapes and attacks on children (which are analyzed separately). In the courtroom, as we have seen, women who were assaulted by strangers were the most likely to be believed. In the community, cases of assault between strangers often created intense furor and condemnation. In investigating these stories, we can begin to unravel the historical and cultural construction of rape myths and stereotypes.

The unpredictability of male sexual violence is one of its most potent weapons; in a sense women must always be on guard and are thus never on guard enough. This is especially true in the case of attacks by strangers. Most of the out-of-doors assaults occurred as women were traversing the roads and fields of rural Ontario, but not, as myth might have it, at night, and also not only when women were alone. Seventeen-year-old Janet R., for example, was walking to the post office at Brown's Bay in Muskoka District in the early evening one September in 1905 when Alexander S., a local carpenter, appeared on the road, dragged her into the bushes, and began to rip at her clothing.[6] Olive D. was out one evening with her sister near the village of Desbarats in Algoma District when Andy C., in the area to work with a Canadian Pacific Railway gang, came up from behind them and grabbed Olive's throat and "private parts."[7] One of the few cases which conforms to the stereotype was that of Maria J. of Lambton County, who was walking to her neighbor's house one Saturday night to return some smoothing irons when, she claimed, she was raped at gunpoint by George M.[8]

Isolated berry patches were particularly dangerous places. Berry picking provided children and couples with summer recreation and sometimes offered dating couples a rare moment of sexual privacy. For adult women, berry picking was an enjoyable domestic task, the product of which became a source of household income when sold or part of the family diet.[9] Because berry patches were remote and frequented mostly by women and children, they were also the site of a number of sexual assaults. Typical is the case of Mabel S., an "attractive and modest" eighteen-year-old, who was attacked by John F., a "tramp from Montreal" (another popular cultural symbol of sexual danger) at a berry patch near her farm on the outskirts of Belleville.[10] In several other cases, children and young teenagers were lured into more remote bushes by men offering to pay them to find berries.

Yet while legal records indicate the potential sexual threat in berry patches and rural roads, it seems that no such popular association was ever constructed. Only once did a legal commentator remark on this; in 1924 a judge warned women in northern Ontario about "the dangers of such occurrences on secluded roads in the sparsely settled sections of this county."[11] It is no doubt not coincidental that this warning was issued on the heels of a berry-picking incident which had as its protagonists Native men and Anglo-Saxon women and took place in a region 'known' for its immorality.[12]

The urban equivalent of the tramp in the berry patch was the street masher. And, contrary to the rural experience, social concern about urban street harassment was commonplace. A popular plot line of early U.S. motion pictures, for example, depicted women outsmarting annoying 'dudes' on the street.[13] In Ontario the labor press as well as the commercial press took up this concern. In Hamilton, for example, the *Palladium of Labor*, a Knights of Labor newspaper, commented regularly on the gangs of "dudes" and "loafers" who set upon female factory operatives on their way to and from work.[14] Street harassment was a problem not only in big cities. As Lynne Mark's recent study of leisure in small-town Ontario reveals, "loafers" and "loungers" who stood on street corners chewing tobacco and harassing female passersby on their way to church or work concerned the 'respectable' townspeople, who would have far preferred to see young men pursuing more refined amusements in churches, Mechanics Institutes, or sports teams.[15]

Serious physical abuse on the street did occur, but such events were rare. Usually street harassment in cities and towns involved men grabbing women or making insolent remarks. In Stratford in 1919, for example, eighteen-year-old Irving H. followed fourteen-year-old Agnes M. on her way home from work at a local glove factory, pushing her and taunting that her undershirt was showing. Similarly, Martin C. greeted Agnes S. with a "Hello, dearie" as he attempted to stop her on the street one evening in North Bay; for his "smart remarks" he was fined twenty-five dollars (after Agnes hit him over the head with her umbrella).[16]

The willingness of women to pursue criminal charges of street harassment by strangers suggests that women took these incidents seriously. Yet in this period the creation of urban streets as zones of moral danger dovetailed perfectly with anxieties regarding the influx of single women to the cities as well as a more generalized concern about the often raucous and public culture of the street.[17] The speed with which one or two incidents became sexual panics was startling. In at least five separate communities between 1894 and 1916, incidents of street harassment became full-blown community crises, complete with a popular villain—Jack the Hugger. Jack the Ripper, of course, has long been a symbol of sexual terror. The fact that the real Jack was never caught left behind a space, which, as Christopher Frayling suggests, has been used ever since to "accommodate the 'beasts,' 'monsters,' and 'maniacs' of the moment."[18]

Jack-the-Hugger scares were first reported in Windsor and Brantford in 1894. According to the press in neighboring Stratford, "feminine Brantford" was badly scared over the actions of Jack, who has been "carrying on his rascality for nearly two weeks." The ubiquitous umbrella surfaced again in Brantford, as one lady broke her parasol "over the scamp's head." In Woodstock in 1897, the town council offered a fifty-dollar reward for the arrest of their Jack, a man "in the habit of molesting ladies on our streets at night."[19]

The Jack scare hit northern Ontario somewhat later, and when stories began to circulate they took on the characteristics appropriate to their community. In 1907 a man who wandered immigrant neighborhoods in Port Arthur trying to kiss women was nicknamed the "Italian hugger." When Emma B. noticed a man following her in Sault Ste. Marie in 1916, she—alerted to the Jack stories circulating in her community—turned on to a more populated street, but not before the man grabbed her and told her she looked like she would "make good fucking."[20]

The contrast between the ease with which urban street harassment by strangers became a socially recognized problem and the near total public silence respecting such incidents in rural environments illuminates one central contention of this study: that the focus by turn-of-the-century social reformers on city life as synonymous with sexual danger not only obscured the class, race and gender anxieties about sexuality, but also overlooked dimensions of sexual danger in rural communities. Indeed, in the case of out-of-doors attacks by strangers, the reverse appears to be true: the women in most of the berry patch stories describe incidents of forcible sex, while the urban cases of street harassment involve relatively milder sexual conflicts; women in the city streets reported being chased, taunted, or sometimes grabbed at. But the Jack-the-Hugger scare is significant in that it was created out of what must be seen as fairly thin air. The 'script' followed by the participants in the Jack drama—along with other incidents of harassment by urban street mashers—can be read to uncover more about public responses to sexual conflicts.

Commentators often noted the effect such incidents had on women's freedom of movement. In the Brantford case the press noted that "very few of the fair sex will venture out after dark." In a strongly pitched call for stricter punishment for mashers (including the lash), a judge in North Bay insisted that "the streets must be made safe for womankind night and day."[21]

There is a curious sense of entitlement here—that women have a right to the streets—in contrast to the conventional view that good women shunned street life. Of course our context is different. A woman walking down Algoma Street in Port Arthur set off a rather different set of responses than her counterpart strutting through the Bowery district of New York City (though, to a girl from an outlying village, of course, Port Arthur might hold untold opportunities for adventure). Why, when women were harassed in the street by strangers, was the response to blame male 'loafers, scamps, and idlers' rather than to blame the victim, which in other circumstances was the more typical response? Why were no moral aspersions cast on 'brazen' street-walking women?

These questions alert us to the historical construction of masculine sexual morality. Changing patterns of leisure and amusement had an effect on both sexes, and some men's public behavior came under moral scrutiny.[22] Men had far greater latitude in negotiating a range of morally sanctioned behaviors, but here too there were limits. In a thundering sermon in 1894 about the evils of that "gregarious amusement," dancing, Reverend Mr. Salton of Stratford compared the "degree of familiarity" permissible on the dance floor with that allowed on the street:

> When a man on the street the other day, opposite the Bank of Montreal overstepped the bounds of conventionality and dared to do that which should be reserved for our intimate relations

and friends, he was rightly arrested. . . . But a person might take similar privileges in the ball room. What was lawless opposite the Bank of Montreal was lawless in the ball room. After every ball there should be a dozen "Jack the Huggers" in prison.[23]

The 'problem' of young men in public meant different things to different people. The labor movement saw such public idleness as a threat to its attempt to forge a common brotherhood through the "dignity of toil." Religious folk worried about the missed opportunities for elevation through instruction. All, however, agreed that the presence of young men in public was indeed problematic. Lynne Marks suggests that at the same time as the problem of the morally adrift single girl in the big city was vexing urban reformers, a parallel social problem in small-town Ontario was the 'wild' young man.[24] When this problem took a sexual form—the harassment of either 'maidenly working girls' or 'respectable townswomen'—women's fears were legitimated.

Yet women's morality became an element in some street harassment scenarios. One of the most effective means for a man to defend himself against any sexual crime was to suggest that the woman in question was a prostitute. One unusually vicious street masher thus defended himself against rape charges from a woman he described as an "old whore," Hattie O. Despite the fact that police found her "bruised and bloody," it appeared his version of events held sway; police investigating her background discovered that during her frequent "drunken fits" she "has the reputation of being a strumpet."[25] But what did Hattie O. in this time was not solely her reputation for immorality. Medical evidence suggested that Hattie was, in fact, raped. This fact upped the ante in her case, opening Hattie to more scrutiny and condemnation than most victims of ordinary street harassment. Most women involved in urban street-masher incidents were not touched by their assailant. One explanation, then, for the alarm bells about street mashers is that—rhetoric aside—they were seen as annoying but basically harmless fellows. They were in this sense safe targets for moral outrage. To act in a similarly forthright fashion against perpetrators of overt sexual violence—fathers, boyfriends, neighbors and bosses—was much more problematic.

Consider, too, the image of female resistance evoked by street masher stories. Clearly some women displayed a sense of street smarts, immediately turning onto more crowded streets or even fighting back with whatever weapon came to hand. Yet such stories do not convey an unambiguous image of female strength. A parasol, after all, is a flimsy, frilly instrument of self defense. There is something near comical in this image, a tension in these stories between the assertive and resourceful urban woman who defends herself and a cowering, scurrying figure, fleeing an ominous villain. Two stories from the labor press illuminate this tension nicely.

Hamilton's *Palladium of Labor* recounted the story of a woman for whom street harassment had literally fatal consequences. This woman was continually followed to and from work each day by a particularly nasty dude, who would pass and repass her on the street and "peer insolently into the girl's face." The young lady was described as having a "timid disposition" and became "much frightened." In time the woman became ill and died. According to the *Palladium*, "her death was certainly not directly caused by her fright, still there can be no doubt that the shock she received weakened her system and had a very bad effect on her illness."[26]

This story is perhaps the epitome of Victorian sexual sentimentalism. The message seems clear: women are so pure and so vulnerable that any besmirching of their honor, real or implied, could be fatal. Yet contrast this to a second story, published in the same newspaper six months later. Another girl was making her way home from work and was beset by a crowd of loafers on a street corner. One of them sidled up beside her and remarked: "It's a fine evening for a walk." Her reaction? "The response came perhaps a little more hasty and forcible than the masher anticipated. With the back of her hand, the lady gave him a whack that brought blood from his lips and probably dislocated a few teeth."[27]

These stories speak volumes about the often-contradictory sexual politics of the labor movement of the day. But they also reveal a more generalized ambiguity about women's presence in public life as well as their capacity to take care of themselves in situations of legitimate sexual danger when confronted by strangers on the street.

Another popular stereotype of strangers who might do sexual harm was the taxi driver. Judge Emily Murphy helped fuel these fears in her 'expose' of Canada's drug problem, *The Black Candle*, published in 1922. Murphy suggested that taxi drivers were moral culprits twice over: the majority of these men were "pedlars of drugs" as well as "lascivious lechers." She even produced statistics to back up her claim. Taxi drivers, she argued, made up the most numerous occupational group of fathers of illegitimate children in the province of Alberta.[28]

Like all stereotypes, this one contained a grain of reality. Four cases in this sample involved women traveling, and in three of these cases the assailant was their taxi or coach driver. Taxi drivers were also involved in cases of seduction and sexual assault in pickup and dating situations. In 1927 Hazel B. was in Fort Frances from her home at a nearby railway stop to buy supplies for her husband and family when she decided to join some friends at a dance. She arranged a ride there and back with taxi driver Francis H. On the return trip, however, Francis, after dropping off other passengers, drove Hazel past her hotel, out of town, and raped her in the back seat of the car. Thirteen-year-old Maude M. was a lone passenger on the way to visit her uncle in Perth County when the driver, thirty-one-year-old "smart looking" John H., attempted to assault her. (She was rescued when another rig pulled up.)[29]

During this period, concern about taxi drivers was part of a more widespread fear for the safety of women traveling alone. That travel might lead to harrowing sexual disasters for women was a familiar theme in social purity literature, so much so that one women's group, the YWCA, established Travelers' Aid booths at ports and railway stations to greet and protect incoming females.[30] Travel in cars or, in an earlier period, buggies often enhanced dating couples' opportunities for sexual privacy. But cars also proved potent weapons in cases of sexual assault: they could be quickly moved to the most isolated of areas, and they were difficult to escape from. Taxi drivers were hardly the only men to discover this.

The final scenario of attacks by strangers were what we would now consider breaking-and-entering stories. A significant proportion of these incidents occurred in remote corners of Ontario, while husbands were working in nearby lumber, railway or mining camps. Joseph L., for example, came to the home of Adeline D. outside Spanish Station in Algoma District, asking for a drink of water. He offered her two dollars for sex, which she refused, calling him a pig. He then attacked her. Perhaps out of some perverse acknowledgment of the fact that she was eight months pregnant, Joseph offered Adeline a choice between oral and vaginal intercourse.[31] Announcing himself as Jack the Ripper, James R. entered the home of an older woman, Jane B., in Norfolk County, beat her severely, threw her on her bed and raped her.[32] While the vast majority of assaults that took place in women's homes were perpetrated by male family members or friends, strangers sometimes abused women they found at home alone and often did so with particular force.

GANG RAPE

If rape itself is emblematic of terror for women, then gang rape is its apotheosis. Clearly much of this fear stems from the impossibility of resistance or escape from such situations. Today this crime evokes a moral revulsion comparable to that usually reserved for assaults against children or the elderly. During the late 1800s and early 1900s, however, there was a surprising matter-of-factness about gang rape, related perhaps to the 'sort' of woman—young, single, often alone—who was victimized.

Few crimes illustrate the relationship between female dependence and sexual violence so clearly, for the victims of gang rape tended to be particularly vulnerable women. Seventeen-year-old Mary T., for example, had been in Kingston two months, after leaving her home in Elgin. She had worked at a series of domestic and factory jobs, but one evening in February 1908, jobless and desperate, she was sleeping in an abandoned steamer in the harbor and had not eaten for some time. She explained her predicament to James C., whom she met one Saturday evening on Ontario Street. James gave her fifty cents, and she promptly went out and bought herself two restaurant meals. She then accompanied him to a coal shanty. Sex was likely the price of James's earlier largesse, but it is just as likely that Mary had not anticipated that anyone else would be involved. When they entered the shanty, however, there were three other men waiting, who kicked and slapped her into submission. She was raped by the four of them.[33] Several other gang rape victims were homeless girls who had recently been banished (for committing minor moral infractions) by angry fathers; one was a deaf mute cook on a schooner in Lake Ontario; one was a domestic servant raped by her employer's son and his friends. Whether the women were 'good girls' or 'bad,' a common characteristic was vulnerability.

A significantly high number of gang rape victims were 'bad.' Mary T., as we have seen, transgressed several moral boundaries: she was a young girl alone in a city, she was poor, and she probably traded sex for money. Velma S. was caught having sex with her boyfriend in his car on a deserted stretch of road outside Sarnia by a gang of men who had just ended an evening of beer and baseball. Initially pretending to be police, four of them beat up Velma's boyfriend and raped her.[34] Addie W. was forced by her boyfriend to row with him and another man to an island off Gananoque where she was attacked by eight men, some of whom she had been caught socializing with by police, in a "deserted place," earlier. Helen K. broke a cardinal rule of sexual safety by accepting a car ride home from her waitress job in Fort William. She extracted a promise from the two men driving her that they would not "do anything bad," but they raped her anyway. It was, she told police afterward, her first chance to ride in an automobile.[35]

Necking in a car, socializing with a bad crowd, or accepting a ride from a stranger—any of these might be as injurious to one's character, and as dangerous, as being homeless and hungry. It was not, as the *Brockville Recorder* sniffed, that a jury should be skeptical of the testimony of Addie W., "who was willing to go in a boat with two men in the middle of the night."[36] Bad girls were no more willing victims of gang rape than good girls; but bad girls, who took more risks and hence had a more tenuous grip on respectability, were easier prey.

PICKUPS AND WHITE SLAVERS

Sexual assaults against women arising from what today we would call pickups formed a small (fourteen instances) group of cases. Pickup situations shared some of the features of street attacks by strangers and some of the features of date rape. They might involve couples who met at a dance or party and left together or, more often, men who met women on the street or in a park. Unlike attacks by strangers, assaults in this scenario were preceded by some degree of sociability: a walk, a car ride, maybe a dance. Yet unlike date rape, these were not the result of friendship or courtship. Like some of the women who had been gang raped, women who were assaulted after a pickup broke a crucial social convention for which they paid dearly: they talked to a stranger.

Mary P. was an eighteen-year-old factory worker, recently arrived in Peterborough from England, to join her parents. One Friday evening at the end of May 1907 she had a date with a fellow to go to a concert. She waited for him for an hour outside the opera house, but, according to Mary, he stood her up. She had started for home when she was approached by Hubert M., who asked her for a walk. She accompanied him to Jackson Park, where he raped her. He chided her for resisting, telling her that "all the girls do it." At her request he then walked her home and asked her for another date. She refused, telling him she thought her father would not allow it.[37]

As this story illustrates, cases of pickup rape contain many conflicting overtones. It is indeed likely that this story would not have become a case at all, but for Mary's mother discovering her stained chemise the next day and "charging her with committing herself." It is possible, as Hubert told police, that Mary was "willing enough" and changed her story when caught by her parents; this was and remains a common male defense. It is also possible that what Mary was looking for that evening was some companionship and flirtation, particularly after being disappointed by her date. Her desires may or may not have included sex in a park.

Similarly ambiguous was the case of Agot D. and Julia O., two Swedish immigrants. They approached James B. one evening on the streetcar in Ottawa, asking him for directions to a friend's house. He offered to walk them there, and on the way invited them to warm themselves with "hot scotches" in his hotel room, which they did. The numerical balance of power in favor of the women ended when the three were joined by Walter R., the hotel's proprietor, in James's room. When Walter locked the door behind him, sociability ended and coercion began.[38]

Sexual assault was not the only dangerous outcome of accepting a social invitation from a stranger. Several pickup cases were reported explicitly as stories of white slavery. Mary S., of Victoria Mines, outside Sudbury, was approached by two men who promised her twenty-five dollars a week if she'd join them in New York and "go on the stage" (both—New York and the theater—potent yet thrilling signifiers of danger). Mary played the part of hapless victim well, and she agreed to join the men. In order to avoid detection, she walked from Victoria Mines to the next town to catch the train. This melodrama, however, had a happy ending. Somehow Mary's plans were detected and she was rescued by a Victoria Mines constable before—to quote the magistrate who charged her with vagrancy—"she was swallowed up in the hungry pit that engulfs young girls, with an ever increasing appetite."[39] At the height of the social purity movement, newspapers abounded with similar stories, of immigrant girls held captive in hotel rooms or girls lured to the wilds of northern Ontario under the guise of respectable employment. Whether these were the fanciful speculations of reporters, tales crafted by women to make their stories more believable in the courtroom, or, for that matter, the gospel truth, the popular flurry of white slave scripts put a new spin on an old story and indicates once again how the prevailing sexual climate might influence both social and self-definitions of sexual conflict. I have already noted that the general conviction rate for crimes of sexual violence in this sample increased considerably during the height of the white slave panic, as did arrests of women in urban centers for prostitution and vagrancy. What is interesting about moments of moral panic such as the white slave scare, as many historians have noted, is not whether white slavery really existed, but rather how a moral panic becomes so spectacularly successful in changing the sexual climate of the day.

Like some of the women in gang rape cases, women who were picked up were very often women alone—sometimes just for an evening downtown, sometimes alone in a new country. This gave them unprecedented freedom and allowed for a rich and varied social life. But it also made their lives, and especially their social lives, more complicated. It has always been difficult to judge strangers. Who could be trusted? How could a woman tell who might offer her an evening of fun, or a ticket out of a stifling small town, from someone who might rape her in a locked hotel room? What would she do if her sexual secrets came under the prying eyes of her mother? As Christine Stansell notes, "the working girl who made known her independence or even her aloneness could still be interpreted as issuing a sexual invitation. . . . A woman alone on the street might really just be asking for directions—but then again, she could be looking for some kind of sexual adventure."[40]

DATE RAPE

Sexual assault perpetrated by boyfriends included many of the ambiguous complications of pickup rapes and added a few new ones. In six of the forty date rape cases, for example, the women became pregnant. In many incidents, charges were pressed by anxious parents; the women themselves were reluctant witnesses. The introduction, in 1886, of seduction legislation in Canada contributed to this confusion. Often no clear distinction existed between an incident that might result in a rape as opposed to a seduction charge.

Legal classifications aside, we can discern two broad types of date rape: those with some overtones of consent (which often existed alongside other contradictory concerns, such as pregnancy, age differences, parental or community judgment, and the man's marital status) and those whose predominant overtones indicated assault. This categorization raises many potential problems. The argument that women lie about their experience of rape—particularly when telling the truth might compromise their own moral or social standing—has been made by accused men and defense lawyers for generations. Contemporary feminists identify this argument as a classic rape myth. In suggesting that some stories of date rape contain overtones of consent or mutuality, I do not intend to reproduce one of many misogynist stereotypes that have arisen about the crime of rape. I am also aware of the difficulties of using language containing words such as 'consent.' This discourse, steeped in liberal notions of self-determining individuals, is clearly out of step with the realities of nineteenth-century women's experience of sex.[41]

The belief that women lie about rape to protect their sexual reputation is not of recent origin; it was a powerful shield that saved many of the men in this study from jail. Thus one must probe court records carefully. Often the suggestion of consent or mutuality arose solely as a legal defense, and no evidence of it existed in the testimony of the woman or other witnesses, nor would an interpretation of consent seem to correspond to the situation described. Often two distinct versions of the story could be found in both the legal recording and the press accounts of the sexual assault. And both were noteworthy in their formulation of completely helpless females and completely villainous men (or the reverse). However, glimmers of contradiction also emerged from the melodramatic facades of purity and villainy. These complications make these tales more troublesome to sort out, but they are vastly more interesting than straightforward stories of men claiming consent and women claiming force, in as much as they open out into wider meanings of sexuality and gender relations. Finally, these ambiguities alert us once again to the difficulties in coming to terms with the historical meaning of rape.

The story of Einaria K. and Taimi M. of Levack (near Sudbury) is a case in point. The two left a dance together one July evening in 1929, Einaria having offered to walk Taimi home. They ended up spending several hours together, walking around town, kissing on empty doorsteps, and finally having sex in the bush. When Taimi arrived home late and disheveled, her foster mother immediately whipped her, learned her story, and called the police. Einaria was arrested within an hour.

This story contains several complications. Even on the witness stand, Taimi described their time together as mutually desired: she left the dance with Einaria because she liked him, and she agreed under questioning that she was "infatuated" with him. She did not object to his kisses and didn't yell when he was "putting it in" because she "liked it." Asked the defense lawyer: "You wanted to be with him . . . you wanted him to fondle you and love you and all kinds of things didn't you?" "Yes," she replied.[42]

The problem was this: Taimi was a fourteen-year-old girl, and Einaria was an older, married man with children of his own. The age difference did not transgress the standards of the Finnish community of the time. But in the eyes of the law, Einaria's marital status made both of them morally culpable: she for seducing and attempting to "steal away" a married man (his version of events), he for failing to show proper "chivalry and protection" to an "innocent young girl" (the judge's version).[43] Einaria was found guilty.

A more clear-cut story of sexual assault is found in the case of Ila G. and Percy B., a couple who dated in the summer of 1927 in Orangeville. Ila and her friend (and fellow mill worker) Alice met Percy and his friend one evening at the Gem Theatre. Percy and Ila had met each other previously at a dance and had dated since then. After the show the couples paired off as they walked toward the girls' boardinghouse. As they approached a stretch of woods, Percy pulled Ila down and threatened to choke her if she yelled. According to Ila, he "did not stop until he satisfied himself." Despite a barrage of hostile questions from the defense lawyer, Ila maintained her story that she had not wanted sex: she had not promised sex during an earlier date, she had warned him before "what would happen if he touched me," and she did not invite him to continue walking her home after the rape. (She responded coolly, "I did not walk with him. He came with me.") She was, according to the *Orangeville Sun*, a "splendid witness."[44]

Other interpretive issues must be considered when contrasting these two stories. We should not overlook the fact that the first one involved Finns in northern Ontario, a setting ripe for wrongs, touching on a region and an ethnic group with equally 'bad' reputations. Taimi's first sin was to admit to feelings for a married man, though as a young immigrant (and likely orphan) girl, she was also no doubt susceptible to the badgering of her foster mother, then police and defense lawyers. All of this marked her in particular ways. Ila G., in contrast, was clearly a respectable working girl from a southern Ontario farm family. Perhaps due to these cultural advantages, she pursued her case quite purposefully, returning three or four times to the home of the local police officer before she found someone who would hear her complaint. On the witness stand she kept her head and displayed a remarkable sense of control.

In attempting to understand the place of sexual conflict in heterosexual romance, the two stories indicate some basic themes. When the couple was known to each other through a romantic relationship, sexual assault was not likely to be the surprise attack it might be from a stranger. As British historian Francoise Barret-Ducrocq also found, working-class youth in this period socialized in a "climate of mingled love and mistrust."[45] Conflict and negotiation around sex informed the social lives of many young couples. Some of these stories reveal clear instances of sexual violation. Then as now, many men had a hard time understanding that no means no. But in the patriarchal and rigidly moralistic world of turn-of-the-century Ontario, yes could only safely mean yes in tightly proscribed situations, typically marriage. Otherwise, women's own desires could get them into trouble. It was not that women cried rape out of vengeance, malice or mischief. Rather, involvement in a sexual altercation with a boyfriend made women targets for public moral scrutiny and humiliation. Even a guilty verdict could not completely erase this image.

NEIGHBORS/FAMILY FRIENDS

Neighbors accounted for forty-six sexual assaults, and friends of husbands or of families accounted for another twenty-three. Women were assaulted by men they knew at social events such as picnics, in vehicles after accepting a ride home from work or school, at the home of family friends, or at their own homes when friends were visiting them. Assaults by neighbors shared similarities to attacks by strangers: they happened out-of-doors, in streets, roads, railway tracks, cow fields and berry patches.

In many such situations, sexual violence was part of a campaign of harassment by neighborhood bullies against young women. Mildred D. was dragged to a field and raped by Albert B. one evening on her way home from church in 1896, despite the fact that, having been chased by him before, she always made a point of running when she got to his farm. Bessie B., a fourteen-year-old girl from outside Brockville, was similarly terrorized by her neighbor, James M. Several times he hid behind his fence and jumped her as she was walking home from school. After a struggle, she always managed to break away. On one such occasion he grabbed her and threw her down in a field of clover, exclaiming, "by Jesus, I will fuck you if I die." He released her when he spotted someone approaching down the road, but he threatened to get her again the next day. She had not told anyone about these assaults before because she was so afraid of him, but this time her fear of attack prevailed; she told her aunt (with whom she lived) as soon as she got home.[46] In cities and towns, doorways, alleyways or shared outhouses offered convenient and private hiding places for neighborhood bullies to lay in wait.

Rarely was a neighborhood bully demonized to the extent that a menacing stranger might be. When an errant neighborhood man did catch the attention of the community, his actions were perceived as troublesome, but not overly dangerous. Frank A.'s habit of "loafing around" and begging had earned him the nickname of Charlie Chaplin in his hometown of Alexandria, near Cornwall. He was, according to the justice of the peace, "not all there," but essentially he was a "harmless fellow." When Agnes Q. complained that he followed her home from church and succeeded in knocking her down and molesting her, he was arrested, but local authorities suggested that he "was not fully responsible for his actions" and should be given "good employment" rather than a jail term.[47] The difference between this case and the Jack-the-Hugger stories illustrates the exaggeration of strangers as sources of sexual harm. Frank A. was known by everyone in the community. Despite the fact that his actual behavior was as intrusive as that of many of the Jacks (much more so than some), he was not turned into an object of fear (except, of course, by Agnes Q.). Charlie Chaplin, after all, was a popular and folksy figure, evoking none of the sexual terror associated with Jack the Ripper.

Assaults by men who were friends of husbands or families are more difficult to analyze. A significant number of these occurred between married women and men who were former boyfriends, or who had flirted with these women in their husbands' absence. Many of these men claimed in their defense that they were having affairs with these women and that criminal charges were merely a ruse to placate jealous husbands. While this defense constructs women as 'bad girls' twice over—as sexual beings and as cheating wives—it is not inconceivable that married women engaged in extramarital sex. One case near Whitby involved a married woman who was pregnant as a result of her liaison; she stated flatly that she would not have told her husband or the police about her relationship if she had not become pregnant. Similarly, Martha O. admitted she brought charges against Benjamin A. because her husband had seen Benjamin leaving her bedroom and threatened to divorce her. She took legal action, she said, to "set things right."[48] Bigamy and murder cases also tell stories of women who took the risks involved in becoming an unfaithful wife.

A second pattern of assaults in this category were those involving men who knew the woman's husband in a work context. These could be either co-workers or, more ominous, the husband's employer. Lewis T. was in a position of authority several times over vis-à-vis Regina S.: he was her husband's boss, and he was landlord to the family of five. After Lewis attacked her (in view of her children) while inspecting their Ottawa apartment in

1915, Regina's husband insisted she remain silent about it. It was only after her husband lost his job (and she contracted venereal disease) that charges were laid.[49]

The reactions of husbands figure prominently in assessing the experience of assault on married women. In one sense it scarcely matters whether consenting overtones were real or not, for exposure to one's husband was a serious threat. The consequences for women caught in an extramarital affair were severe: moral condemnation, abandonment, even, as we shall see, murder. Much like parents of unmarried women, husbands acted as the first judge of these cases. Their reactions helped determine whether the story was framed as an assault demanding criminal charges or an affair ending in divorce or revenge. Husbands also determined whether to pursue punishment through the legal system. Years after the law was changed so that the aggrieved party in rape cases was no longer the father or husband but the woman herself, male family members continued to exert an enormous influence.

WORK-RELATED ASSAULTS

The sexual danger of the workplace was a familiar topic to social reformers of the period. What we would call sexual harassment never quite received top billing in social purity campaigns; prostitution, racial purity and commercial amusements all proved more sensational items. But the links (both real and imagined) between women's paid work and a variety of moral dangers is a recurrent theme in the history of women's labor.

The labor movement was a prolific commentator on the sexual dangers of the workplace and, not surprisingly, saw the issue exclusively through a class lens. Highlighting the extent to which prostitution eclipsed other sexual dangers, some in the labor movement sketched a parallel between workplace immorality and other vices. "It is no wonder," exclaimed Hamilton's *Palladium of Labor* in 1885, "that wealthy libertines and those who pander to their lusts find in the shops and factories where the hellish avarice of soulless capitalists has ground down wages to starvation point, recruiting grounds for the great army of unfortunates."[50] Throughout the 1880s, Leonora Barry, women's organizer for the Knights of Labor, made it part of her job to warn fathers and brothers to protect 'their' women from the advances of unscrupulous bosses. Similar sentiments were voiced in subsequent decades by other labor and socialist parties.[51]

Mainstream moral reformers also took up the question of sexual danger in the workplace. Members of the federal government's Royal Commission studying "Relations of Labour and Capital" in the 1880s were especially concerned about such moral problems as separate washroom facilities for women and men in factories.[52] The difference, however, between working-class and dominant discourse about workplace sexuality was that working-class men claimed 'their' women did not like it.

There has long been a popular association of working-class women and sexual immorality. This image of working-class women as "moral pollutants" can, according to historian Frank Mort, explain the obsessive concern evinced by state investigative bodies about the moral tenor of factories. Such moral regulation, argues Mort, formed a "middle-class bid for cultural hegemony over key areas of personal and domestic life."[53] In their construction of the exploitative libertine boss, labor spokespeople began to articulate a sexual discourse that resisted hegemonic notions about working-class, and especially female working-class, depravity.

This helps explain a curious dimension of working-class discussions of sexual danger on the job, which have generally focused strictly on factory employment. Indeed, when the Knights of Labor campaigned in the 1880s to expand the seduction law to cover seduction in the workplace, they suggested specifically that the law apply to factories and workshops. Potential sexual dangers in the most populated female employment, domestic service, were eclipsed by concerns about the factory. More attention was paid to the moral suitability of a prospective servant than her employer.[54]

Domestic service, while well populated, was not well liked. Domestic labor on farms was especially disliked. The combination of overwork, low pay, boredom, and lack of privacy and amusements took its toll; by the late 1920s the Ontario government described farm domestics as a "genus extinct."[55] Yet rarely, it seemed, did commentators include sexual harassment as a factor in the declining popularity of domestic service.

Legal records tell another story. In this sample, domestic servants accounted for over one-half of the victims of workplace assault. Contrary, it would appear, to the British experience, most of these assaults took place between servants and their employers (or sometimes brothers or sons of employers). Only a few occurred between fellow laborers.[56] Yet few of these employers corresponded to the labor movement's image of the exploitative capitalist. In rural Ontario, domestic servants were often recruited from among neighboring farm families of similar class background. Most of these servants were young women, often called in by a neighboring family for a short period, to assist, for example, during an illness or pregnancy.

Neighborliness, however, was no guarantee of sexual safety. Rural live-in domestic servants found themselves in a position of extreme vulnerability. Seventeen-year-old Alice H. was repeatedly harassed by her employer, William M., who would wake her up each morning by entering her bedroom, shaking her shoulders, and sometimes climbing into bed with her. She complained to his wife, who dismissed it as "teasing." After one encounter, during which he both "knocked her around" and "hoisted her clothing," Alice decided she'd had enough. The two families were neigh-bors, but Alice had no means of traveling the five miles home until her next regularly scheduled visit, when her parents came to pick her up. The next Sunday Alice tearfully told her mother her story and insisted that she was so afraid of her employer that she would not return.[57] Many other domestic servants were forced to stay in similar situations, either because they needed to collect unpaid wages, or they had no job or home to go to, or their isolation made escape impossible. Tochka K., a Ukrainian immigrant, spent the winter of 1914 literally trapped in a lumber camp north of Nipigon, where she was employed as a cook. The first evening she spent there she was raped by her boss, Louis S., who threatened that she would be "eaten by wolves" if she tried to leave. Four months later she escaped, pregnant, and filed charges.[58]

Domestic service was not the only employment situation that might re-sult in sexual conflict. Waitresses and secretaries also reported incidents of assault, and several women were assaulted in their workplace as a result of encounters with grocery delivery clerks, store keepers and peddlars. Two cases involved doctors and patients, and one involved a teacher and his stu-dent. But the predominance of assaults involving domestic servants and their employers in this survey is striking, particularly when set against the relative public silence surrounding this particular sexual liaison.

Part of the reason for this pattern emerges from the history of domestic service itself. Structural and ideological constraints have historically hin-dered domestic servants from organizing on their own behalf (with the exception of women from highly organized and politicized ethnic commu-nities, such as the Finns).[59] In part, then, the sexual exploitation of domestic servants did not emerge as an issue because domestic servants themselves did not emerge as a collective force capable of articulating their own griev-ances.

The boisterous factory girl became a symbol of female independence and, sometimes, immorality. Historically her life appears to have been quite different from that of the deferential and closely supervised domestic ser-vant. Neither, however, was immune from unwanted sexual advances from her employers. It is difficult to know which occupational group experienced more harassment. But factory girls were able to draw on an array of individ-ual and collective measures to resist employer harassment: they gathered support from female co-workers; they attempted to have their unions take up the issue; sometimes they even used sexual grievances as the basis for strike action.[60] Failing any of these, they could simply move on and not show up for work the next day. Domestic servants, particularly those in farm households, were thought to be safe, protected from the rough world of the factory. Yet living in close proximity to their employers, often some distance away from family or friends, and socially isolated from the people with whom they worked, rural domestic servants had little protection from unwanted sexual advances. Since the prevailing sexual ethos did not recognize families and households as sites of sexual danger, we should not be surprised that this received minimal public airing.

CHILDREN

Childhood is a relatively recent phenomenon. And the association of children with sexual innocence was a key stage in the historical formation of a distinct concept of childhood.[61] Michel Foucault has argued that changing perceptions of child sexuality were accomplished not by simple repression or avoidance, but through the proliferation of new "discourses of sex," directed at ensuring that what he terms "youth's universal sin" would not be practiced.[62]

Canadian history shows that the extent to which children's sexual innocence was believed and protected depended very much on their class and gender. For example, a major task of the movement to 'rescue' needy children in nineteenth-century Canada was to attend to their moral needs. Children's health, education or other aspects of their social welfare took a back seat to concerns about their moral environment. The class dimensions here are clear; the child rescue movement represents another example of what Frank Mort identifies as the intrusion by the middle class into the lives of the poor. For poor children, immorality and delinquency were inextricably linked, as though the poor, by being poor, were more prone to sexual deviance. Yet the morality of poor children was sexualized in gender-specific ways. Poor boys had a number of ways to go astray, chief among them thieving, truancy, trespassing and public vandalism. Female juvenile delinquents were defined predominantly in sexual terms: they became pregnant or they became prostitutes.[63]

It is telling that in this study almost all of the charges of sexual assault against children were brought after 1893, after establishment of the Children's Aid Society. Yet to view this trend solely as unwanted intrusion is to ignore the reality of sexual exploitation experienced by girls and the complexity of relations between the state and the family. Middle-class rescue agencies, despite their obvious class and race biases, could provide real assistance, and as other historians have shown, their intervention was often actively sought by working-class mothers.[64]

Sexual assaults against female children conform to the general pattern of assaults: mostly they were committed by men the girls knew. Of the 39 assaults against children, 26 were committed by neighbors, farmhands or family friends, 10 were committed by strangers. When one includes assaults against children committed by family members (examined below), the number of cases in which the girls were acquainted with their assailants increases even more dramatically. I have (somewhat arbitrarily) defined as children those twelve years of age and under. The youngest child in this sample was three years old.

One striking similarity among many of these cases is that men used money or other goods, rather than force, to extract sexual compliance from children. Sixty-seven-year-old John O., for example, offered twelve-year-old Marceline S., the daughter of his tenant, anything she liked in the Eaton's department store catalog in return for sex. Joseph S., a fifty-five-year-old single paper-mill worker in Sault Ste. Marie, regularly had sex with eight to ten young girls (all under the age of twelve) in return for nickels and trips to the movies.[65] Such scenarios often reveal a matter-of-factness about sex on the part of children. Rarely did children rush home tearfully to recount stories of sexual assault to their parents. Rather, children's sexual activity was usually discovered inadvertently. Sometimes a child's money or new goods caught the attention of parents; seven-year-old Vera N.'s experience was uncovered when she came home with a nickel and offered to buy her parents ice cream.[66] Other times, mothers noticed their daughters' irritated vagina or stained clothing, or venereal disease.

This matter-of-factness could be read as evidence of the triumph of childish sexual innocence. Perhaps children were so removed from the sexual world that they could not recognize sex even when it was happening to them. There is, however, much conflicting evidence. How, for example, do we understand the experience of eleven-year-old Ellen M., who described willingly accepting her adult neighbor's offer to "come down the hill, have a good time, and look at his big thing," and admitted that she would not have told her mother had she not been spotted by another neighbor? How can we account for the fact that several children reported, when caught, that they had had several previous sexual experiences? How are we to understand mothers such as Elizabeth H., whose initial response to the hired man was to give him a "talking to" when she caught him with her four-year-old daughter Lucy, her clothes unbuttoned, in the outhouse? (Criminal charges were brought some time later, after Elizabeth caught him atop her daughter in a field.) What should we make of George T., who attempted to defend himself from indecent assault charges by claiming he had been "seduced" by two six-year-olds; or the crown attorney in Joseph S.'s case, who acknowledged that "no harm had come" to any of the girls he had bribed into sex?[67]

Children, declared concerned novelist Susanna Moodie in the early nineteenth century, did not exist in Canada. A boy quickly became a "miniature man," and a Canadian girl was a "gossiping flirt, full of vanity and affectation, with a premature love of finery and an acute perception of the advantages to be derived from wealth."[68] Working-class children were subject to some of the same moral stereotypes as their parents. Those children who found themselves in the criminal courts and child rescue agencies at this time had yet to learn a critical tenet of patriarchal sexual ideology—shame. This was not because, as some would have it, their parents were neglectful or 'depraved' themselves. Rather, it reflects more widely held notions about working-class childhood. Despite legislative reforms in the areas of compulsory education and child labor earlier in the century, the notion that children were merely small workers had not ceased, particularly in working-class families.[69] And in this culture, working-class children's bodies were not sanctified in the realm of labor or sexuality. We can glimpse in these cases a multifaceted struggle, between girls, their parents, the courts and accused men, over competing definitions of children's sexuality and respectability.

Many of the contradictions and double standards surrounding children and sex were highlighted in a particularly scandalous case which took place in Cochrane in 1928. Ward W., the town's Anglican minister, was accused of having sex with two young girls from the community, in the church basement. According to twelve-year-old Theta H., Ward initiated the sexual encounters, offering her a dime in return for a kiss. Gradually their physical relationship grew to include intercourse, for which he paid fifty cents. Theta described how she and her ten-year-old friend, Grace B., would visit Ward at the church when they wanted money to go to the movies. It is unclear how the relationship ended, though Theta admitted she was afraid it "might get us in wrong or something." It is also unclear how the affair came to light. Theta's family moved out of the province shortly after the encounters ceased, and Theta's mother first knew of it when two police officers arrived at her home to question her. The minister's defenders hinted darkly at a conspiracy: the charges, according to the Anglican bishop, were "a work of spite on the part of an enemy of a year's standing."[70]

To this point, the story seems to fit the conventional script about sexual encounters with children: an older man bribes a sexually precocious, calculating young girl. The story, however, took on significant class overtones. Less than a week after his arrest, the minister's congregation jammed the parish hall to hear the town mayor and the bishop sing his praises. The mayor pronounced the accused man "one of the best men and hardest workers the Church ever has had" and called his detractors "the devil." Over three hundred dollars were raised for his legal defense. Theta H. and her family were portrayed as immoral, unrepentant liars. Attempts were made to portray Theta as a classic 'bad girl,' who smoked, got low marks in school, and had lots of boyfriends. Theta's teacher reported on her poor grades and spotty attendance record. Many members of the town's middle class came to court to speak on W.'s behalf, including Mrs. Ivy, wife of the mayor and leader of the church's women's auxiliary, who announced she was satisfied to leave her daughter in the minister's care. Following the popular stereotype linking poverty, overcrowding, and incest, Theta and her mother were questioned at length about the number of beds in their household, to which Mrs. H. replied coldly, "you cannot always have big accommodations if you are a poor family."[71] The subtext was clear: whatever had transpired in that church basement, Theta H. was to blame. She accepted money; she was an incorrigible girl; she was poor. The crown attorney's suggestion that the Anglican bishop used his power over the dispersal of Mothers' Allowance benefits to force Grace B.'s mother to drop her charges, and to silence other mothers who might have corroborated Theta's story, got nowhere. The minister was found not guilty.[72]

Notions of propriety and sexual innocence affected girls and boys differently. Most prosecutions for same-sex sexual offenses (variously, charges of gross indecency, indecent assault and buggery) involved adult men who had had sex with boys usually between the ages of ten and fourteen. These cases share some similarities with heterosexual encounters. Boys were always rewarded with cash or goods, often sports equipment. The tenor of the stories and the treatment of the victims, however, were markedly different. Ten-year-old Allan R., for example, a newsboy in Sault Ste. Marie, calmly described meeting Charles B. on the street corner and being asked if he wanted to earn a nickel. Allan followed the man to his hotel room, where Allan fondled his "tool." Eleven-year-old Ernest J. told the court about meeting Alex W., who "asked me for a fuck. I said I would give him one" (in return for a hockey stick).[73] Like many of the girls, these boys were remarkably matter-of-fact about their experiences. Yet the boys were treated differently on the witness stand: they were asked few badgering or shaming questions in court. The boys were never asked about their sexual or moral pasts, there was no attempt to position them as the seducer, and their willingness to exchange sex for money did not overshadow the crime itself. Homosexual offenses were not, of course, treated with lenience in this period. But male children were much more likely than females to be believed and taken seriously when they reported a sexual encounter with an adult.

Women had to fit rigidly circumscribed boundaries of victimhood, so it is no surprise that female children too faced misogynistic sexual double standards. But whether assaults were committed by respectable pillars of the community or single laboring men in their own working-class neighborhoods, whether girls were left severely traumatized by the incidents or merely a few pennies richer, poor girls neither experienced themselves nor were they treated as sexual innocents.

FAMILY AND HOUSEHOLD MEMBERS

Assaults committed by one household member on another account for the largest single category of sexual crimes in this study—sixty-six instances. One-third of these cases involve such household members as boarders and farmhands; the rest are family members. Uncles, stepbrothers and cousins accounted for one-third of these assaults, while fathers, stepfathers and adoptive fathers made up the rest.

Assaults by men who were farmhands, boarders or extended family members share some of the features of attacks by neighbors or friends. Farmhands and boarders took advantage of the temporary absence of husbands or parents (who were away working or in town for supplies) to assault wives or daughters. The potential for sexual harm from men living in close proximity was clearly on the minds of many parents. Helen L. never left her twenty-seven-year-old "weak minded" daughter Ella alone on the farm without either locking her in the house or leaving her sixteen-year-old son to supervise. Despite these precautions her farmhand Sylvester S. managed to talk his way into the house one afternoon while Helen was in town and the boy was working in the fields, and attacked Ella.[74]

The flip side of the danger of hired men and boarders was their romantic promise, particularly for women living on isolated farms. Some of these cases began as flirtations between the men and daughters (or sometimes wives) of the family. The moral problem posed by the presence of unmarried male boarders in families, particularly female-headed single-parent families, became a concern for social reformers. Officials in child rescue agencies in Boston during this period frowned on the practice of taking in boarders on the grounds that they might prove an "immoral influence." In Ontario, architects of the first Mothers' Allowance policy considered adopting a clause, which some U.S. policies included, disqualifying from benefits single women who took in boarders.[75]

When men and women were related by blood, however, little moral concern about the mingling of the sexes arose, either from state officials or within individual families. The presumed moral safety of families afforded cousins, uncles and in-laws unsupervised access to female relatives. Eighteen-year-old Agnes C. traveled to her brother-in-law's home in a neighboring town to take over management of the household during her sister's absence. While she was housecleaning, Kenneth M., her brother-in-law, claimed what he clearly deemed his right of sexual initiation: he raped her and afterward told her she had been "broken in." Marie A., who lived with her mother and stepfather in an isolated mining camp in Algoma District, was assaulted by both her cousin and uncle during one of her mother's periodic absences.[76]

It is in the sexual relations between fathers and daughters that we most clearly see the connections between the privacy and presumed moral sanctity of the family and its capacity for secret sexual abuse. Linda Gordon, in her sensitively written account of the history of incest, has argued that the experience of incest puts female children in an impossibly contradictory position: they must reconcile the demands of being chaste and virtuous with the equally strong cultural imperative to obey one's father.[77] Most women dealt with this dilemma through silence.

In a few instances, incestuous assaults appear to be unplanned attacks. One evening William E.'s alcoholic rage forced his wife to flee the family home, leaving him alone with their five children. After he quieted down and the rest of the family went to bed, William accosted his fifteen-year-old daughter, Loretta. He shoved her onto his bed and raped her, threatening to cut her throat if she screamed.[78] Yet such scenarios were in the minority. The more typical pattern of father/daughter incest was a sustained and secret period of sexual relations, which might last several months or many years. Such relationships look very different from usual sexual assaults and pose a number of difficult interpretative problems. Gordon has suggested that historians must accept a certain amount of ambiguity in coming to terms with cases of incest from the past. "One of the most complicated and painful aspects of incestuous sex," she writes, is that it cannot be said to be motivated only by hostility or to be experienced simply as abuse."[79]

A case in point is the story of fifteen-year-old Ruby B. and her stepfather, Samuel S. Samuel had married Ruby's mother when Ruby was three years old and had, she said, been "using her as a woman" since she was nine. Their sexual relationship continued on and off for six years, even after Ruby left home to work, when she and Samuel continued to exchange sentimental post cards. Margaret W.'s father, John P., had been sexual with her "ever since she could remember," but she felt safe enough to lay charges only after two other significant events in her life: her marriage and the death of her mother. Neither marriage nor adulthood necessarily freed women from sexual obligations to their father. The most long-term case of incest involved William F. and his forty-one-year-old daughter, Florence, who had remained at home to keep house for him after the death of her mother. A sexual relationship, she finally told a neighbor, had been maintained for eleven years.[80]

Some men took advantage of the periodic absence of mothers to initiate sex with their children, and some mothers took immediate action when daughters revealed their stories. But not all relationships occurred in secrecy, and not all mothers chose public disclosure and punishment as a solution. Ruby B.'s mother, for example, had seen Samuel S. hugging, kissing and lying on the bed with her daughter, but assumed it was "all in fun."

Josephine F.'s mother refused to believe her daughter when she confessed that her father, Angus, had "made a woman out of her." "I did not believe it" she testified, "I could not believe it." (The jury, in this instance, sided with Angus and released him. Two years later the family was back in court; Josephine had become pregnant by her father and had killed the infant at birth.) Eva V.'s mother probably spoke for many when she explained her silence over her daughter's abuse: "I was" she said simply, "powerless to stop it."[81]

A mother's silent complicity could serve, in the eyes of the community, to displace culpability from the man involved. Ellen M. and her daughter, Penny, lived for many years with Allen B., a farmer in Perth County. Ellen worked as a domestic servant; she was also, in the words of the press, his paramour. In 1894, twelve-year-old Penny blamed Allen for her pregnancy, claiming they had been having sex regularly in the barn. Penny insisted her mother knew about these liaisons, but in court Ellen denied it, hinting instead that a passing peddlar was responsible for Penny's condition. It was rumored Ellen was worried that legal intervention would deprive her and her daughter of a home, but authorities saw only immorality. The crown accused her of "heartless neglect of and unnatural indifference to her child," and the judge denounced her conduct in "scathing terms." The Stratford press regretted that no legal punishment would come to Ellen, for "bad and all as was B.'s crime, it did not approach in heartlessness that of the girl's mother."[82]

Mother blaming in instances of incest was (and remains) persistent.[83] The most extreme case of a villainized mother—and of child sexual abuse— was that of the Robinson family who lived outside Sudbury. It provoked an enormous hue and cry, in the press, in judicial circles, and among women's groups, and I return to this story in my investigation of sexual scandal. The basic story is as follows: James Robinson, his wife Annie, and their ten children lived in a two-room farmhouse on an isolated stretch of land near the village of Warren. Some of the children went to school, and they all attended church, but otherwise the family lived a life of complete isolation. James was considered a respectable man by the citizens of Warren, but to his family he was a tyrant who used physical abuse to dominate his sons and sexual abuse against his daughters. Over a period of several years (beginning when one of the girls was age five), James maintained a sexual relationship with three of his six daughters. Annie Robinson described watching him go into the bush from time to time with one of their daughters, but it was not until her daughter Ellen was pregnant that her suspicions were confirmed. The first child was born in 1906, followed by two more, a second one to Ellen and one to Jessie, both in March 1908. The latter two children did not survive. During labor, Jessie finally broke the long family silence, crying, "if I had not been made to do this, this would not have happened," and begging her mother to "keep this hid." Jessie was Annie's favorite daughter and was described as the "weakest" of the children. Jessie's pleas proved too much for Annie (who performed all of the deliveries). She was in such a "state of sorrow" for her daughter that she smothered the infant as soon as it was born. When Ellen's second baby was born several weeks later, she did the same. (The deaths had no effect on the sexual relationships; when they came to light in August 1909, Ellen was pregnant again.) Annie's act of kindness to her daughters was not so interpreted by the law: she was arrested in August 1909 and charged with murder. Several days later, after a chase, James was also arrested. Twice the jury returned a not guilty verdict in Annie's case, but both times the judge refused it. Finally they found her guilty, and the judge sentenced her to hang. After a widespread campaign on her behalf, organized in large part by the Women's Christian Temperance Union and local Councils of Women across Ontario, her sentence was commuted and she spent less than two years in Kingstons Prison for Women. James was found not guilty of accessory to murder, but pled guilty to a variety of rape and incest charges and was sentenced to twenty-eight years in jail.[84]

While there is no question Annie Robinson broke the law by murdering two infants, her arrest and initial severe sentence also stemmed from a judgmental evaluation of her failings as a mother. Justice McGee, who presided at her trial, suggested to the jury that she also bore responsibility for the crime of incest: "it is difficult to realize that she could for so many years have allowed her husband's misconduct toward his own children to continue without doing something to end it . . . it would almost give the impression of callous indifference or absence of moral sense." Officials in the Justice Department who deliberated over her death sentence also found this point "difficult." Annie answered this charge in court quite simply. It was fear of disgrace, she said, which silenced her, and the impossibility of providing for her ten children alone which made her stay. "There was too many of them," she said, "too many of them for me to take, and I couldn't go and leave any behind." The one time she tried to send Jessie away on her own, James found out and chased her back home.[85]

While this case was horrible, it was not absolutely unusual. Other incest and infanticide cases brought to light massive evidence of sexual exploitation in families. In Thessalon, outside Sault Ste. Marie, a sixty-six-year-old adoptive father and two of his sons were revealed as having sex regularly with their ward, age fourteen. Henry D. of Blind River was charged with having sexual relations with his three daughters and forcing them into acts of prostitution with his friends. Jessie W. gave birth to a baby (later murdered by her brother) after an incestuous relationship with her father and brother.[86] Local commentators and the press were quick to dub these stories of "depraved families," and mothers were condemned just as stridently as fathers. What "depraved families" seemed to have in common, in this rendering of the story, were not solely brutish fathers and degraded mothers. The isolation of these families and their location in the backwoods of Ontario were often used to explain the sexual abuse. A clergyman and old family friend of the Robinsons, for example, in a letter on Annie's behalf written to the minister of justice, spoke at length about their upstanding family background. How, then, could one account for the horrific turn their lives took? The answer, according to the clergyman, was that they left their hometown in southern Ontario to move north, "where the influences were not the most elevating."[87]

We explore this association of immorality with isolation in more detail in later chapters. What is significant in understanding the history of incest is how this notion also helped displace responsibility away from patriarchal family structures. In urban centers the crime of incest was often portrayed by middle-class social reformers as a result of overcrowding of the working class. The issue was thus read as a housing question or a poverty question or a question of working-class morality, all of which served to reinforce one set of relations of domination—class—and erase another, gender.[88] This formulation, of course, also leaves unexamined questions of sexual violence within middle- and upper-class families, which rarely caught the attention of the legal system or other agencies.

In incest cases, a family's rural isolation might serve to perpetuate sexually exploitative relationships. As in the abuse of domestic servants, such isolation might also make the possibility of escape that much more difficult. In an urban environment, on the other hand, crowded tenements could serve as safety valves and watchful neighbors could unite to assist women against abusive men.[89] While we should not underestimate the neighborly links of interdependence and intervention in rural and small-town Ontario, clearly things could go very wrong in isolated families before 'help' arrived.

Defining urban incest as a problem of overcrowding and rural incest as a problem of isolation not only results in tautological nonsense. A federal Justice Department administrator assured the minister of justice that the "revolting" Robinson case was "absolutely abnormal." While few cases match the Robinson story in terms of its intense abuse and pain, one is struck by the sheer ordinariness of most families in which incest was reported. Sexual abuse does not, of course, characterize all Canadian families, but privacy and the ideology of the moral sanctity of the home do.[90] 'Normal' patriarchal families, whether located in downtown Toronto or the wilds of northern Ontario, can be experienced by their dependent members as sexual prisons.

The discourses of danger which dominated turn-of-the-century Canadian society did not reflect the actual place of sexual abuse in women's lives. Cultural stereotypes of the men or situations harmful to women left unexamined vast areas of private life. As many domestic servants, daughters, nieces and other relatives learned, the patriarchal, hierarchical household often locked danger and exploitation *in*. Outside the family, assumptions about female sexuality and dependence ensured that the 'wrong' sorts of girls who happened into the 'wrong' sorts of situations wound up legally and socially powerless.

CHAPTER THREE

Maidenly Girls and Designing Women: Prosecutions for Consensual Sex

OVERT SEXUAL DANGERS—ACTS OF UN-wanted, physically coerced sex between a man and a woman—were processed and under certain conditions punished by the legal system as crimes such as rape and indecent assault. Yet historically, these dangers were not the sole ones a woman was thought to face. In this chapter I examine prosecutions of voluntary sexual relations that did not generally involve physical coercion and were often, as far as can be determined from the limited information in legal records, mutually satisfying to the men and women involved. How then did such romantic involvements find their way into the criminal court?

Perhaps the key insight of those who advocate a social construction approach to sexuality is that the meaning assigned to human acts, values and behavior is constantly shifting.[1] In today's sexual discourse, neither seduction nor abduction exist as criminal categories. Rather, in the language of popular culture, seduction conjures up images of erotic flirtation, a sexual adventure in which one party is 'in charge' but the other surrenders at her or his will. In the hands of nineteenth-century moral reformers and the legal system, however, the distinction between coercive, forced sex and sexual play was not so clear. In a culture that denied full political and economic citizenship to women, it is not surprising women were denied cultural and legal control over their sexuality. Then as now, women and men did not face each other as equals in the bedroom (or, in our context, the berry patch or the kitchen) any more than they did in the factory, the street or government institutions.

The criminalization of voluntary sexual activities between women and men reveals something of the force of the double standard of sexual behavior, a cultural imperative of remarkable durability. But the sexual double standard was more than a powerful social prejudice. Legislation that made certain types of sex illegal (whether because sex was coerced, or because of the age or relationships of the individuals) was always framed to prevent men from acting against women. Men do, of course, act against women's physical wishes, often. But the entire weight of Anglo legal tradition rests on the patriarchal assumption that, as Rosalind Coward puts it, "only men have an active sexuality, therefore, only men can actively seek out and commit a sexual crime."[2]

The double standard of sexual behavior is thus linked to the historical construction and regulation of desire. Female desire has rarely been regulated overtly; it was men, after all, who were forbidden to have sex with certain types of women. State sexual regulation, premised on such assumptions about women's and men's differing sexual natures, helps on the one hand to construct, channel, or sometimes limit male sexual desire, while on the other hand leaving vague questions about female desire.[3] Women's bodies and desires are indeed a site of regulation, but this tends to take place in a more diffused and indirect fashion. Women are more immediately regulated by families and husbands, and at the level of the state, policies as varied as those on birth control, abortion, and even welfare act to shape women's sexual possibilities.

An appreciation of the gendered complexities of sexual regulation and desire helps us to understand why certain types of voluntary sexual relations between women and men became the subject of legislative debate and criminal prosecution in late nineteenth-century Canada. Laws that regulated seduction and abduction were, in their conception and application, based on an assumption of the oppositional sexual natures of men and women. As illustration I begin this chapter with an overview of the legislative campaign in favor of the seduction law, as waged by one firebrand member of Parliament. The law was supported by the moral reform movement and the labor movement, and passed into law by the late 1880s. The rest of the chapter focuses on criminal prosecutions of two types of voluntary sexual activity: seduction and abduction. Prosecutions under the law allow us to contrast the intentions of moral reformers with both the opinions of legal authorities and the actual experience of young heterosexual couples. Further, I explore how the criminalization of voluntary sexual activity served to entrench the legal and parental regulation of women and punish women who transgressed cultural prohibitions of female desire.

THE CAMPAIGN AGAINST SEDUCTION

A tribute to John Charlton, delivered in 1897 by the Norfolk County Liberal Association on the occasion of Charlton's twenty-fifth anniversary as M.P., perhaps overstates his fame, but it certainly captures Charlton's sense of himself and his political mission:

> The name of John Charlton, as orator, economist, financier, moral reformer and deadliest foe of vice, is a household word in every Canadian family. There is no citizen in the country at large who does not regard his life, his property, his privileges and above all his sacred family ties, as more safe, more assured and more free from touch, by reason of that honoured name.[4]

Charlton was an M.P. representing Norfolk North and a successful entrepreneur. During his political career (1872–1904) he piloted an amazing array of morals legislation through the House of Commons. Sabbath observance, temperance, censorship of 'obscene' literature, and opposition to abortion and birth control were all causes embraced by Charlton, but it is in the area of the criminalization of certain sexual offenses that, as he opined in a published collection of speeches, his "name will be remembered."[5] (And in this instance, hyperbole was not without substance. Charlton was so associated with seduction offenses that it was common for both criminal indictments and newspaper accounts of trials to refer to seduction as "offences against the Charlton Act.")

Charlton's diaries and unpublished autobiography reveal no particular insights into why—save deeply held religious convictions—the cause of moral legislation was so important to him. His constant and often-stated concern was to protect women, especially young women, from unspecified moral dangers. He was far more alert to the consequences of immorality. "It is surely a crime," he told the House of Commons in his second attempt to introduce seduction legislation in 1883, "to blight a home, to ruin a life; to make an innocent person an outcast of society, and to drive her to prostitution, when this is done by the exercise of wiles and false promises."[6] Thus Charlton, like other moral reformers of his day, had a dramatic and paternal vision of the lives of 'seduced' women.

Another constant theme in his speeches, one that united his major moral preoccupations, namely, seduction and Sabbath observance, was the relationship between a strong morality and a strong state. In a major address in the House of Commons on Sabbath observance, for example, he argued that by bringing more people "under religious influence," a strong Sabbath observance bill would reduce crime, win the favor of the working class, and, by placing Canada "on a higher moral plane . . . will strengthen the nation and make it more powerful and prosperous."[7] Similarly, in another speech in the House of Commons on seduction, he put the issue in melodramatic terms:

> The degradation of women is a crime against society. The pure Christian home is the only safe foundation for the free and enlightened State. Vice in the shape of social immorality is the greatest danger that can threaten the state, and the duty of the Legislature, the duty of the Government, is to take measures, so far as it can, to punish infractions of morality and to conserve the morality of the public.[8]

Claims such as these, made about issues such as the publication of Sunday newspapers or sexual relations outside matrimony, appear exaggerated and absurd to late twentieth-century observers. However, if one sets these issues in an expanded conception of the meaning of moral regulation, Charlton's grand statements make more sense. Historians have tended to interpret the turn-of-the-century moral reform movement as an Anglo-Saxon, middle-class response to increasing fears about immigration, the growth of the working class, and the changes in social and family life brought on by industrialization and urbanization.[9] Yet, as Valverde and Weir note, moral regulation also involved the attempt to create a particular kind of citizen. The emerging state in nineteenth-century Canada was concerned not just with the formation of political and economic "subjectivities," but also with "the formation of a moral subjectivity that would not only be congruent with but also would provide the psychological basis for what was known as nation-building."[10]

The link between moral building and nation building can be glimpsed in the way Charlton chose to express his opinion on the Pacific Scandal, a railway-financing venture which embarrassed the ruling Conservative government. Never a fan of Prime Minister Sir John A. Macdonald (a "bad old man" whose morals were "not above reproach"),[11] Charlton blamed Macdonald and the Tories for "betraying the interest of a young nation for the benefit of a body of speculators and capitalists."[12] In Charlton's view, young nations, like young women, needed protection lest the strong (speculators, capitalists, or blackguardly men) betray the weak.

An expanded definition of the meaning of moral regulation also helps make sense of another of Charlton's favorite themes, Canada's moral reputation or standing in the world. A peculiar form of 'moral boosterism' was common when people reflected upon incidents of sexual crime in their midst. Judges at assize court, for example, would congratulate or condemn an entire community, depending on the number of sexual crimes on the docket. When reporting on serious sexual crimes in Britain or the United States, Canadian newspapers would often smugly point out that Canada's purer moral atmosphere would make the commission of such a crime unlikely here. Alternatively, when sensational crimes did occur in Canada, commentators would find convenient scapegoats in geography. Border towns would blame their proximity to the United States, and rural areas would blame nearby towns. When Charlton, in making his case against the publication of Sunday newspapers, argued that "we do not want this American institution in Canada," he spoke in a language common to other moral reformers, designed to blend community or patriotic fervor with good behavior.[13] Moral standing was thus not simply a matter of individual reputation. A common standard of morality was a community concern, and the community—in concert with the state and the legal system—had an interest in ensuring the maintenance of that standard by all. Yet morality, conceived of in abstract national or geographic terms, was applied to existing communities with rigid social hierarchies, and often served to reproduce those hierarchies in new ways.

Charlton introduced his seduction bill in 1882, and by 1886 a version of it became law.[14] The salient features of the bill were that it introduced the concept of seduction—as opposed to forcible, coercive attack—into Canadian criminal law. Consent was not an issue in seduction cases. The law proclaimed that in certain situations, consent to sexual relations could not exist. The situations specified changed throughout the period under investigation, but in general they applied to heterosexual relations in which the female was (1) between the ages of fourteen and sixteen; (2) under the age of twenty-one when sex was accompanied by the promise of marriage; and (3) under twenty-one and the ward or employee (in a factory, mill, or workshop) of her 'seducer.' In all cases, the law applied only to women "of previously chaste character." The maximum penalty for those found guilty of seduction was two years in prison. Even after the law was passed Charlton continued the campaign to expand its scope, mainly by attempting to raise the age limits for women, so throughout the 1880s and 1890s many amendments were added. These provisions in the criminal law were predated by a civil seduction law, however; the right to sue for seduction had existed throughout this period. Unlike the criminal suits, civil seduction suits could not be initiated by the woman involved; her father had to seek damages. As a result we see very different patterns of both prosecutions and verdicts, which I contrast below.

Charlton's bill was initially ignored in the House, but as he persisted, the arguments against criminalizing seduction became vociferous. The fear that women would use the law to blackmail men was repeated by many through the years of debate on this topic, and when the workplace seduction provisions were introduced, this concern reached new heights. Many members of Parliament seized on the popular stereotype of the 'designing woman' to make their case against the bill. According to one M.P., employers would be at the mercy of a "designing woman, who would throw herself very much in his way, and who would do what has been done again and again in the history of the world, namely, seduce him." The promise-of-marriage provision might prove tempting for women, who "might find it profitable to fall." Others worried that even the stipulation requiring previous chastity would not guarantee that the law would be used to help respectable girls, since "chastity, like the phases of the moon, is very changeable." Still others spoke candidly as men, arguing that "we have the right to protect ourselves; and it is our duty to see, not for ourselves alone, but as representative men, that legislation is not placed upon our statutes which is unfair or unjust, and likely to lead young men into trouble improperly."[15]

Charlton's bill was supported by one of the major players in the moral reform movement, David A. Watt and the Montreal Society for the Protection of Women and Girls. Like Charlton, the Montreal Society had a far-reaching concern with protecting women from all moral dangers, though in general Watt's own preoccupations, revealed in his voluminous correspondence with the federal Justice Department, were in the area of prostitution and procuring offenses. The Montreal Society did advance one significant criticism of the seduction bill. In reference to the employer/employee section of the legislation, the society argued that a woman's "previously chaste character" should not be a criterion for successful prosecution. An employer, they argued, "should not be in a position to take advantage of the weakness or previous faults of those whose moral welfare he should be in an important sense the custodian."[16] This suggestion was not acted upon by government, but it is an interesting reversal of the more typical discourse of the period, in which fallen women fell permanently. In this articulation of the moral obligations of employers, Watt gave voice to the protective practices of many nineteenth-century factory owners, who attempted to protect the good name of female employees by "claiming common cause with their fathers and husbands."[17]

The seduction law also had a less well known source of support, one not generally regarded as a participant in the movement for social purity. The nineteenth-century labor movement displayed a significant concern for the moral hazards of women's working lives. The Ontario branch of the Knights of Labor was a staunch supporter of the seduction law and was credited by the minister of justice, John Thompson, with convincing him to introduce legislation prohibiting seduction in the workplace. Unlike middle-class proponents of seduction legislation, the labor movement had a precise notion of the sorts of moral dangers requiring protection.

In Hamilton, for example, a Knights of Labor stronghold, the Knights were first drawn to the problem of seduction through the case of Maria McCabe, an Irish immigrant convicted of the murder of her illegitimate infant. The Knights read this case as a clear sign of the vulnerable position of working-class women and participated in a successful community campaign to commute McCabe's death sentence. Katie McVicar, one of the most active women in the Canadian branch, added the McCabe case to her arsenal of arguments in favor of women's suffrage, noting that at present "girls have nothing to do with the making of the laws by which they are governed."[18]

McCabe's case served as a local springboard for an even more sensational incident which captured the Canadian Knights' attention a few years later. The Knights followed the story of William Stead and his "Maiden Tribute to Modern Babylon" in Britain with avid attention. Stead's discovery in Britain of a huge network of white slavery, consisting primarily of working-class "daughters of the people," as well as his subsequent prosecution for abduction confirmed for the Knights that capitalism and morality were incompatible. As labor journalist Phillips Thompson explained: "The main cause of the moral rottenness of the English upper classes—and of the same class everywhere—is the inequalities of conditions which prevail; the corrupting influence of unearned wealth and idleness on the one hand, and on the other the degradation caused by overwork, poverty and wretched homes."[19]

For Thompson, aristocratic exploitation of young women was simply an extension of capitalist domination of workers: "Sensuality is naturally begotten by luxury, overfeeding and laziness, and fostered by the entire spirit of English institutions which make the poor slaves of the rich."[20] Thompson's words were more than good polemics. This argument, which clearly located vice in the upper class, was the opposite of the dominant association of immorality with the working class.

Both the McCabe story and the Maiden Tribute revelations served to make the Ontario Knights keen supporters of Charlton's attempts to introduce seduction legislation. Hamilton's *Palladium of Labor* drew attention to the "special interest" workers had in Charlton's bill, since working women's dependent position "places them at the mercy of lecherous employers." The labor press also reminded its readers that if women had the vote, "as they rightfully should," the issue would be dealt with quickly. In the wake of Stead's findings, it seemed clear to the Knights that Canadian legislators were stalling Charlton's bill. The "notorious libertines" on Parliament Hill, claimed the Knights, had "strong personal reasons for wishing the defeat of the measure."[21] This time, however, the workers had the government's ear. In 1889 the Canadian Legislative Committee of the Knights met with Minister of Justice John Thompson and convinced him to include a limited amendment on workplace seduction in the next round of changes to the criminal code.

The Knights saw *one* of the particular ways in which the power relations of capitalism victimized women. Sparing themselves the painful business of self-reflection, they did not examine the distribution of power *between* women and men in the working class. Yet as British historian Barbara Taylor has argued in another context, "the men were as bad as their masters."[22] This construction of sexual danger clearly let working-class men off the hook. Furthermore, like others in the progressive wing of the social purity movement (including most feminists), the Knights continued to reproduce the dichotomy of good and bad womanhood, and offered little space for positive or autonomous female sexuality. Yet unlike some social purity activists, the Knights did not blame working-class women themselves for their proximity to vice. Rather, they located the problem in women's dependent economic and political position, and used this issue to reiterate their support for female suffrage. They also made a significant discovery: notions of female purity, passionlessness and innocence were clearly out of reach for most, especially working-class, women. It seemed to the Knights that capitalism forced working women into daily battle with vice: in fending off advances from employers, in the temptations of sin which grinding poverty created, or even in the simple act of walking home at night from work. As such, these women were denied their right to chastity and morality. A seduction law provided an opportunity to claim these virtues for all, to democratize morality.

Such were the expectations of the proponents of the seduction law. Whether one saw the issue in class terms or not, seduction law advocates expected that their legislation would help innocent and victimized maidens claim redress against wiley, powerful men. The law was constructed such that age or economic relationships, not force, were the determinants of the sorts of sexual liaisons women were to be protected from. Once seduction entered the realm of the legal system, however, some very different stories emerged.

THE SEDUCTION STORY: PROSECUTIONS UNDER THE LAW

Canadian legal historians have done valuable research reconstructing and interpreting the legislative framework of nineteenth- and early twentieth-century sexual morality. John McLaren studied the seduction law in the context of a larger examination of the movement against white slavery in Canada and thus explained seduction in terms of the generalized concern of the middle-class moral reform movement to regulate the sexual activities of the working class.[23] Constance Backhouse looked at seduction in the context of rape and other sexual assault legislation. Noting the overwhelmingly paternal nature of the seduction law, she also locates it in the general movement toward the consideration of sexual assault as a crime against women themselves, rather than in the earlier notion that rape damaged women only in so far as they were considered property of their fathers.[24] Graham Parker studied seduction and other sexual crimes in which physical force was not a criterion (such as 'carnal knowledge' of young girls, and abduction). According to Parker, laws governing voluntary sexual behavior served to reinforce the double standard of sexual morality and the cult of chastity for women.[25]

My survey of seduction prosecutions reaches similar conclusions. Studying the law from this perspective allows us to view the sorts of sexual entanglements thought to require punishment as well as the way the legal system determined guilt or innocence in these situations. This approach yields rather different results than studies that rely primarily on legal commentary and interpretation. In this sample, seduction was not primarily about rape or other nonconsensual sexual acts; nor was it about prostitution or commercial sexual exchange. Well over half of the seduction cases in this survey were the result of ongoing and mutual relations between two lovers. As such, the seduction law often acted to contain the sexual behavior of women as well as men.[26]

The sexual situations resulting in prosecutions reveal that the law was interpreted by many complainants as a means of channeling sexual behavior into 'appropriate' institutions, namely, marriage; it was about ensuring childbirth in wedlock. Seduced women, and often the parents of seduced daughters, attempted to use the law to enforce what historian Christine Stansell calls the barter system between the sexes—where a woman traded sexual favors for a man's promise to marry. But as Stansell also notes, this exchange was not between two equals. A woman "delivered on her part of the bargain—and risked pregnancy—before the man came through with his."[27] Thus the power which male seducers held did not arise primarily from their advanced age or their economic relationship to their conquest; their power resulted from their more favored position in this system of sexual exchange. These men had power because they were men, in a society in which the dominant moral climate punished pre- or extramarital sexual activity on the part of women. The seduction law did not change or improve women's standing in the sexual barter system, because, despite the chivalrous rhetoric advanced by proponents of the new law, women's stories of sexual betrayal were simply not believed by the legal system.

Over fifty Ontario women who had been wronged by their lovers took the law at its word and presented the court with stories in which consent to sex arose from false or unmet promises. A typical case was that of fifteen-year-old Charlotte S. and her boyfriend Henry S. They met when Henry, a farmer's son in Fitzroy Township near Ottawa, came to Charlotte's father's farm in fall 1889 to help with the threshing. According to Charlotte, Henry "appeared to desire to induce me to be his companion." Henry began to visit regularly, and they "kept company" in the kitchen of Charlotte's family home, while the rest of the family was upstairs asleep. Charlotte's mother, Jane, saw "nothing improper in their company keeping" because she presumed that his "object was marriage." After a time, Henry "coaxed" Charlotte into having sex. In a grand declaration of love, Henry told her that "if he owned the whole world . . . he would not think it too much to give it to her," and asked for her hand in marriage. The family kitchen continued to be the site of their visits; they would lay down on the bench and have sex at the kitchen table. This arrangement lasted until Charlotte got pregnant, and her mother began to hear "stories" about her. When questioned, Charlotte confessed her situation to her mother. Charlotte's parents confronted Henry at his father's farm, and, standing in a cow field, the two families had it out. At first Henry denied any responsibility for Charlotte's pregnancy, but when pressed, he admitted that "he could not put hand to heart and answer to God that he had no freedom with Charlotte." He insisted, however, that he would not, and had not promised to, marry her. Charlotte's distraught mother begged him to do "what was right" and offered the couple a home in a neighboring farm. At this Henry relented and promised to return to Charlotte and her family later that week, but his father disagreed. Telling the girl's family to "go to hell," Henry's father refused to let Henry leave, saying there was too much work to do on his farm. Thus the affair ended up in court, where Henry was found not guilty.[28]

Reading seduction charges from the bottom up, that is, from the complaints filed by women which they thought demanded legal punishment, reveals two general categories of seduction scenarios. Contrary to the intention and language of the legislation, seduction charges were filed when sex was both forced and voluntary. In the former case a number of other charges (rape, attempted rape, indecent assault) would have been appropriate, but this confusion in legal categorization reflects in part the uneven development of the justice system in this period, particularly in rural areas. The difference between, for example, what might be termed rape, indecent assault, and attempted rape was (and is) always a judgment call on the part of authorities, and there was a great deal of regional variation in legal classifications. Such confusion cut both ways. Even after the seduction law was well in place, rape charges continued to be brought in cases that read like seduction tales, for example, pregnant women who stated quite clearly that they consented to sex after their boyfriends promised to marry them.

Yet, as American historian Mary Odem has pointed out in her study of statutory rape prosecutions, the practice of categorizing stories of physical coercion alongside stories of seduction also reveals the ambivalence of the legal system in accepting the assumptions behind the seduction law. In a sexual climate that drew rigid lines between good girls (who were not sexual) and bad, any woman who admitted to sexual relations outside proscribed boundaries was suspect.[29] The sexual culture of turn-of-the-century Ontario, which informed the opinions of judges and the decisions of juries, held little sympathy for a girl who had the misfortune to fall voluntarily for the wrong sort of man.

Stories of forced, unwanted sex, sometimes between strangers (what we would today call pickup situations), more often between neighbors or household members, form a minority of cases in this study, fewer than 20 percent of all charges filed under the seduction law. Such sexual encounters usually occurred only once or twice, and, according to the women, physical force by the man was what led to sex. Even when women used the language of seduction to tell their story, it is clear they were often describing acts of rape. As fifteen-year-old Edith H. from Parry Sound told it, her neighbor William J. came by to borrow a drill one afternoon, and, finding her alone in the house, he "shoved me up against the door and seduced me."[30] Such cases were sometimes accompanied by other charges, such as rape, attempted rape, or indecent assault. These types of cases have two elements in common: they were rarely the result of sexual relations between lovers, and they were much more likely to be believed than seduction stories; most such incidents resulted in guilty verdicts. The exception to this rule was the pickup situation, which never resulted in a guilty verdict.

The voluntary incidents always involved sexual relations between lovers, often those who had dated for a period of one or two years. The lovers could be neighbors, co-workers, boarders, farmhands or old friends. The women in these situations admitted to having sexual relations with their boyfriend, usually claiming that a promise of marriage was what led them to consent to sex. These are stories of courtship gone awry, either because the woman got pregnant and the man reneged on his commitment to marriage, because the man ended the relationship in favor of pursuing another, or because the woman discovered the man was already married. Many of these sorts of cases were pursued when the woman discovered she was pregnant, and often the complainant's parents played a significant role in the prosecution. The men involved were rarely found guilty.

Charlotte S.'s case was typical of seduction stories in which the young man's refusal to marry his pregnant girlfriend was the main reason the case went to court. The suit of Kenneth C. and Margaret F. was typical of a second type of voluntary case, in which courtship ended when the man's previous marriage was discovered. Kenneth and Margaret were co-workers at the Martin Manufacturing Company in Whitby, in 1917. They dated regularly, every Wednesday and Saturday evening, and he would also pick her up from night school other evenings. They usually had sex in his vehicle. Margaret began hearing rumors at the factory that he was married, which he laughed off. When her mother got wind of the same rumors, she forbade any more contact between the two. Their attempt to run off to Toronto (to marry, according to Margaret) was stopped when Margaret's mother caught them in a hotel room in Oshawa and immediately brought charges against him. Kenneth wrote his wife from jail, telling her she would be surprised about the "scrape" he had gotten into and asking for her help. He requested that she bring along their son to court, for "if you and him come it will help me out," and also asked for money. The crown attorney was outraged by the case. Margaret may have acted "imprudently," he told the judge, but "the law was made to protect young girls from men like him." Kenneth's cavalier attitude irked the courts; he was found guilty, but received a suspended sentence.[31]

These cases share many similarities with other seduction stories. The principals appear to be relative social equals, and clearly sexual activity took place in the context of a romantic relationship. Most of the men and women involved in these cases were from similar working-class or farm backgrounds. A few domestic servants charged their employers (a work relationship that, until 1920, fell outside the scope of the law), but no cases in this sample involved employers in the specified "factories, mills or workshops." Nor were there cases in which the seducer matched the Knights of Labor vision of aristocratic libertine. The nineteenth-century workplace was hardly free of what we would today call sexual harassment. As American labor activist Rose Cohen remembered, the first words of English she learned in her job in the garment industry were, "Keep your hands off me, please."[32] Then as now, women used both individual and collective strategies to negotiate their way past unwanted sexual attention at work. Yet given women's often precarious position in the labor force, it is hardly surprising that the criminal court system was not how they chose to deal with these problems.[33]

These cases reveal that young men and women were relatively free to pursue a relationship that included a sexual component; only when they got caught, either by an unplanned pregnancy or breaking the rules of monogamous marriage, did the relationship come to an unhappy conclusion. Often it was then up to the woman's parents to determine how to proceed. These cases reveal a variety of patterns of parental involvement in their children's sexual lives. In Charlotte S.'s case the parents took the side of their wronged daughter. Similarly, Elizabeth S. told the court that her mother was "managing" her case against her boyfriend, George D., for her. Elizabeth testified that she "thought enough" of George to marry him still, even though he had "used her so mean," reneging on his promise of marriage after she became pregnant. Elizabeth's mother freely admitted that she laid charges against George "to compell him to marry my daughter."[34] Yet other times the interests of parents and children conflicted, and the legal system might be used to assert parental authority in other ways.

Some parents clearly undermined their daughters' desires. In 1903, fifteen-year-old Mary Ellen T. became romantically involved with Patrick C., an Oshawa ironworker and boarder at Mary Ellen's family home. Their sexual affair became known when Patrick took off a half day from work to go berry picking with Mary Ellen and the next day bragged about the "good time" he'd had with her to his co-workers. News of his sexual exploits reached Mary Ellen's father, Hiram, who then began to watch the couple. He told the court the remarkable story that he watched them one evening having sex in the kitchen. "I saw him sitting on her knee with his arm around her neck and they were kissing each other. In a few minutes they changed places and he raised her clothes and unbuttoned his trousers . . . he accomplished the act . . . he seduced her." Hiram did not interrupt them that night, because he "wanted to keep cool until I had my man arrested." This he did the next morning. It is unlikely Mary Ellen was a party to the prosecution; it does not appear she was pregnant, and her father took his story to the police without telling her. The court heard no testimony from her. It appears that in this case, prosecution acted to punish Patrick C. as well as his 'wayward' girlfriend by ending what appears to have been a mutually desired relationship and by exposing her intimate life to public scrutiny.[35]

Like Mary Ellen T.'s father, the parents of Beatrice A. of Woodstock used the legal system to challenge their daughter's relationship with a man of whom they disapproved. This case also illustrates the double standard of justice delivered to blacks in late nineteenth-century Ontario. Beatrice, a "prepossessing mulatto," had been dating a "coloured" laborer named Thomas M. for a year and a half. She became pregnant after several sexual encounters with him, most of which took place outside her father's house, after their evening walk. Thomas wrote Beatrice's father a letter apologizing for his "indiscretion" and asking his permission to marry Beatrice, but Mr. A. had long objected to this courtship; he refused permission, opting instead to take Thomas to court. Beatrice would have preferred marriage. In a melodramatic rendering of the story, the Woodstock press described how, in court, the "wronged girl fell upon the neck of her lover, and he, in turn, clasped her in a fond embrace." The scene was referred to in a jocular and breezy tone, which contrasts with the tragic language used to describe most other seduction trials, as "full of pathos and not without a tinge of humour." Thomas's color likely also accounts for the verdict; despite his admission of responsibility, Beatrice's admission that she consented to sex, and Thomas's willingness to 'fulfill his obligation' by marrying Beatrice, his case resulted in a guilty verdict.[36]

Thus the seduction law could be used to regulate the sexual behavior of both parties, sometimes putting an end to a relationship not sanctioned by a woman's parents, other times channeling sexual activity into its only acceptable form, conventional marriage. The desire to avoid unwed motherhood was clearly what fueled many prosecutions for seduction. Historian John Gillis has termed illegitimacy the "moral litmus test" of Victorian society.[37] While some studies suggest a degree of community and family tolerance for unwed mothers in Canada, these cases reveal that this was not a fate young women or their families accepted willingly.[38] In several of these cases, the threat of court proceedings served to force the men involved to uphold their part of the sexual bargain by marrying the woman. Three days before his trial for the seduction of Alice M. in 1917, Thomas L. of Thessalon ensured that the proceedings were halted by marrying her. (In this case, however, marriage did not mean the end of their troubles. Five years later Thomas was back in court pleading guilty to assaulting his fifteen-year-old niece.)[39] Thus despite the low conviction rate, the law gave some women a degree of bargaining power to make men uphold their part of the sexual bargain.

The stipulation requiring "previously chaste character" on the part of the woman was one reason so few seduction cases resulted in guilty verdicts. This clause, unique in Canadian law, certainly provided an out, which accused men used to their advantage. The meaning of this clause was subject to a continuing debate among judges and other legal commentators. Some judges interpreted it narrowly, and simply looked for evidence of whether women had had previous sexual relations. Others interpreted it more broadly and allowed evidence on all "acts and that disposition of mind which constitute an unmarried woman's virtue or morals."[40] A wide interpretation was allowed in many of these cases. The most common defense was to suggest that the man charged was not the first or only man to have been involved with the woman. Thus William W., for example, successfully defended himself against seduction charges laid by Beatrice M. by producing two other men in court who, according to the *Orangeville Sun*, "with brazen and brassy faces, told of their illicit relations with the girl."[41] In other cases, the mere suggestion of other boyfriends seemed to be enough to raise doubts about a woman's chastity. Many women were cross-examined about their past relationships with men, and even when there was no evidence that these had involved sexual intimacy, their stories were rarely believed. Over time this clause drew the ire of Canada's largest feminist group, the National Council of Women. Simultaneously reinforcing the hierarchies of class as she attempted to deconstruct those of gender, Lady Julia Drummond, president of the Montreal Local Council of Women, argued in 1896 that "in the class of life where such offences are most frequent, girls thus defiled are not likely to be able to substantiate a good character" and lamented that accused men "may stand before a jury whose sympathies are invariably with their sex."[42]

A woman's sexual history was not the only criterion for determining character. When a woman alleged that she consented to sex under promise of marriage, she was asked to carefully reconstruct the precise timing of the proposal. If it came after the first sexual liaison, clearly she had not been seduced. Women were also questioned regarding how long they had been dating before they consented to sex. Being "coaxed" is how many women described their sexual initiation, and even here one could display degrees of morality. Elizabeth P. admitted that John H. seduced her on their second or third date, but hastened to add, "I required a great deal of coaxing."[43] Mary C. of Sault Ste. Marie insisted that her boyfriend, Paul C., faithfully promised to marry her before sex took place, but in court she also pointed out his stature: "Do you think I could fight a big fellow like that?"[44]

Other areas of cross-examination show how broadly conceived notions of morality could be. As in sexual assault trials, women who pressed seduction charges were interrogated about their church or school attendance, their employment history, and sometimes their parents' moral conduct. William T., for example, produced as his witness a previous employer of Margaret V., who testified that he had dismissed her two years previously from domestic service at his home in Stratford because she repeatedly stayed out past her 10:00 P.M. curfew.[45] Elizabeth P.'s mother, Lydia, was subject to a barrage of questions regarding her illegitimate child, her poor supervision of her daughter (allowing her to stay downstairs alone with her boyfriend), and her own alleged flirtation with the accused, John H.[46] Similarly, Mary S.'s mother, Martha, was repeatedly grilled about the extent of her supervision and control: Did she ever attempt to stop her daughter from going out? Did her daughter have a lot of friends? Did she warn her daughter to be careful with boys?[47]

Finally, financial transactions could be used to suggest poor character on the part of the woman or her family. One type of transaction suggested prostitution, the other blackmail. Women were regularly asked if they accepted money from their boyfriends before or after sexual relations. And while it does not appear that any of these cases involved outright commercial exchange for sex between strangers, we see evidence of what historian Kathy Peiss calls "charity girls"—women who agreed to continue sexual relations with their boyfriends in return for money or gifts.[48] Celestine L. admitted to accepting five dollars from Emile C., whom she had been dating for three months. She used the money to buy herself new boots and stockings. Bob C. swept young Henrietta M. off her feet: he bought her clothing, jewelry, paid for her music lessons, and even settled some of her father's debts.[49] Accused men used such instances to allege prostitution—a sure defense against a woman's claim of previous chastity. Yet given that in all situations where money or gifts changed hands the couple had been romantically involved for a time, it seems more likely that money was simply a part of the barter system, particularly when women were taking the risk of premarital sex.

Like men accused of acts of sexual violence, men accused of voluntary sexual transgressions also attempted to exploit the cultural stereotype of the designing woman. Sometimes a conspiracy on the part of the woman's family was suggested. When Margaret V.'s father took the stand in the case he was pursuing against William T., the first question he was asked was whether he brought this action "for the purpose of getting money." (He denied it, and further denied knowing that William's father was a wealthy man.) Margaret B. no doubt increased her moral standing as a noble wronged woman (and helped secure a rare guilty verdict against her seducer) by returning the money her boyfriend's wife had offered her for silence and instead pressing criminal charges.[50] The courts frowned on financial negotiations, often interpreting such bartering as evidence of extortion. As in rape cases, however, financial transactions in cases of voluntary sexual activity were not necessarily sinister, but rather part of traditional, extralegal patterns of community social regulation.

The argument that financial negotiations were not the malicious plot they were made out to be by the courts is strengthened when we recall that the right to take civil action for a monetary reward in cases of seduction existed throughout this period. Similarly, women whose boyfriends backed out of a commitment to marriage could sue them for breach of promise. Yet even when women pursued their legal right to sue a man for damages, cultural stereotypes about women's maliciousness prevailed. Judges and legal commentators villified women who brought such suits, casting them, as one judge put it, as "hungry spinsters and designing widows."[51]

Despite these prejudices toward designing women, civil prosecutions for seduction were popular and remarkably successful. Seduction cases were the most litigated cases involving women, and an astounding 90 percent of cases between 1820 and 1900 in Ontario went to the plaintiff.[52] In civil trials, 'previous chastity' was not a condition of successful prosecution, although Backhouse found that it could determine the amount of the award. Across Canada, between 1900 and 1910 the average yearly conviction rate in criminal cases of seduction was 9 percent, and it increased to 34 percent yearly between 1911 and 1917.[53] The conviction rate in my Ontario sample is 35 percent (increasing to 45 percent if we add incidents of physical coercion). It seems that seduction stories were believed much more readily in the civil courts.

Civil courts are, of course, different from criminal courts. In the criminal courts, persons accused of a crime are presumed innocent; the state must prove them guilty beyond a reasonable doubt. In civil courts, responsibility to prove culpability rests on a balance of probability, which changes the odds. Due to the differing requirements of proof, wronged parties generally receive a more sympathetic hearing in civil rather than criminal courts.

The civil seduction law stipulated that actions must be brought by the woman's father; women could not bring suit themselves. The tort of seduction was, Constance Backhouse has argued, a relic of feudal ideology which held that some individuals (men) hold property interests in others (women, children and serfs). Backhouse does not compare the success rate in civil versus criminal seduction trials, but she does contrast the high success rate of civil seduction prosecutions with the much lower rate of convictions in rape trials, which, for the 1880s, she calculated at 34 percent. "The stark difference," she argues "relates to the visible presence of the woman's father in the seduction trial, a factor which turned the competition into one between two males."[54]

As we have seen, however, fathers often played prominent roles in criminal seduction prosecutions, and the presence of a father or mother did not appear to increase the chances of a guilty verdict. The direct and overtly paternal role of the father as the wronged party in a civil trial may be part of the reason for its higher rate of success for the plaintiff; one suspects that traditional differences between the two court systems as well as the question of previous chastity also came into play.

Class shaped one's choice of legal venues and also helps explain different patterns of prosecutions. Backhouse suggests that civil prosecutions were a "working-man's lawsuit," though most defendants were wealthier than the plaintiffs who brought claims.[55] Obviously there would be little point in taking a poor man to civil court for financial compensation. In the criminal courts it appears that more often the defendants were of at least similar economic circumstances to the plaintiffs; men who were farmhands, boarders or co-workers were often younger and less financially established than the woman's family. The relatively low conviction rate in criminal trials should also serve to underscore that those who did press charges took their experiences seriously. Clearly many of these women (and/or their families) felt they had been dealt with unfairly and brought their cases to the criminal courts in order to right a wrong.

ABDUCTION

The charge of abduction amplifies my contention that laws governing voluntary sexual activity acted to regulate the behavior of women as well as men. Looking at prosecutions for abduction also allows us to probe the sexual conflicts that arose between parents and their children because in these cases the protagonists were positioned differently than in seduction cases. Rather than a wronged woman teaming up with her parents to attempt to use the legal system to punish an errant boyfriend, in abduction cases the parents generally acted against their daughter's will and sought to punish both her and her boyfriend.

The roots of this law lay in England, where the abduction of a "girl of property" against the wishes of her father had been criminalized since the thirteenth century. Canada imported this legislation in the 1840s, expanding its provisions to include all women under the age of sixteen. Heiresses, however, were covered under this legislation until age twenty-one. This obvious class bias irked D. A. Watt and his Society for the Protection of Women and Girls. He argued throughout the 1890s for an extension of abduction provisions to "poor and friendless" girls over the age of sixteen. He was unsuccessful in this demand, but he did achieve his goal in raising the age provisions for women who were 'abducted' or procured for the purposes of prostitution. Like the seduction law, this statute assumed that girls under the age of sixteen could not consent. Unlike the seduction law, however, previous chastity was not a legal requirement.[56]

Abduction was not a widely prosecuted crime; only thirteen such case files exist in these counties. One apparently nonsexual charge involved a man who helped rescue his niece from an orphan's home in which she was not happy. In another case the law was used (rather innovatively) by a jealous husband to punish a man who ran away with his wife and children; the abduction charge pertained to the children. The remaining charges involved lovers who fled their community together because the girl's parents disapproved of the relationship. Thus the abduction law allowed parents to retrieve their daughters and end unsanctioned relationships. The law did more than permit parents to override their daughters' romantic wishes, however. In several cases the girl as well as the boy suffered legally; sometimes she spent time in a children's shelter or was even charged with vagrancy. Thus even more than seduction cases, abduction prosecutions reveal how both parents and the courts might punish girls who had used their sexuality 'irresponsibly.' The abduction law was the most obviously interventionist of all sexual laws, and abduction cases were pressed most often when one or both of the protagonists were non-WASPs—immigrants or Francophones. Most cases in Canada were prosecuted during the height of the white slave panic, between 1910 and the 1920s.

Samuel W., a twenty-one-year-old mill worker, met Cecile V. on the street one evening in Blind River. They dated for two months, usually ending their evenings at her home, having sex in the kitchen while her family was asleep upstairs. Cecile's father disapproved of the relationship and only allowed his daughter out twice a week. Samuel joined the Roman Catholic church in hopes of convincing Cecile's father to allow the two to marry, but to no avail. One afternoon in August 1928 the two made their escape. Samuel finagled one hundred dollars from his boss (telling him his sister needed an operation), and the two purchased a suitcase and a train ticket to Toronto. They amused themselves in the city, staying in a hotel, shopping, and eating in restaurants. When their money ran out they moved in with Cecile's older sister, who eventually told her father where the two were. Three weeks after their departure from Blind River, the Toronto police paid a visit to Cecile's sister's house on Church Street. Cecile was promptly placed on a train back home, and Samuel was arrested.[57]

It is obvious that this relationship was desired by both parties. Cecile wrote Samuel several letters while he was in prison, keeping him appraised of her father's thoughts on their relationship and telling him how much she missed him. Mutual affection was apparent in most other abduction cases. Florida B. met Joseph G. when they were both working at the Ottawa Exhibition; after a week of meeting each other during their breaks, she left with him for Quebec. Vera C. became quite smitten with George Y., a boarder at her home in Oshawa. When he left to seek work in Toronto, he sent her money to join him. Santa T. also met her boyfriend, Nicolas P., when he boarded with her family. She received sustained beatings from both parents for defying their orders not to see him; they had another man picked out for her to marry. She left with Nicolas and another boarder to seek work in Guelph.[58]

Sometimes abduction charges were resolved amicably. When Cecile V.'s father discovered that his daughter was pregnant, he relented in his opposition to the marriage, provided that the two were married by a priest and "did not expect any expenses from him." Three other abduction charges were withdrawn when the parents gave their permission for marriage. Yet eight abduction charges resulted in guilty verdicts. George Y., for example, was convicted and spent six months at hard labor in Toronto's Central Prison, while his girlfriend, Vera, was charged with vagrancy and spent time in the Toronto children's shelter. Bob C. received an astoundingly harsh sentence of ten years in prison for his conviction on the combined charges of seduction, abduction, and carnal knowledge of Henrietta M.

Bob, a man in his forties who was a "frequent visitor to the local courts," admitted that his relationship with Henrietta began when she was eleven years of age. Shortly before his trial she gave birth, causing the judge to claim he had "blasted a young girl's life." Bob's sentence was also no doubt attributable to the fact that he drew a gun on a police officer when he was arrested and that he attempted to escape from jail.[59]

Race and ethnicity influenced abduction prosecutions in a number of ways. An unusually high percentage of the protagonists in abduction cases were eastern and southern Europeans and Francophones, which itself testifies to the way the white slave panic stirred up concerns about the 'disappearance' of young women to 'foreign' men. Distinct abduction scripts emerged, depending entirely on ethnic configurations. When an immigrant man 'abducted' an Anglo-Saxon woman, the story was read in such a way as to confirm fears of the perilous sexuality of male immigrants, or, as one newspaper put it, "the fascination of the foreign races for Canadian girls." Vera C.'s mother had long objected to her daughter's relationship with their boarder George Y., on the grounds of both age and race. Fifteen-year-old Vera was, she claimed, too young to accompany George to hockey matches, but, she added, "of course, he doesn't talk very good English." The two dated secretly for a time, and when George secured a better job in Toronto, he left town. Several weeks later he sent Vera his address and train fare, and she joined him in Toronto. For a week they lived together in a boarding-house, and he bought her a number of gifts. After they were caught, Vera admitted to police that she joined George on her own accord, he told her she could return to her mother at any time, and she was still quite willing to marry him. Despite all this, the press cast George as a foreign dandy who manipulated a naive Canadian girl. "Oshawa Maid of Fifteen runs off with Assyrian Blacksmith" ran one headline. It was George's "slight foreign accent, his strength and, if the truth be told, his good manners" which made a "big hit" with Vera. Vera's mother, so the story went, presumed George was a respectable boarder and had "been in Canada long enough to learn the language and become Canadianized." What she hadn't counted on was that "George, being an Assyrian, does not see anything unusual in the performance, as in the country from which he comes it is quite the thing for young ladies to enter matrimonial bondage at the age of even less . . . than that reached by Vera."[60]

When both the man and the woman were non-WASPs, the discourse of protection was replaced with one of punishment. In the trial of two of the few Native peoples whose stories surfaced in these records, it came out that Joseph P. took Margaret P. to an island off the Parry Sound Indian Reserve for a week. The judge disbelieved Margaret's story that she had been held against her wishes, stating that the tale "sounded so unlike an abduction even as told by her, that it would not be safe to convict."[61] The *Sudbury Star* characterized Olga S., a young Finnish girl who left town with her boyfriend, also a Finnish immigrant, as "half witted and unruly," and the judge refused to marry the couple, arguing that it would be "a shame to let this simple minded girl marry anybody."[62] 'Canadian' girls involved with 'foreign' men were uniquely protected under this law, whether they desired assistance or not. The simple fact of a girl's Canadianism determined that she would be framed as a hapless, somewhat silly maiden who had fallen under the spell of a manipulative foreigner. When a non-Anglo-Saxon woman was involved with a man of similar racial or ethnic origin, however, the naive waif became a culpable, 'unruly' bad girl.

The judge's pronouncement on Olga S.'s lack of fitness for marriage alerts us to another feature of the abduction law—the power it granted legal authorities to shape, encourage or discourage relationships. In chapter 5 I explore the forms of social and moral regulation that obtained in this period, mainly those of the family, the community and the state. Legal prosecution of abduction reveals the covert and overt dimensions of state regulation. The law itself was unapologetically interventionist and gave wide latitude to parents and police wishing to end liaisons of which they disapproved. But within the broad powers of the law, legal authorities could and did exercise other forms of moral power. Alfred Cuddy, an OPP inspector who tracked down Cecile V. and Samuel W. in Toronto, did not hesitate to express to their hometown police his opinion of the couple's relationship. Samuel, according to Cuddy, was "what I would describe as a snivelling cur, who has not the slightest intention of marrying the girl." "It would be a shame," he went on, to try to encourage marriage to such a "weakling."[63]

Relatively few young couples in Ontario fought out their problems in criminal court. It is difficult, especially in the absence of Canadian studies of working-class and rural courtship, to say how typical these cases were. We do not yet fully understand the contours of the sexual 'barter system' in Canada—how many other women risked a sexual relationship or defied parental wishes so drastically as to leave town with an unacceptable boyfriend. Nor do we know much about what happened, beyond these criminal trials, to those who were caught. We will never know if seduced and abandoned women lived the "ruined and blighted" lives Charlton and others warned of, what fate lay in store for small-town girls who arrived back home after a brief, heady sexual adventure in the big city, or whether the romantic desires of fifteen-year-old girls resulted in happy adult marriages. The problem of unwed motherhood continued to vex moral reformers, particularly those in the expanding field of social work. The Ontario government tacitly admitted the failure of the seduction law to solve the problem of illegitimate children when, in 1921, it took the decision to pursue charges against fathers out of the hands of the women involved.[64]

We do know, however, that the criminal law was unhelpful in either punishing men who reneged on romantic promises or changing the social ethos that made premarital sex disproportionately risky for women. Protection, especially of the powerless, slid easily into surveillance.

The suppression of women's sexuality historically has taken many forms. Through limiting women's sexual autonomy, creating artificial categories such as maidenly girls and designing women, or through more obvious forms of abuse such as rape, patriarchal ideas and practices about sexuality, desire and gender were entrenched.

CHAPTER FOUR

Spectacle, Scandal, and Spicy Stories

On 11 August 1881 James Weatherly, a moderately well-to-do produce dealer, wed Margaret Dougherty, a storekeeper, in Mount Sherwood, a village outside Ottawa. Both their ages and their marital histories set this couple apart from other newlyweds of the day. James was sixty-five and embarking on his third marriage. Margaret was forty-five, the mother of four children, and marrying for the second time.

Their unusual liaison did not go unobserved. At about eight o'clock on the evening of their wedding, a crowd of boys appeared outside their home, beating tins, ringing bells and shouting. One of the Weatherlys' friends who was visiting went outside to investigate. Shouting "charivari," the boys demanded money from the couple, and the Weatherlys agreed to give them a dollar in hopes they would leave. They did, but returned a short time later with a larger group (this time a mix of young and old men), again demanding money and throwing stones, breaking windows and cracking the plaster on the house. Mr. Weatherly refused to give in to the "blackguards," and the crowd continued its noisemaking for several hours. After the crowd thinned out, Mr. and Mrs. Weatherly ventured outside, in order, Mrs. Weatherly claimed later, to "chase the boys away from breaking down the house." They were met by a "shower of stones," and Mrs. Weatherly ran back home. Mr. Weatherly was last seen chasing the boys down the street. Several hours later his body was discovered on the side of the road near his house.[1]

The "fatal charivari," as it was quickly dubbed, occurred as the popularity of this nineteenth-century spectacle was beginning to fade. Yet such rituals did not simply die out through community disinterest. Charivaris and other community-based practices that served as forms of moral regulation were ultimately replaced by the state, particularly the legal system. But this process was slow and deliberate. Legal hegemony, as Douglas Hay has argued in his analysis of the operation of the criminal law in eighteenth-century England, rests in part on coercion (the "raw material of authority") and in part on consent, organized by the majesty, justice and mercy exhibited in the courtroom.[2]

Social and sexual life in rural and northern Ontario around the turn of the century was regulated by a shifting combination of families, communities and the state. In this period and in these regions the state had yet to assume predominance in the eyes of many as the sole legitimate forum for the settlement of sexual grievances. Many were reluctant to give up individual and collective means of solving disputes or enforcing community standards. Courtrooms did not, after all, spring up overnight. Calling the police, hiring a lawyer, and going to court were learned processes. In this chapter I investigate how, in cases of sexual conflict, the lines between public, popular forms of problem solving and the impersonal, bureaucratic state were negotiated.

Reactions to the "fatal charivari" provide an example of how respect for the law was instilled. The actions of the crowd in this case were condemned across the province. Most commentators framed their outrage by counterposing the outmoded brutality of the mob against forces of progress and civilization. Respect for the law and for a particular conception of privacy figured centrally in this discourse. The *Ottawa Citizen* immediately declared that "it is high time that the charivari business was put down with a strong hand. It is a gross outrage that quiet and respectable persons cannot change their circumstances in life without being subjected to the insults of a mob of vagabonds."[3] The *London Advertiser* suggested that charivaris were relics of the past, "when means of entertainment were few, and a wedding was the occasion of a social jollification." Now, however, the custom was "only a display of rowdyism of the worst kind."[4] The *Hamilton Spectator* called the charivari "the lowest form of vulgarity" and engaged in a bit of regional moral boosterism. The practice, claimed the paper, had declined in the western part of the province, through the "advance of more refined feelings and the indignant frown of public sentiment, but it appeared to be more or less a custom to the eastward."[5]

All called on the federal government to pass legislation outlawing the charivari, and many pressed their case for stronger legal machinery in the 'backwoods.' The *Montreal Herald* suggested that the "spirit of ruffianism" (exemplified by both the charivari and the increasing "outrages against women") was kept in check in cities and towns, but was "too frequently manifesting itself in rural districts, where there are no police." The *Citizen* heaped praise on the Ottawa police in quickly rounding up the leaders of the gang, but argued that the cost of bringing the perpetrators to justice "will be more than would have been paid policemen, who would have been able to prevent the whole riot."[6]

Some historians suggest that it was the working-class character of the charivari which ultimately led to its demise. Such displays of rowdyism were at odds with bourgeois notions of justice and public decorum. In this sense, decline of the charivari was linked to shifting values in public life. Similarly,' religious groups such as the Salvation Army also drew fire from mainstream churches because of their overwhelmingly public, raucous, and resolutely working-class nature.[7] Large crowds, whether throwing stones at neighbors who had breached community moral codes, or parading and chanting in the name of the Lord, represented a working-class challenge to dominant conventions of proper public behavior.

The twin themes of rural and working-class immorality and the need for a stronger system of policing were echoed throughout the closing decades of the nineteenth century, and this discourse united several disparate concerns. The immorality of remote regions was attributed, at least in part, to the sparseness of the judicial system. Lack of this more preferable, 'civilized' system left space for mob rule (or, in communities with a high proportion of European immigrants, 'peasant' lawlessness). Part of what made a community modern—a sign that it had emerged from the backwoods—was a full fleet of police officers, an attractive, imposing courthouse, and an obedient populace.

When the assize court visited smaller communities, the presiding judge, the grand jury, and the local press did their best to create a dignified atmosphere, sometimes in the face of formidable odds. Small-town grand juries often expressed alarm at the physical deterioration of local jails and courthouses. In Timmins the jail was located in the basement of the town hall, where prisoners could converse and pass notes to passersby on the street. A grand jury in Fort William was shocked to learn that the physical conditions of the jail were such that "the vile conversation of the prisoners could be heard distinctly in other portions of the city hall, particularly in the library, which is visited daily by many of the women and children of the city." Local boosters in Rat Portage were pleased to report, in their 1897 *Souvenir Diamond Jubilee Guide*, that the local police force had that year been outfitted in a smart new uniform, "which adds much to the neatness of its appearance, as well as to its usefulness on behalf of law and order."[8]

The process of teaching respect for the law was part ideological and part material. Legal historians agree that, due to such tangible factors as insufficient police and limited funding for the criminal court system, court records yield only a "partial picture of the settlement of criminal disputes and the punishment of offenders."[9] Prosecutions of sexual crime illustrate well the uneven development of the criminal justice system, especially given the private nature of most incidents and the ambivalence of many authorities about prosecuting such cases. Often, for example, a great deal of confusion surrounded legal classifications. As we have seen, the difference between what might be termed rape, attempted rape, indecent assault, or even noncoercive crimes such as seduction and abduction varied widely throughout the province.

A person might encounter any number of problems when trying to take a case to the police. Lillian P. claimed she was told by the police not to bother pressing charges against John H., an acquaintance who offered her a ride home in his buggy and attempted to assault her, because of the "trouble and notoriety" of a criminal trial. Martha C. immediately went to the justice of the peace to press charges against two men who broke into her house and raped her, and she informed him of their whereabouts (they were staying at a hotel outside Parry Sound). The official, however, had run out of the appropriate forms and insisted on traveling to the next town to secure more. By the time he returned, with a constable to arrest the men, they had fled.[10] W. D. Logan, a magistrate in the Thunder Bay District, reported in 1881 that during the first sittings of his court in Rat Portage a property dispute was resolved in favor of the plaintiff when he seized the item in question "by superior force" out of the hands of the bailiff. "After the Bailiff had thus failed to enforce the process of the court," Logan reported, with perhaps a hint of irony, "little business has been transacted since."[11] Respect for the law in northern Ontario was no doubt dealt a further blow several years later when the Ontario Provincial Police constable H. P. McGrath was convicted of extorting money, in exchange for protection, from a woman who ran a brothel near North Bay.[12] Problems, large and small, which beset the legal system in remote areas of the province evoke an image of Canadian policing which owes more to the Keystone Cops than the national icon, the Royal Canadian Mounted Police. Such problems were not lost on social critics of the day. Edmund Bradwin, a reformer who studied the condition of logging towns in the 1920s, cited the rudimentary legal system as a key social problem. Magistrates, he claimed, "do not always receive their appointments because of fitness or particular capacity for their work," and the local police, he stated primly, "do not rise higher than the public life about them."[13] Insufficient decorum on the part of legal authorities was one problem. Excessive friendliness was another. In small towns the legal system had yet to establish itself as a distant and bureaucratic machine, completely removed from the community. As a crown attorney in Ontario County complained to the provincial attorney general in 1881, a lack of time and money, combined with the "unpleasant nature of their duties in having examinations and committing their neighbours for trial," hindered local magistrates.[14]

All of these incidents suggest there were indeed some significant spanners in the workings of the turn-of-the-century legal system in remote areas. But alongside the problem of establishing an impersonal and efficient legal system were important ideological tasks. Authority works best, after all, when it is recognized as legitimate.

THE THEATER OF THE COURT

Historically the criminal court operated as much like a theater (and perhaps a church) as it did a place of justice. The general fanfare accompanying the arrival of the assize court in eighteenth-century English towns, the crowds that turned out to watch the trials and executions which sometimes followed, and the sermonlike pronouncements by judges in passing sentence (directed as much at the audience in the courtroom as the accused) all contributed to an atmosphere of awe and reverence as powerful as that found in any religion. This spectacle, Hay claims, was particularly significant in rural areas, for it was "the most visible and elaborate manifestation of state power to be seen in the countryside."[15] Paul Craven found little of the majesty and pomp of the English institution in his study of the mid-nineteenth-century Toronto police court. But in the spectators' active participation and the extensive and sensational daily reporting of the court's proceedings Craven saw a close relationship between the court and theater, particularly the "secular morality" of melodrama.[16] Extending the comparison between criminal trials and the conventions of theater, Ruth Harris argues that the popularity of such melodramatic roles as the 'good' heroine, whose virtue was besieged by the villainy of a man, helps explain why so many women in turn-of-the-century France were found not guilty of 'crimes of passion' against men who had wronged them.[17] In many countries the ritualized and dramatic aspects of the criminal court lent an air of majesty to the proceedings, which in turn helped solidify support for the rule of law.

It is common sense among contemporary feminists that our generation has helped politicize sexual violence by talking about it, after previous decades of silence. While this notion may be true of recent times, in the long view it is incorrect to suggest a history of only silence and denial of sexual violence. Some trials for sexual crime were enormously popular in this period and served to educate people about 'proper' sexual behavior. Always well publicized and well attended, such trials unfolded as miniature morality plays, complete with heroes, villains and audience. Sometimes art imitated life. A popular local amusement in this period was the mock court trial, community theater performances of courtroom drama which were staged as benefits for church groups and featured local personalities as actors. Many of these performances had as their theme a 'mild' sexual crime such as breach of promise.[18] In real life, judges and other legal commentators often took the opportunity afforded by sexual trials to make statements about appropriate sexual conduct, gender roles and morality.

When the courtroom was used as a forum for settling sexual disputes, its theatrical aspects were not without their own set of problems. Publicity sometimes threatened to change the dynamics of the story itself and other times was thought to reflect badly on the community. When testimony was considered particularly revolting, a judge would order the court cleared— less out of compassion for the victim and her privacy, more out of the judge's own sense of the hierarchy of 'evil' crimes. Courts were cleared most often in cases of same-sex buggery, gang rape, incest and bestiality.

The presence of an audience often had an immediate impact on those required to retell their stories of sexual crime. Many women reacted like Bridgit C., who burst into tears when she saw "so many eyes upon her" as she took the witness stand in an indecent assault trial. Others, like Minerva T., a young woman who accused four men of gang raping her, flatly refused to testify until the court was cleared. One young woman who had been assaulted by a man she met one evening as she was strolling through downtown Oshawa insisted that her case be tried in the relative quiet of the county court Judges' criminal court. Because she was engaged to be married, she wanted to avoid the publicity of an assize court trial.[19]

Men and women reacted differently to publicity, and gender intersected with class in turn-of-the-century concerns about public decorum in several interesting ways. Middle-class distaste of the Salvation Army, as historian Lynne Marks has argued, stemmed from the prominent, public role the church gave its women members as well as concerns that the mingling of the sexes in the Army fostered an atmosphere of "sexual looseness." When Katie McVicar, a young factory worker in Hamilton, wrote to the Knights of Labor in hopes of encouraging them to begin organizing Hamilton's working women, she expressed her anxieties about union activism in similar terms. If a girl made herself "conspicuous" by union involvement, she worried, her peers might think she was "angling for notoriety or something else besides organizing." Women, particularly those in the working class, were unaccustomed to having their voices heard or opinions listened to in public. Amelia Turner, a Calgary labor activist, remembers that "it was an ordeal for me to say 'present,'" at her first socialist study-group meeting. This hesitance to take on a public role reveals more than simple shyness, however.Making oneself conspicuous carried with it moral overtones, which held whether a woman was speaking out at a union meeting or recounting her rape on a witness stand.[20]

Men, for whom sexual reputation had more fluid parameters than it did for women, sometimes approached notoriety with a certain playfulness. Martin B., awaiting trial on an attempted rape charge in Gananoque, passed his time in jail by entertaining the crowds that gathered outside his cell. The cell was visible to people on the street, and Martin apparently attracted quite a crowd by "dancing, singing and [making] remarks intended to be witty." In return, passersby gave him tobacco and liquor. The arrival in Brockville of Malcolm A. to face a charge of rape also drew a large crowd to the train station. Some of the more curious even boarded the passenger car and "evinced the wildest desire to get a glimpse of the prisoner."[21]

It was the presence and behavior of an audience inside the courtroom which increasingly bothered authorities. Community morality was suspect when large numbers of citizens displayed an interest in sexual trials. The following editorial from the *Woodstock Sentinal Review* expresses typical concern:

> The Fall Assizes for the County of Oxford this year might have been called the filthy assize. . . . There were three seduction cases, two slander cases and one charge of indecent assault, not a creditable showing, truly, for this county. . . . Another thing that was unpleasant to notice was the eagerness to hear the cases. His lordship took special notice of this indecent anxiety on the part of visitors to the court and on one occasion administered a fitting rebuke to those, who having no business to transact, came to satisfy their prurient tastes by listening to the details of such cases.[22]

Such rebukes were administered regularly by judges and the press. An Ottawa judge, commenting on the large crowd in attendance at the particularly sensational trial of a doctor charged with raping his patient, also stated that such cases should not be tried in open court, "as the effect was most demoralizing."[23] These concerns eventually reached the ears of the federal government. The Toronto Children's Aid Society took up this question in a series of letters proposing changes to the federal criminal code in the early 1890s. As a means of preventing an "education in crime," the justice minister was urged to prohibit all women, men and children from entering the criminal courts "unless they can prove that business takes them there."[24]

When women entered the courtroom as spectators, eyebrows were raised even farther. Many judges refused to allow female observers in court and used either shame or direct intervention to escort them out. Before the trial of a doctor charged with performing abortions in Sault Ste. Marie commenced, the judge, noting the number of women present, appealed to their sense of community morality: "The ladies present would sustain the wholesome reputation of the ladies of the city of Sault Ste. Marie by leaving the courtroom." The press noted the large numbers of women who crowded in to observe a well-known murder trial in Goderich, lamenting that "women as well as men, were in possession of a morbid curiousity."[25] A sure indicator of the spiciness of a story was when it was reported that the testimony drove the women out of the courtroom.

For all its moralizing about curious spectators, the press itself was an important purveyor of information and opinion on sexual crime. Local newspapers announced the arrival of the assize court in town with all the fanfare accorded a traveling circus, including dispensing information on which cases were expected to be controversial and interesting. Press coverage of sexual crime varied by county and region. A few newspapers were circumspect or even silent about sex crime, but most, particularly those in the north, gave ample space to the crime, the investigation, and the trial and did not hesitate to create heroes and villains in the process. In casually noting community sentiment regarding the character of the parties involved, a reporter could easily play his own favorites among the protagonists. Like judges who periodically cleared the court, some newspapers deemed certain stories unfit for publication, usually those involving infanticide, abortion and incest.

When faced with the charge that press attention sensationalized crime, the press championed the reformative power of publicity. The *Sault Ste. Marie Star*, for example, told the story of a woman raped by a man answering an advertisement for boarders. Some time later the same man struck again, raping a second woman. "Had publicity been given to the first crime," the story went, "there is a strong probability that other ladies would have been on their guard."[26]

The public, it would seem, generally ignored tirades from a judge or outraged editorials in the press and continued to flock to the criminal court in search of spicy stories and scandal. Such publicity clearly affected female defendants, and especially their desire to go public with their experiences. For victims of sexual assault, the civilization of the courtroom might not look very different from the brutality of the mob. Promotion of the legal system as a place to settle sexual scores helped skew the odds in favor of men. Men's stories were more readily believed, and men generally had less to lose in a public airing of private life. The construction of sexual trials as unwholesome, forbidden regions of popular amusement further stigmatized women who had been seduced or assaulted, portraying their experience as beyond the interest of polite society.[27]

Illicit interest in trials of sexual crime proved embarrassing to those attempting to construct the courtroom as a place of sober authority. The courtroom audience was not passive—the observers booed villains, cheered heroes, and shed tears of relief at popular verdicts. If the regular sessions of the criminal court were reminiscent of working-class theater, the trials of those charged with sexual crime resembled the bawdy atmosphere of early burlesque or cabaret. Trials of sex crimes joined the dance hall and saloon as popular but risqué sites of entertainment.

Despite the antics of spectators, the 'theater of the court' helped instill respect for the law. Given the choice between an armed and unruly mob on the street and the same crowd noisily observing a criminal trial, the latter was preferable because it was containable. In spite of its rowdiness, once inside the courtroom the crowd essentially was rendered mute; the proceedings themselves were firmly in the hands of the state.

Prurient public interest in sexual crime also helped create a popular consensus about what constitutes 'normal' sexuality.[28] In the same way that today's "spectacle of AIDS" is carefully stage-managed as a sensational didactic pageant, furnishing the general public with dramatic evidence of what 'we' already 'know' concerning the dangers of sexual promiscuity, sexual scandals in the past acted as moral parables, warning eager spectators of a host of forbidden dangers.[29] Good girls were not raped, but if they were, they were not supposed to talk about it in public.

Sexuality and Scandal

Sexual crimes took place in private, but once reported they quickly entered the public domain. Stories in the local press, the public's attendance at trials, and community gossip ensured that most sexual secrets received a wide airing. Some cases, however, attracted more than average attention. Sexual crimes became sexual scandals when they involved powerful or famous men, when they involved acts deemed particularly horrific, or when they involved certain types of women.

Some sexual crimes became famous not only because of the nature or quality of the act. Sensational sexual murders, committed by young working-class toughs such as Edward Jardine, or by transient French Canadians or blacks such as Amede Chattelle and Frank Roughmond, sent communities into a panic and certainly acted to underscore and solidify existing class, gender and race anxieties.[30] But murder itself did not necessarily inspire such fear or condemnation. Cases of fatal or near-fatal wife abuse, for example, tended to attract much less attention within the courtroom and in the press. Similarly, while most abortion trials tended to receive a great deal of publicity, when the abortionist was a woman or when prominent medical men were involved, public interest was much stronger.

Despite the fears of legal authorities and community leaders, extreme public interest did not necessarily imply moral laxity or suggest a community's propensity toward vice or violence. The messages conveyed to a packed courtroom or emblazoned in newspaper headlines were profoundly conservative. Women who achieved fame as criminals did so as broken, pathetic victims. Working-class and non-Anglo-Saxon men who achieved sexual notoriety helped entrench dominant sentiments about the sexual depravity and 'otherness' of marginalized men. And powerful Anglo-Saxon men were generally able to employ the cultural prejudices of class and gender, which usually allowed them to escape punishment, their reputations intact.

Sex Lives of the Rich and Famous

Privacy was, in important respects, class and gender bound—the rich could afford more privacy than the poor, and men could afford more than women. Public forms of work, entertainment and social life, cramped housing and neighborhoods, as well as the dominant association of the working class and immigrants with vice and crime, made all aspects of working-class life, including sexuality, open to community and legal scrutiny. Similarly, given the sexual double standard, women had much more of an interest in attempting to keep their sexual lives private than did men. It is not surprising, therefore, that most of the sexual relations reflected in criminal trials took place within one class, the working class.

Class boundaries were rarely traversed in sexual relations, and sexual misconduct in the middle and upper classes tended to remain secret. Thus upper-class men were often protected from more overt forms of regulation and supervision. When detected, however, class was no hedge against publicity. In fact the reverse tended to be true: 'respectable' men experienced less than their share of policing, but more than their share of publicity. Once a doctor, teacher, politician or businessman was caught, even the most routine sexual wrong became the subject of extreme community ferment. It was almost as though a trade-off were in effect: a few prominent men were exposed to the glare of exaggerated public scrutiny in return for the privacy of most others. As Douglas Hay has suggested, part of what made the manifestly unjust and class-bound system of English criminal justice appear democratic was the occasional "victory of a cottager in the courts or the rare spectacle of a titled villain on the gallows."[31] In her feminist analysis of the Yorkshire Ripper case in England, Wendy Hollway claims that the 'mad' (biological) versus 'bad' (social) debate over Peter Sutcliffe's motives obscured the more widespread ramifications of sexual violence and "exonerates men in general even when one man is found guilty."[32] Certainly one effect of widespread publicity about past upper-class sexual crimes would have been to render invisible the sexual privileges of most upper-class men.

While the occasional story of upper-class sexual misconduct received more than its share of headlines, the effect of such publicity on the men involved is ambiguous. The limited historiography of sexual scandal in high places in Canada suggests a remarkable level of community and legal tolerance for errant famous men. The stories of two 'respectable' men in nineteenth-century Ontario demonstrate that an unsavory sexual reputation did little to thwart public men in their pursuit of electoral or other ambitions. Schuyler Shibley, a Tory politician from the Kingston area, managed to win reelection to a number of political positions in the 1860s and 1870s, despite his proximity to a scandal involving the beating death of his illegitimate child. And D. I. K. Rine, a leader of the Gospel Temperance movement, shrugged off indecent assault charges brought by a fifteen-year-old servant girl as "a little playfulness"; he returned to the temperance lecture circuit to large and supportive crowds.[33]

When sexual scandal touched the lives of men in public life, they (and their supporters in the press) tended to suggest that the real story lay elsewhere, usually in the conspiratorial motives of their political enemies. Thus when the estranged wife of the newly appointed police magistrate of Oshawa turned up to press a bigamy charge against him in 1913 (having left him nine years previously), the Oshawa press instantly suspected that "the rabid politicians who have been fighting Mr. Watson are believed to be behind the prosecution." In her testimony, Mrs. Watson admitted that a certain Oshawa doctor had suggested that she return from her home in California to press charges, but she hastened to add that she "thought it would be a good thing to save the town from having a Magistrate to dispense justice who had no idea of it himself."[34]

In an even more sensational and involved case in Goderich, Malcolm Cameron, a sitting Liberal member of Parliament, was the subject of an extended rumor campaign alleging that he seduced his young servant, Ellen Lomas, who died in childbirth. The scandal apparently cost him reelection, and in the course of the 1892 libel charge he successfully pressed against James Mitchell, editor of the *Goderich Star*, the affair was framed completely in partisan terms. According to the *London Advertiser*, for example, the rumor was circulated solely by Cameron's "political opponents," who lacked "the manliness to make the accusation boldly on the platform, where they could be held responsible for it." The rumor was picked up by "a section of the Conservative press, much to their discredit."[35] Further into the trial, Robert Gore, Cameron's former gardener, confessed that he and his lover,

another former domestic servant in the Cameron household, conspired together to frame Cameron and that he "never would have said or written a
word against Mr. Cameron, had I not been urged to do so by the Conserva-
tives of Goderich," who, he claimed, paid him for his trouble.[36]

It is, of course, entirely possible in both of these cases that political motives lay behind the prosecution and rumor-mongering. But the substance
of the story gets lost amid all of these accusations, particularly in Cameron's
case since Ellen Lomas herself was conveniently unable to intervene. Political maneuvering eclipsed the stories themselves as the greater crime, and
thus the men involved could be portrayed sympathetically, as victims of a
disreputable press or political enemies. Indeed, when the presiding judge
found Robert Gore guilty of perjury, he used the sentimental discourse of
home and family to underscore Cameron's victimization: "I know of no
charge which can affect a man so grievously, even if untrue, as inconsis-
tency and unfaithfulness with reference to his home. Every man should
have a home, inside of which he can go and where the tongue of slander
cannot reach him."[37]

The story of Arthur Brown and Dorothy Turner of Oshawa illuminates
the other major line of defense used by men involved in high-profile sexual
scandals—imputing malicious, evil motives or character to the woman
pressing charges. Arthur Brown was a former Salvation Army preacher
who in 1926 held the position of relief officer for the town of Oshawa. In this
context he met Dorothy Turner, a client applying for relief. Turner could
have been a sympathetic character. She was the mother of two children, and
her first husband was killed in action in World War I. Her second husband
was also a war veteran, but was suffering from a heart condition and was
confined to a military hospital in Toronto. Brown and his wife befriended
Mrs. Turner and her children. The two families often visited each other,
and several times the Browns drove Mrs. Turner to Toronto to visit her husband.

When Dorothy Turner accused Mr. Brown of raping her during one family visit (in the presence of his wife, she claimed), the story became front
page news in Oshawa. Brown admitted having sex with Dorothy Turner,
but claimed the two were having an affair, of which his wife knew
nothing—a story that earned him the label "dirty, slimy hypocrite" from
the crown attorney. Despite this hyperbole, Brown was able to go Turner
one better, and the respectable war widow quickly became a designing
temptress. The headlines in the *Oshawa Daily Reformer* illustrate the moral
positioning of the two protagonists. "Former Relief Officer's Trial is Proceeding," ran the largest story, followed by "A. W. Brown of Oshawa
Stands Charged with Serious Offence." After this, the stark "Woman Testi-

fies" told of Dorothy Turner's contribution. Simply identified as "woman," she was denied the respectability Brown's occupation and community status conferred upon him.

Dorothy Turner was not just a woman—she was a woman with a past. In the course of the trial Brown's lawyer made a series of allegations against Turner: that her second child was fathered by her first husband's brother (who, she said, "forced her" to have sex after her husband's death), that she had once taken her second husband to court on a "serious charge," and that she herself had been a Barnardo child. If these allegations (some of which she denied in court) were true, they indicated that Dorothy Turner had been orphaned, raped and beaten. Yet in the courtroom these were serious blemishes, no match for the sterling record of Arthur Brown and his wife. Mrs. Brown testified that the two had been married for forty-six years, had eight children, and had lived in the same house for fifteen years. Not surprisingly, the jury believed Arthur Brown's story, and with a stern reprimand for "tralloping around after other women, displaying a weakness rather than wickedness," the judge let him go. [38]

Probing a woman's past or current moral character was a strategy used by men of all classes to defend themselves against sexual assault charges. But when such arguments were used by prominent men with obvious social credentials, their stories were believed much more readily. Of all of the cases involving men from a significantly higher social class, only one, a teacher charged with raping his student, resulted in a guilty verdict. Thus while their location on the class spectrum did not always protect upper-class men from publicity, it acted as a powerful shield against punishment.

Notoriety of a Different Sort: The Sex Murder

Sexual fame was also achieved when one's crime was particularly heinous. The stories of doctors or laymen who performed (botched) abortions, groups of young men who ganged up to rape women, a Children's Aid Society superintendent who had sex with several boys in his care, and a 'depraved' father who raped and forced prostitution upon his daughters were described as revolting and nauseating, rather than the customary, playful epithet 'spicy,' but they too received enormous public attention. Stories of sexual murder, however, not only received the most publicity but also generated the most explicit moralizing.

Two cases of sexual murder, both of which took place near Stratford within several years of each other, rocked the community and the nation and, due to the particular protagonists of each, illustrate well the combined gender, class and race prejudices of the period. Both crimes were indeed grisly, and certainly of all sexual crimes in this period (or in our own, for that matter), rape and murder are ultimately the most brutal. Yet these cases stand out not solely because of the viciousness of the crimes. The race, class and sexual secrets of the men in these stories instantly identify them as monstrous, subhuman villains, and the deaths as well as the ages of the women (one very young, one very old) frame them as saintly martyrs.

In October 1894 the body of thirteen-year-old Jessie Keith was found by the railway tracks near her home in Elma. She had been returning home in the afternoon from posting letters and shopping in nearby Listowel. Hers had been an awful death; she was raped, knocked unconscious, and her body severely mutilated. Several witnesses reported seeing a suspicious stranger—an unshaven Frenchman, carrying a black valise, near the scene. When the abandoned valise was discovered, full of women's clothing, authorities knew they had their man. Amede Chattelle, a sixty-year-old transient from St. Hyacinthe, Quebec, was arrested several days after the murder and initially confessed to the crime. When he went to trial in March 1895, he denied his confession and insisted on defending himself without a lawyer. The jury hardly deliberated, finding him guilty instantly; he was later hanged.[39]

Frank Roughmond was also a transient, a thirty-three-year-old itinerant black fortune teller who, in September 1908, came to Stratford looking for work and lodging. Finding neither, he continued on, stopping at the Peake family farm, several miles outside of town. Sixty-six-year-old Mary Peake was home alone that day; her husband was in town, and her two sons were working in the fields. Roughmond apparently entered the basement through an unlocked door and surprised Mrs. Peake in the midst of domestic chores. Her sons found her body in the basement. She had been killed when her head hit the concrete floor. Curiously, Roughmond lay sleeping beside her, making it easy for her sons to tie him up and hand him over to the police. In this case the medical evidence of sexual assault was ambiguous. Roughmond said nothing to authorities, either during his arrest or at his trial. A hastily appointed lawyer put up a lame defense, but Roughmond too was found guilty and was hanged in June 1909.[40]

Both of these cases became huge community scandals, and attracted national as well as local attention. The Stratford press hailed the killing of Jessie Keith as "the first crime of its kind in North America." In Listowel the crime "aroused the people to a dangerous level of excitement" and made women "afraid to stay in a house alone without being well armed." Hundreds of people flocked to the railway tracks to get a glimpse of the scene, scooping up as mementos bits of barley which the girl had been bringing home. Fourteen years later the Stratford press reported the killing of Mary Peake as "probably the most brutal murder ever committed within the confines of Perth County."[41] Hundreds of people attended the funerals of the victims (at Jessie Keith's, women "cried bitterly and strong men shuddered") and later the hangings of the convicted men. Two years after Jessie Keith's death the community raised funds to erect a twelve-foot-high marble statue depicting a woman dropping a flower at the girl's grave. Inscribed on the monument were the words "While defending her honor she lost her life." Over sixty years later the crime continued to resonate in the community. After another sensational murder in the area, in 1967, the *Listowel Banner* retold the Jessie Keith story and published, for the first time since the slaying, Chattelle's confession.[42]

The evidence suggests that both men were indeed guilty of the crimes, though it appears likely that Chattelle (who had spent several years in an asylum) was insane, and Roughmond could have killed Mrs. Peake accidentally. Yet as transient, non-Anglo-Saxon outsiders, both men were punished for a host of other evils: they were tramps and strangers, malevolent infiltrators of rural harmony. While they both may have been guilty, both undoubtedly received completely inadequate legal assistance. In neither case did the press observe the niceties of the criminal justice system. By the day after his arrest, Chattelle was referred to as "the murderer and mutilator of Jessie Keith," and in Roughmond's case the papers outdid themselves in thinking up new ways to refer to the prisoner. In the first news story alone, Frank Roughmond was referred to as a "husky brute," "big negro," "burly negro," "inhumane monster," "black fiend" and "coloured brute."[43] The judge allowed an obviously disoriented and incoherent Amede Chattelle to proceed with his own defense, and Frank Roughmond waited months in jail before a local lawyer could be found to take his case, a man who was no match for the crown prosecutor A. E. Du Vernet brought in from Toronto.[44] Both men were badly mistreated by the courts. Yet the major moral conclusion reached in each case was a smug satisfaction with the superiority of the Canadian justice system.

In Chattelle's case, the interpretive tone of the story was set immediately. In the first of many Jack the Ripper allusions, the Stratford press reported the crime as "Whitechapel Outdone." The only difference was that Jessie Keith was "an innocent girl." Indeed, there were some who suspected that Amede Chattelle was the London murderer himself.[45] The Jack the Ripper comparison signified more than creative headline writing, however. The danger represented by this crime was on a scale so great the community insisted it must have been the work of an outsider. Echoing the common perception that linked sexual danger solely to urban life, the *Evening Beacon* declared: "it is inconceivable that the wretch who committed the deed could have, even for a limited time, been brought under the comparatively refining influences of the most isolated part of Canada. Such a monster is clearly the product of the most degraded resorts of a large city."[46] Cities took the blame for a host of evils, in part because of who lived there. German historian George Mosse argues that cities were home to outsiders—Jews, criminals, the insane, homosexuals—while the countryside was "the home of the native on his soil."[47]

The suspects in these stories were not only outsiders, they were tramps. In small communities, tramps and strangers, both popular symbols of danger, were often scapegoats in cases of sexual assault. In the days between Keith's murder and Chattelle's arrest, there was, according to the press, "no rest for the tramps." Several such suspicious characters were arrested in Perth County, and others were reportedly chased out of town by irate citizens. Employing a discourse that would warm the hearts of contemporary neoconservatives, the press urged the government to pass stricter vagrancy laws to rid the countryside of "this tramp nuisance." "Idle, useless and improvident men" who would rather beg than work should be "set to work road-making or at some other occupation that would contribute to the public welfare."[48] Tramps, one police constable argued, were particularly well suited to a life of crime, since they "tend to look alike and it is difficult to identify them."[49]

When Chattelle was arrested, these fears seemed vindicated. Amede Chattelle was the ultimate tramp. Born in Quebec, he had spent his life wandering and had worked primarily as a sailor. The story of Chattelle's life was recounted as a warning of the dangers that can beset persons who stray too far from home. According to the *Evening Beacon*, "Attracted to the outer world as he was by a desire for adventure, there is no doubt that during the many years in which he wandered over the earth, Chattelle had many an experience with which the ordinary traveller to eternity never comes in contact."[50] Chattelle's status as an outsider was exacerbated by his strange sexual habits. He had stolen the valise of clothing from a woman in a neighboring town, and when he was arrested he had been wearing her undergarments. Unfortunately for Chattelle, his crime predated the emergence, in the 1920s and 1930s, of the psychiatric diagnostic category 'sexual psychopath.'[51] And in the absence of a defense lawyer, there was no attempt made to patch together even the most superficial suggestion that Chattelle was an insane "sex pervert." The most skillful lawyer, however, would have had trouble winning acquittal in Stratford, which saw the case in straightforward moral terms. The newspapers declared that "the wearing of female apparel is the only thing that points to any weakness of intellect in him . . . and that can be attributed as much to licentiousness as to insanity."[52]

There was less need to explain Frank Roughmond's background, motives or sexual proclivities; his color alone was sufficient to account for his supposedly violent nature. The range of descriptive epithets deployed against Roughmond broadened in the course of his trial to include "lustful negro" and "notorious negro." His physical stature was constantly mentioned in menacing and disapproving tones; one story reported that he stood "fully, if not over, six feet." The wild and "restless" nature of Roughmond was contrasted to the placid tranquillity of the Peake family. Roughmond, it was declared, was attracted to the farmhouse by its "air of peace and stillness," and disturbed Mrs. Peake in the act of that most homey of domestic tasks, baking bread. The cause of death was debated by several doctors, yet medical evidence was scarcely necessary. According to one doctor, Mrs. Peake died from shock caused by "the appearance of an uncouth negro."[53] Estelle Freedman argues that even into the 1930s, when sex criminals were explained in psychiatric rather than moral terms, black men were still more likely to be imprisoned or executed. As she puts it, "white men who committed sexual crimes had to be mentally ill; black men who committed sexual crimes were believed to be guilty of wilful violence."[54]

It was hardly surprising, therefore, that Roughmond's lawyer's attempt to appeal to the mercy of the court failed miserably. Roughmond, claimed J. J. Coughlin, "was an outcast with no friends and a negro, so that he would excite little sympathy at the hands of the white race. Hence there was a need of setting aside all prejudice and judging entirely from the evidence submitted." Only in death did Frank Roughmond lose some of his savagery. His expression on his way to the gallows was described as "simple and child-like"; he was much thinner, and "his hands and wrists were slim and almost lady-like in size."[55] In death Amede Chattelle also lost some of his villiany. In 1896, at the ceremony held to unveil the monument to Jessie Keith, the presiding town official reminded those gathered that Chattelle "was once 'a mother's darling,' and we do not know the whole history of the rough and thorny path of life along which he travelled from the cradle to the grave of infamy and dishonor."[56]

Despite such appalling treatment by the press and the courts, both men were believed to have received exemplary trials. The proceedings were complacently described as preferable to mob rule and underscoring the superiority of Anglo-Saxon law. In both cases, however, intense community ferment had led to widespread rumors of lynching. In Chattelle's case the press initially reported these rumors half approvingly. Fully "two thirds of the community" were known to have expressed the sentiment that "I don't believe in lynching, but I'd make an exception in this case." Several days later, however, the people of Listowel were congratulated on "the good sense and the healthy respect for law and order they displayed in withholding their hands from the prisoner." In Roughmond's case the rumors were put down immediately. The "common expression of regret that Roughmond was not strung up on the wind mill at the Peake farm when captured" was deemed "unseemly in this country, where the vilest criminal is given a fair trial."[57]

When the verdicts were announced, more testimonials to the fairness of the legal system poured forth. Justice Ridell told Roughmond that "you differ from most of us in colour but no man can say you did not have a fair trial." Furthermore, he announced, he was "glad that my Canadian people have refrained from violence and have let the law take its course. That is a great object lesson to others, and to people of your race, Frank Roughmond." The *Stratford Daily Herald* editorialized happily that "the majesty and solemnity of a British court of justice" helped "put aside" the thirst for revenge which had been present in the community. "It is good to live in a country where its people wait for the law to exert its power. It proves the quality of self-control and education."[58]

In Chattelle's case, defenders of the British system of justice were stung by criticism from some lawyers and the press in Quebec that Chattelle had not received a fair hearing, particularly that an obviously insane man had been allowed to conduct his own defense. A petition circulated through the Montreal legal community asking that Chattelle be examined by a "panel of experts" to determine his sanity. The people of Stratford put little stock in the allegations of racism which accompanied this campaign in Quebec, claiming that had Chattelle "been an Englishman, Scotchman or Irishman, his treatment would have been the same."[59]

Supporters of Amede Chattelle and Frank Roughmond (if indeed Roughmond had any) could be forgiven if they failed to see a substantial difference between lynching by an angry mob and the proceedings of the Anglo-Saxon legal system. Both crimes touched profound anxieties in rural Ontario; as nonworking, transient strangers, the two men reached a level of 'otherness' which made their rapid convictions a forgone conclusion. In cases of sexual murder, unlike 'average' sexual assaults, it was the behavior, character and motives of the men which went on trial. Little was ever said about the female victims; their deaths ensured that their character remained intact. That the women and men were strangers to each other also helped, since the less well acquainted the victim and perpetrator were, the more likely a conviction. Similarly, these cases draw out several familiar feminist arguments about sexual violence: that linking sexual danger solely to evil strangers obscures the magnitude of harm done by friends, lovers and family; and that the image of male 'sex villains' looming larger than life over cowering, defenseless females reproduces a set of assumptions about male violence and female victimization which simplifies the complexity of violence, resistance and gender.[60] Finally, the sanctimonious rhetoric regarding the fairness of the trials indicates an awkward attempt to present the legal system as neutral, just and removed from the prejudices of the mob, which, in these cases, it was not.

Murder in the Name of Motherhood: Angelina Napolitano and Annie Robinson

So far, women have remained rather shadowy figures in this discussion of sexual scandals. The women who were the objects of scandal in cases involving prominent men tended to be eclipsed by rumors of political maneuvering and blackmail, and the women who died at the hands of sex murderers were quickly canonized and forgotten. It was only on the rare occasion that women acted as the subject of crime that their lives and motives were probed.[61]

Two women in northern Ontario during this period became celebrated, internationally known criminals. Angelina Napolitano was an Italian immigrant from Sault Ste. Marie who admitted killing her husband in retaliation for his prolonged physical abuse and insistence that she become a prostitute. We have been introduced to Annie Robinson already: she was the woman from outside Sudbury who, at the request of her daughter Jessie, murdered at birth two offspring of her husband's incestuous relationships with two of their daughters. Both women were found guilty of murder and sentenced to hang, and both were granted clemency after an enormous public campaign on their behalf, waged in large part by the women's movement.

Both women were, before being catapulted into criminal notoriety, ordinary women. Yet within weeks of their conviction their relationships with their husband and children, their family history and sexual morality were the subject of gossip and scrutiny. The social meaning of these women's lives, and the interpretation of their crimes, differed dramatically according to who was doing the looking. Angelina Napolitano and Annie Robinson acted as mirrors: in their stories feminists in the early women's movement saw reflected back their own concerns about marriage, motherhood, and the inequities of the legal system; others saw the dangers of stiletto-brandishing foreigners, the moral hazards of life in northern Ontario, the effect of drunkenness on good men, or the sexual immorality of immigrants. In the state's response to the clemency campaigns we see the continuation of a familiar debate regarding legal authority.

Of the two, Angelina Napolitano's story drew the most publicity and involved a larger, more controversial campaign of support.[62] Angelina and her husband, Pietro, had left Italy together in 1901, spending seven years in New York and a year in Thessalon. Since 1909 they had been residents of Sault Ste. Marie, where Pietro worked as a laborer. In Thessalon they had owned a home, but the family fortunes declined while living in the Soo, and they and their four young children resided in a rented four-room home in an alley in the town's little Italy. Pietro and Angelina's relationship began showing signs of strain shortly after they moved to northern Ontario. According to Angelina, Pietro became jealous when he saw "lots of other people having houses and money" and complained that he was working too hard for too little. His solution was to put Angelina to work; he began pestering her to "do bad business" with men in order to earn extra money to build the family a house. Angelina continually rejected his demands, sometimes asserting female virtue (insisting she simply "was not a bad woman") and other times expressing a fear that such a life would be bad for her young children. The trouble between the couple worsened, and Pietro left her temporarily in fall 1910. With four children and ten dollars in savings, Angelina took in a boarder who paid the rent and with whom, she admitted, she became sexually involved. Several weeks later Pietro returned and the trouble continued. During one argument, in November 1910, Pietro repeatedly stabbed Angelina, sending her to the hospital for two weeks. He received a suspended sentence for this assault. Several more months of arguments ensued, exacerbated, Angelina complained, by Pietro's increasing alcohol consumption. Finally, on Easter Sunday afternoon 1911, Angelina had enough. The two quarreled that morning, and Pietro threatened that if Angelina did not make twenty or thirty dollars for him by the evening, he would kill her or take her children away. He then went upstairs to his bedroom for a nap. Deciding that she "could not stand this trouble any longer," Angelina followed him some hours later and killed him in his sleep, striking him several times with an ax. She was seven months pregnant at the time of Pietro's murder, a fact which became the most significant and sentimentalized of all the arguments her supporters made in her defense.

Angelina confessed her crime immediately to neighbors, and there was no question in the mind of the trial judge, Justice Britton, that this was, as he put it, "a simple case." He balked at the defense lawyer Uriah McFadden's attempt to draw out evidence regarding Pietro's previous conviction for assaulting his wife as well as their many arguments about prostitution. According to Britton, "if anybody injured six months ago could give that as justification or excuse for slaying a person, it would be anarchy complete." He questioned that there had been any provocation on Pietro's part, particularly since he'd been killed in his sleep, "lying in bed, in a perfectly helpless condition." To the jury he was straightforward. Angelina, he said, was a "free agent" and had always been "at perfect liberty" to leave her husband. Her attempts to claim virtuous, 'wronged woman' status were marred, in his opinion, by her relationship with her boarder, whether this developed "for the board for a week, or for bread and butter for the children . . . or simply as a matter of lust and . . . animal desire." Her act, he claimed, was one of "deliberation," which could find no justification in law. Her pregnancy he dismissed as "a matter of detail which it is not necessary to deal further with," but he assured the jury that, if she was found guilty, her hanging would wait until after the child was born.[63]

Annie Robinson's story of her husband's repeated sexual assaults upon her daughters, his constant drinking, and her isolation and shame also failed to move legal authorities.[64] Twice the judge rejected a verdict of not guilty by reason of insanity, sending the jury back until they brought in a guilty verdict. Annie Robinson's failure to leave or report her husband's wrong doing drew harsh criticism from Justice Magee.

So while the actions of Annie Robinson and Angelina Napolitano condemned them in the eyes of judges and juries, it was precisely their injured womenhood and maternalism which captured public attention and ultimately saved them from hanging. The justice minister received literally thousands of letters and petitions on behalf of both women. Annie Robinson's case was taken up by the WCTU and local Councils of Women as well as by many citizens and clergymen acquainted with her family in southern Ontario. Angelina Napolitano received even more attention; as well as the WCTU and national and local Councils of Women, she received support from the national and international suffrage movement and the Left and the labor movement. Petitions were received from England's Women's Social and Political Union; the American Socialist Party; suffrage groups in the United States, Austria, Hungary and Poland; and many Canadian suffrage groups. The Canadian labor press also supported her; a petition on her behalf was circulated by the *Winnipeg Voice* and *Cotton's Weekly*. Individuals wrote for her as well. Famous feminists such as Flora MacDonald Denison and a more lukewarm Helen MacMurchy expressed their concern, and unknown women in unhappy or abusive marriages wrote candidly of their own experiences. One of her countrymen offered to provide a home for her and her children, and in Annie Robinson's case one woman offered to go to jail in her stead. Robinson received more support from the mainstream press and local community. The *Sudbury Star* helped publicize her campaign. Angelina Napolitano received more ambiguous support from her own community. Her lawyer in Sault Ste. Marie continued working on her behalf, collecting petitions and writing letters for years, and hundreds of members of Toronto's Italian community, as well as the Italian consul in Montreal, wrote to support her. The press in the Soo, however, a faithful adherent of the belief that armed foreigners were ruining the community, displayed mixed feelings about her case. There were also reports that the Italian community of Sault Ste. Marie believed her to be an immoral woman and rejected her story that she had acted to save her own and her children's honor.

Responses to the sad tales of Angelina Napolitano and Annie Robinson provide an unusual opportunity to observe the opinions of individuals and organizations about sexuality, marriage, and especially motherhood. In Angelina's case, some observers also drew predictable conclusions about race. While an air of Anglo-Saxon pity and charity pervaded much of the discussion of the "ignorant" Napolitano family, some commentators were quite explicit. Racism, however, could be used both to support and condemn Mrs. Napolitano. H. W. Brown, a jeweler in Oregon, for example, asked that Justice Minister Alan Aylesworth "have pity on a simple young foreigner," and a woman from Long Island suggested that murder "was the only way her ignorant, uneducated self knew" to protect herself.[65] A Toronto newspaper, quoted extensively in the Sault Ste. Marie press, argued that it would be "dangerous" to suggest that Mrs. Napolitano was justified in killing her husband, since Italians "are all too ready as it is to use the knife, the pistol, or any other weapon that lies at hand, as a means of redressing real or fancied wrongs." The Sault Ste. Marie press remained incredulous about the attention the case received and was one of the few voices to cast doubt on her motives and character. Mrs. Napolitano, claimed the *Sault Ste. Marie Star*, "is not the angel the American press make her out to be"; "Peter" Napolitano "was the better of the two by great odds," continued the paper, concluding that Angelina "richly deserves hanging," particularly since the paternity of her unborn child was, apparently, up for question.[66]

An obvious line of defense in the Napolitano campaign was that Pietro's beatings and threats regarding prostitution constituted legitimate provocation. This was the position her lawyer Uriah McFadden had taken at the trial and was the major argument put forward in a petition he circulated among residents of Sault Ste. Marie. This defense was echoed in other letters and petitions, primarily those organized or signed predominantly by men. The members of Toronto's Bloor Street Baptist Church men's Bible class, for example, argued that "the provocation received, that is the inducement on the part of the husband for her to resort to prostitution for his benefit, as well as his previous attempt to stab her, . . . his threat to kill her on the day of the crime, constitute weighty reasons for the exercise of mercy."[67] A heartfelt personal letter from a woman in Pittsburgh declared, "I am a mother and wife of an able bodied man who will not support me and [am] roaming the street and after years of ill treatment and abuse . . . I know I would have killed him."[68]

British and American feminists were outspoken in pointing out the "masculine bias" of the case. The British suffrage journal *Common Cause* argued that "the law and its administration are both bad, and for the same reasons—that they are exclusively masculine." Emmeline Pethick Lawrence, writing in *Votes for Women*, drew the obvious conclusion: "No wonder," she declared, "women are fighting for the vote."[69] Individual feminists, clearly influenced by the social purity movement, saw in Angelina a hero, one who defended herself valiantly against male privilege and sexual license. Anna Hurtubis from Massachusetts thanked God that "the little woman had the courage (that of a tigress protecting her young) to slay the villain. . . . Oh, if men only knew."[70] Mrs. Napolitano was simply defending her honor, wrote a woman from Philadelphia, and since the law protects men who are assaulted by robbers, why punish her, since "robbing a woman of her character is far worse than any other kind of robbery."[71] One particularly indignant woman in England claimed that "the taking of the corrupt life of her wicked husband was not even murder in Mrs. Napolitano's case it was a dreadful sacred duty" since her crime "delivered of the race from loathsome human ulcers." "The world needs such heroines," she concluded, "to lift it out of the foul rut in which it lies derelict today, the rut of immorality, a far worse crime than murder!"[72]

While hundreds of Canadian feminists signed petitions circulated by their organizations, their leaders showed characteristic reserve. Flora Mac-Donald Denison simply reminded the government that thousands had been involved in the campaign to free Angelina and politely inquired when this would be done. Helen MacMurchy positioned herself as a gatekeeper between the angry popular hordes and the government. She wrote twice to tell the justice minister of the depth of community ferment about the case, agreeing that Angelina's position "was an awful one" and asking him to "carefully consider the requests for clemency." More distressing to her, however, was the fact that everyone, from an unknown working woman who "accosted" her in the post office to the Chicago branch of the American Socialist party (whose "extraordinary allegations" about the case she helpfully forwarded), was in an uproar. The National Council of Women, the country's largest women's organization, refused to call for the woman's release. Delegates to the council's annual meeting in 1911 soundly defeated a motion asking for the commutation of the death sentence, since the council, as delegate Violet McNaughton put it, "should not put itself in the position of interfering with the properly constituted legal authorities."[73]

Yet the single most popular sentiment expressed regarding Angelina Napolitano was not about her status as abused wife or woman who refused prostitution, but rather about her condition as an expectant mother. Both feminist and nonfeminist supporters argued that the death sentence should not have been levied against a pregnant woman, because of the damage it would inflict on her unborn child. The Toronto Suffrage Association, for example, claimed that "every additional hour spent by her in the condition of terror, anticipating her execution . . . cannot but react in a dangerous way upon her unborn, innocent child." "Leading women" in the rural districts of West Huron and Bruce agreed, claiming that the sentence "overlooks the prenatal experience on child-life."[74]

From this argument, many others went on to claim that pregnancy had *caused* Angelina Napolitano to commit the crime. Mrs. David Mills, a woman from Woodstock, Ontario, wrote that "it is a well known fact that a woman is hardly responsible at such a time, being more easy to aggravate, as one suffers so and cannot stand anything harsh, especially from a husband."[75] This argument was put forward by women's suffrage groups across North America. The No Vote No Tax League, for example, stated that pregnancy sometimes produces in women a "mental disorder."[76] This notion was given medical legitimacy by a doctor in Montreal, contacted by the Italian consul general. Dr. G. Villeneuve, medical superintendent of the St. Jean Dieu Hospital in Montreal, agreed that "pregnancy often created in a number of women a morbid condition, both mental and moral, leading to an unbalanced state of mind and more especially to impulsiveness." Even A. C. Boyce, M.P. from Sault Ste. Marie, agreed that the crime had been committed "under the impulse of hysteria, bordering upon madness."[77]

The theme of wounded motherhood pervaded the arguments in support of Mrs. Napolitano, particularly those from women's groups. Most women prefaced their remarks with a reference to their own motherhood. A group of women teachers from Austria, for example, made their appeal "in the Name of Motherhood—the base of all civilization—and in the name of the home." Local WCTU chapters in Canada protested against "the inhuman spectacle of a woman being allowed to live just sufficiently long to rise from child-bed and from thence to the scaffold."[78] Sentimental stories in the press embellished this theme. North Americans were kept informed of the fate of Angelina's four children (cared for by the Children's Aid Society) and read portions of her children's letters to her in prison. They heard of her own mother's reaction to the story, and were no doubt moved to learn that Angelina "turned from her own agony and is giving loving, motherly care to the future of her baby" by hand sewing baby clothes in jail.[79] The Italian consul general to Canada circulated photographs and biographies of the children to women's organizations. The Toronto Local Council of Women took an avid interest in their welfare: members met with J. J. Kelso, superintendent of the Children's Aid Society, to ask that the children not be separated from one another. One council member, Mrs. Powell, even offered to pay the CAS for the maintenance of the children so that they could remain together. In the end they were placed, separately, in foster homes around the province.[80]

Angelina Napolitano's supporters thus drew from an assortment of often inventive arguments. Concerns about defiled motherhood and women's irrationality while pregnant predominated, thus sidestepping the thornier issues the case raised: wife abuse and power relations within the patriarchal family. While some were concerned about prostitution, and a few spoke of their own experiences of male violence, Angelina catapulted to international fame as an ill-fated *mother* rather than an abused *woman*.

Defiled motherhood was also a significant basis of support for Annie Robinson, particularly from women's groups. All the major Canadian women's groups lined up behind Mrs. Robinson, but the tone of this campaign bore less of the feminist indignation which fueled supporters of Mrs. Napolitano. In her trial, Annie Robinson referred to herself as "borne down by shame" as a result of her years of silence and isolation, and this image of a disgraced, weakened creature recurred throughout the campaign for her release. The Toronto Local Council of Women, for example, worried that her daughters were "without a mother's care," particularly since "girls in misfortune are so often marked. . . . Even if she as a mother could not protect them from the evil within the home, surely she could protect them from without." The WCTU echoed this concern, arguing that Mrs. Robinson "is the natural guardian of the children who will need her many times more in the next ten years . . . and, with her help, could work the farm and keep the family together." Few found pity for her daughters. A prim letter from the Imperial Order of Daughters of the Empire remarked that Mrs. Robinson "in her mother love tried to hide the guilt of her infamous husband and irresponsible daughters."[81]

Annie Robinson presented a less heroic figure for Canadian feminists, and some displayed mixed feelings about her case. While a few correspondents spoke of the brutishness of her husband, and the *Toronto Star* opined that he "should be hanged, painfully, and twice," no one suggested that Mrs. Robinson's actions were warranted or deserving of celebration.[82] The ever-cautious Helen MacMurchy was likely more in step with her peers this time when she remarked that "the circumstances of this case are so abhorrent and dreadful one would gladly forget them all." Even so, she went on, she was "not sure that she [Mrs. Robinson] should so suffer."[83]

Luckily for Annie Robinson, she came from 'good stock.' She had been raised in a devout Methodist family in a village outside Ottawa, and her brother Peter Matheson was a Methodist minister. A number of Methodist clergymen from the Ottawa area supported her, all of whom described to the justice minister Mrs. Robinson's background and the "high moral character" of her family. Peter Matheson left his position to take up guardianship of the Robinson children and family farm, and her brothers kept up a steady correspondence with the Justice Department. They never condoned her crime but offered to take care of her upon her release.

While the campaigns for the release of these two women helped keep the cases in the public eye and no doubt contributed to the women's eventual release, the publicity took legal authorities by surprise. The Justice Department did not take kindly to what they deemed interference with the law. In both cases Justice Minister Aylesworth responded tersely to the avalanche of mail he received. His response to a correspondent in Michigan about the Napolitano case was typical: "The agitation the newspapers have worked up in this case," he wrote, "seems to me about the most uncalled for thing I have yet seen." But, he went on, "the case will receive identically the same consideration if there never had been a single newspaper article printed about it."[84] An internal Justice Department memorandum about the Robinson case made the same point, noting that "the whole matter is not to be decided upon the more or less hysterical outcries of the press, or the more or less competent judgment of those superficially acquainted with the real facts, but on the sober common sense of the Privy Council of Canada." Some correspondents anticipated such objections from the government and took care to word their support for clemency without appearing to undermine the authority of the legal system. Reverend Blakely from Renfrew County, who wrote in support of Annie Robinson, argued that "the majesty of law has been adequately manifested by the imprisonment . . . of James Robinson, the initial criminal."[85]

The campaigns worked. Annie Robinson's death sentence was commuted to ten years imprisonment. After spending slightly over a year in Kingston Prison, she was released in March 1911, at the age of forty-six, to her brother's care. James Robinson was found not guilty of murder, but pleaded guilty to a series of rape and incest charges, and received a twenty-eight-year sentence. Angelina Napolitano waited much longer for her release. After her sentence was commuted to life imprisonment in July 1911, she wrote regularly to the Justice Department asking for her freedom. Letters on her behalf grew less frequent over time, but the Salvation Army wrote regularly, offering to care for her if she were released on parole. Finally, in December 1922, thirty-nine-year-old Angelina Napolitano left Kingston Prison. In a final, tragic twist to the story, it appears she was led to believe that she was required to stay in the city of Kingston until authorities allowed her to move. So despite her often-stated desire to reunite with her children, with whom she renewed contact at the end of her jail term, she stayed in Kingston for over two years, working as a domestic servant for a member of the local legal community. When Angelina finally wrote the governor general for permission to leave Kingston to meet her children, she quickly learned that, since "no woman is called upon to report to the police while under license," she had never been prevented from leaving town.[86] After that, no more was heard from Mrs. Napolitano.

Sexual scandals reveal clearly the relationship between legal authority, popular amusement and collective custom. Crime—real and fictional—still contains enormous popular entertainment value. During this period, however, communities were intensely involved in the process of judging, punishing, or saving criminal celebrities. A community's level of involvement in these crimes reflects the relatively underdeveloped state of legal structures and authority of the time. Even after the 'unruly mob' was dispersed, crowds gathered to watch trials, glimpse suspects, or sign petitions favoring those unjustly convicted. Each of these acts was rebuffed by what was then an extremely defensive legal system as unwanted meddling in the lofty affairs of state.

In these years we see a transition in the regulation and judgment of personal life. Community policing, via such rituals as the charivari or tarring and feathering, was supplanted by the legal system, though communities continued to keep watch and express their opinions as audiences in the courtroom, spectators at curb-side jails, or writers of heartfelt letters to authorities about unpopular verdicts. Over time even these acts of community participation waned in favor of the more passive act of reading newspapers and crime novels. We must understand these changes in the broadest of terms since they did not constitute a seamless, chronological advance. Consider the contemporary controversy over the case of Lawrencia "Bambi" Bembenek, the Milwaukee, Wisconsin, woman who many believe was unjustly convicted of murder. Her story has created a minor industry of books and films, and her well-publicized escape to Canada was greeted with delight by her U.S. supporters, many of whom donned masks bearing her likeness to symbolically assist her in retaining her anonymity and short-lived freedom.[87] Active public involvement in criminal cases has not been completely supplanted by the legal system.

The prejudices of the turn-of-the-century mob may or may not have differed from those of the state. It is not my intention to contrast the democracy of the crowd with the narrow elitism of the state, particularly when it comes to sexual crimes. The state, as Frank Roughmond discovered, could be just as brutish as the worst lynch mob. But the fate of James Weatherly also indicates that communities evolved a set of sexual standards which could be hazardous—even fatal—to those who transgressed them. The point, however, is that the establishment of the state as sole authority in the realm of moral and sexual regulation was a long, difficult and contested process.

CHAPTER FIVE

From the Parlor to the Kitchen: Courtship, Popular Mores, and Regulation

During the late 1800s and early 1900s in rural and northern Ontario, the determination of innocence or guilt in the courtroom was a complex process, relying as much on legal interpretation as on popular sexual mores. Judges and juries drew from a vast pool of social assumptions regarding respectability and personal character when weighing the evidence in trials of sexual crimes. In this chapter I explore the moral codes which informed the social and sexual lives of nineteenth- and early twentieth-century heterosexual couples, and ask whether the dominant Victorian sexual ethos bore any relationship to actual sexual practice.

Sexual encounters that caught the attention of the family, the community and legal authorities provide conclusive evidence that Victorian sexual ideology was contested. But to truly understand the complexity of sexual meaning historically, we must do more than contrast convention with rebellion. In this period, as in our own, certain sexual standards became hegemonic and internalized, part of everyday life. The records of sexual crime yield insights on courtship, sexual conflict and negotiation (between men and women, and between parents and children), and the construction of standards of sexual behavior. These standards drew meaning from (and were applied differently to) persons of different sexes, classes, races, and ethnicities.

Stories of sexual crime can be interrogated as historical snapshots of heterosexual intimacy. Studies of heterosexuality itself are hardly rare. An entire branch of social history—the history of the family—is devoted to the study of (usually) unproblematized heterosexuality. What is rare is the study of the process of creating families, that is, courtship, romance, and dating as well as the explicit acknowledgment that one is studying an institution as opposed to a natural, pregiven social unit. The hegemony of heterosexuality has been surprisingly recent, yet historians, as Jonathan Katz notes, continue to use the term uncritically, as a "universal analytical tool."[1]

Most of what we know about the history of courtship and dating is based on personal reminiscences (diaries and letters, for example) of the Anglo-Saxon middle and upper classes,[2] yet reliance on personal memoirs skews history in favor of the dominant. Previous studies also tend to lack conflict or tension, presenting a universal picture of contented couples who passed through courtship as the natural progression toward wedded bliss. Heterosexual coupling is taken as a given rather than as a structured process—one that could indeed result in happy married life but could also go awry at many turns. Not everyone lived happily ever after. Conflict, betrayal and recrimination were as much a part of social life as 'successful' marriage. In failing to probe heterosexuality as an institution, one that has historically demanded near total participation, the many strands comprising the construction of heterosexual hegemony (or, to use an often-quoted phrase, 'compulsory heterosexuality') are overlooked.[3] Whiggish, sentimentalized interpretations of courtship would benefit from a larger context, one that takes into account the experience of all classes and races and also examines the broader meaning of sexuality as a realm of conflict and power.

Kathy Peiss's study of working-class women's leisure in turn-of-the-century New York City, *Cheap Amusements*, is such an attempt to extend the study of coupling and sociability to a broader realm. Similarly, Christine Stansell's *City of Women* examines the dating and leisure patterns of an earlier generation of New York working-class youth.[4] As Stansell and Peiss have both demonstrated, one way of dealing with the lack of first-person sources from working-class and immigrant historical actors is by reading against the grain the records of those charged with supervising their behavior (the police, courts, social workers, reformers). For example, one cannot read the records of criminal prosecutions as straightforward instances of sexual or romantic truths; these stories are mediated by many factors. The involvement or noninvolvement of a woman's parents, the objective in bringing charges, the place she lived and the degree of cultural comfort she felt in using the services of the legal system, plus the fact that these stories were told to an often hostile, all-male and extremely public criminal justice system—all would determine the way a complainant's story unfolded. With these cautions in mind, I use these cases to make some preliminary remarks about the social life, sexual activity, and mores of women and men from rural and small-town working-class backgrounds in this period.

The late nineteenth and early twentieth century witnessed an explosion of new opportunities for what Christine Stansell has called "heterosexual sociability." There were plenty of new ways to have fun. By the beginning of the twentieth century, urban dwellers could amuse themselves in a host of new commercial establishments: the ice cream parlor, dance hall, movie theater, amusement park or Sunday excursion. New private enterprises encroached on traditional working-class forms of sociability such as neighborhood, ethnic group, or trade union social events.

New pastimes produced new terrains of struggle. When temperance advocates, for example, drew up a 'workingman's budget' in order to calculate the financial benefits of working-class abstinence, they intentionally ignored recreational spending, arguing that there was "ample free recreation of the proper moral elevation to be found in the churches and public libraries."[5] Conflicts between workers and authorities over the development and use of community parks, the appropriate way to celebrate national holidays, and even behavior in movie theaters were fought in "class ways"; the battle was about control over life outside the workplace.[6]

The sexual politics of leisure were also contested. Efforts by middle-class social reformers to discourage certain forms of entertainment (such as the dance hall) in favor of other, more socially sanctioned pastimes (such as those organized by the YWCA and other reform groups) had at their root a concern for the threat posed to economic and sexual conventions by the emerging culture of single, urban working-class women.[7] Yet part of the story remains uncharted. Sexual danger, commercialized vice, and immoral influences were seen by most early twentieth-century moral reformers as distinct products of urban life. Feminist historians studying these questions have focused their research on urban settings and have tended, by and large, to accept the notion that the relative freedom provided young single women by wage labor in urban settings also facilitated their participation in the heterosocial world of commercialized leisure. Freed from the watchful eyes of parents and neighbors, able to choose any number of unchaperoned sites of amusement, encouraged by the new entrepreneurs of leisure (such as the movie house) where they had once been discouraged (such as the saloon), women in urban centers during this period experienced, so the story goes, an unprecedented degree of social autonomy and anonymity.

The spread of wage labor and urban commercial amusements expanded women's range of social opportunities. What has yet to be established, however, is how new patterns of leisure among urban women contrasted in a fundamental way with those of rural and small-town women. The form of urban recreation was indeed quite different, but in terms of such issues as the degree of autonomy, privacy and control over their leisure time, rural women's experiences were not qualitatively different from their urban sisters'. Those who stayed on the farm had their share of sexual adventures and mishaps.

PATTERNS OF SOCIABILITY

The pastimes of rural and small-town youth were not, overall, so very different from those of their urban counterparts. By the 1910s and 1920s even towns the size of Sault Ste. Marie, Orangeville and Cochrane had movie theaters, which provided a meeting place for couples. Throughout this period, women and men found each other and entertained themselves at community dances, ice cream parlors, berry patches and circuses. Couples in northern Ontario went ice skating and canoeing; girls in rural Ontario met boys at county fairs and church picnics. When opportunities for such structured amusements did not exist, couples simply 'hung out.' They went driving (in buggies, cutters and, later, cars). Most often they went out walking, the single most popular way to date, get picked up, or flirt. Lynne Marks's rich analysis of the leisure possibilities during this period also challenges the received wisdom that the most fun one could hope for in small-town Ontario was a weekend in Toronto. In her study of three small Ontario towns, Marks uncovered a vast network of homo- and heterosocial entertainments. Churches, fraternal orders and sports teams existed alongside commercial amusements, some of which were sanctioned, such as the roller rink; others, such as the theater, the circus and community dances, raised eyebrows among respectable townspeople.[8]

Historians have advanced competing interpretations of changes in nineteenth- and early twentieth-century courtship patterns. Some suggest that the courting model, in which a man called on a woman in her home, found favor with parents and resulted in less parental and community scrutiny than later forms of commercial amusement, which raised social anxieties (and therefore attempts at social control) to a new level. Historians also disagree on whether city youths or rural and small-town dwellers found more privacy.[9] Still others, such as D'Emilio and Freedman, argue that class rather than geography shaped sexual practices, contrasting what they see as the public courtship practices of rural and working-class youth with the private world of the middle class.[10]

Romantic relationships could begin in any number of places, however, and were facilitated by new ways of using leisure time. Between the 1880s and the 1920s, changes in family life and economic relations gave many women the opportunity to leave home (whether permanently or for a few hours daily), meet new people, and make new choices. Many women were picked up by men they met in the course of their jobs. Waitresses flirted with their customers; hotel chambermaids and cooks met a succession of men new to their communities; store clerks got to know not only their customers but the salesmen who serviced their establishments; and factory workers often worked alongside a number of eligible men.

Even that supposedly respectable and closely supervised form of female employment, domestic service, allowed some women the opportunity to make friends with men. Some domestic servants were assaulted by their employers or their employers' sons; others began voluntary relationships with them. In rural and small-town Ontario, temporary work as a domestic servant might allow a woman to get to know neighboring men. The families of Herman M. and Mary S., for example, had been neighbors in Sombra Township (near Wallaceburg) for ten years, so when Herman's mother needed domestic help while she was ill, she called Mary in for a few weeks. While she was employed there, Mary began a relationship with Herman, which was regularly consummated on the drive home from church, in the barn and sometimes in the house.[11]

Yet girls who 'worked out' were not the only ones able to gain the independence and privacy necessary for heterosexual companionship. Farm girls formed relationships with the hired man or a boy from a neighboring farm; others became involved with men who boarded with their families. Women also found freedom while visiting married siblings. Older sisters in particular allowed visiting younger sisters quite a bit of latitude. Some couples met at parties given by elder sisters, and some elder sisters could be counted on to turn a blind eye to a sibling's sexual rendezvous (sometimes even permitting her to entertain a boyfriend while visiting).

The middle-class models of courtship described by other historians do not generally match the reality of working-class social life, whether in rural areas or small towns. It seems that many women defied social convention and conducted their social lives in public, meeting their dates and 'walking out' through the streets or roads of small-town Ontario. Kathy Peiss has suggested that, among New York working-class youth, a pickup on the street was "an accepted means of gaining companionship for an evening's entertainment."[12] In rural areas this often was the evening's entertainment. Alternatively, 'calling' did not necessarily result in more respectable sociability. As seduction tales reveal, even the most staid Victorian courtship ritual, the social call, could encompass chaparoned tea in the parlor, as well as late-night trysts in the kitchen. Couples who wanted to engage in sex could find the space and opportunity. Many had sex in the woods on their way to and from church, and one couple made love regularly in a buggy on their way home from Salvation Army meetings. As Percy Beale, an English 're-mitance man' who recorded his active social life in Toronto of the 1880s put it, Sundays were his day to "go to church to prey."[13]

Meeting romantic partners did not seem to be a problem, but there was a perceived regional imbalance in opportunities for sociability. Northern and rural southern Ontario bore distinct social reputations. Later I explore in detail the regional dimensions of sexuality, but at this point I need only note that the two regions fell on opposite poles of the recreation controversy of the time. The north was presumed to be a place of too much fun, the south a place of too little. The predominantly male immigrant population of the north was associated with such 'rough' entertainments as gambling, drinking, and prostitution and other forms of sexual licentiousness. In fact, northern schools had trouble attracting young female teachers because parents were concerned about releasing their daughters to the immoral wilds.[14] The rural south experienced the reverse. A steady stream of commentators on the turn-of-the-century 'rural problem' identified the crisis of rural depopulation in the south as the result of inferior opportunities for social life, recreation and companionship.

Accompanying the assumption that rural southern Ontario was a place of too little fun was the suggestion that men were scarce. In particular, the eligible male population in rural Ontario was depleted. An uncredited poem penned in Norfolk County in 1880, titled "An Ontario Girl's Complaint," expresses this sentiment clearly (if badly):

> I make a complaint of a plaguey pest
> That's known by the name of the great North West
> For this wondrous land of the setting sun
> Has taken my beaux away, every one.
>
> Yea, one by one have they all cleared out,
> Thinking to better themselves, no doubt;
> Caring but little how far they may go
> From the poor lone girl in Ontario.

The author went on in this vein (and should at least be given credit for attempting to find rhymes for 'Winnipeg' and 'Keewatin'). She ended with a stirring declaration:

> I'll sling my goods in a carpet sack;
> I'll off to the west and won't turn back,
> I'll have a husband and a good one too.
> If I have to follow to Cariboo.[15]

The opposite held true in northern Ontario. The large numbers of single men who populated northern mining and lumbering communities helped fuel the region's reputation as a zone of sexual danger, but for many women the gender imbalance gave them a high degree of popularity and social choice. As one woman remembered her arrival in Timmins, "It took me four hours to find a man, there was no need to look for them, just pick and choose. I arrived on the four o'clock train and at 8 I left to dance."[16]

Questions such as whether rural or urban couples had greater freedom or privacy or whether pre- or extramarital sex was more common among city or town dwellers cannot be answered with any degree of empirical certainty. Scientific attempts to chart sexual behavior are fraught with difficulty in our own time, and we cannot project these questions back to the past. What is more relevant in understanding the sexual lives of people historically is an appreciation of the forces that might permit sexual liaisons as well as those that turned such liaisons into sites of conflict and struggle. For it was not the dance halls, movie houses or amusement parks which themselves led to sexual temptation. The berry patch could hold the same possibilities for both danger and pleasure as the most raucous dance palace. When sex because part of a couple's social agenda, either by consent or a man's insistance, opportunities for companionship or having one's way could be secured in even the most unlikely places.

Once a man was 'found,' either through traditional social networks (family, community, or church gatherings) or in less respectable settings such as movie theaters, dance halls or the street, the relationship could go in many different directions. Parental and community mores, of course, encouraged particular kinds of social interaction.

FORMS OF MORAL SUPERVISION

The Family

The family was the most immediate watchdog regulating social life and sexual behavior. Most of the women involved in prosecutions for sexual offenses lived at home with parents or a husband. Those who had left home to pursue paid labor clearly often had social lives influenced by their parents. The employment options for young rural women at this time tended to keep them close to home, and they returned there after short stints of paid labor.[17]

In my analysis of seduction and abduction cases I discussed instances of direct parental involvement in a child's sexual life. Parents of pregnant girls were the most likely to take control of the situation and demand marriage, insist on financial redress, or press criminal charges. We have also seen that many daughters lived in fear of informing their parents about their sexual activities, whether the activities were voluntary or forced. Numerous women reported that they did not tell their parents immediately after a sexual assault because they had been warned about consorting with the opposite sex and were afraid of punishment. In many cases this fear was warranted. Christina C.'s father heard her scream when their neighbor Francesco S. walked in on her in the outhouse. Her father saw them struggling and immediately hit Christina, threatening to kill her if she didn't tell the truth about what had happened. Many other girls chose the same route as Hattie W., who told her sister, rather than her father, that their uncle had raped her. Previously her father had threatened to beat his daughters if they 'got in trouble' (which he did, immediately after hearing of his daughter's plight). [18]

As daughters grew up and began to earn their own money, families were plunged into conflicts about the degree of power or autonomy such a wage bestowed. Kathy Peiss has written of the "dramas of control, resistance, acquiescence and subterfuge" which occurred in working-class families as the traditional family economy was eroded by the pull of industrial capitalism. [19] Many such dramas were played out over parents' claims on children's paychecks as well as over their right to control children's leisure time. Both sources of conflict surfaced dramatically in one East Whitby family in 1911.

Eighteen-year-old Marcella C. had been employed in the local woolen mill for three years but continued to live at home with her parents. She paid board and helped out with the chores, but only, she asserted, "when I feel like it." She and her father had a long history of fighting about how much money she contributed to the family. She felt that her regular board and her willingness to help out were sufficient. She often bought clothing for her three sisters and had once contributed ten dollars when a sister had diphtheria. Her father, Adolphus, disagreed. Several times he beat her with a horsewhip during their arguments and once stole money from her coat pocket. After this incident she began depositing her paycheck directly into the bank, "in case of sickness and so no one could take it from me." Conflicts about money and leisure time came together one evening when Marcella entertained a gentleman friend who invited her out to a party. Marcella's social life (coupled with the fact that she again refused demands for more money) enraged her father. Later that evening he called her a "lazy cow" and kicked her so badly she required medical care. Marcella was an unusually defiant daughter; she sought help outside the family. After this incident she contacted the Children's Aid Society and charged her father with assault. [20]

The fear with which tyrannical parents (usually fathers) ruled their daughters was usually said to be for their own good. Yet 'protection' sometimes had unintended consequences. Girls who were afraid of their parents sometimes took extra risks and were thus left more vulnerable than they might otherwise have been. We met Verna J. earlier. She was out in downtown Oshawa one spring evening in 1919 with several female friends when they were approached to go out walking with some young men they knew from school. Verna's father had threatened to thrash her once before when he caught her walking home with a boy and warned her never to be so "indiscreet" again. (Verna was a doctor's daughter, which no doubt demanded a higher degree of public respectability from the family.) Her father's admonition on her mind, Verna accepted Edward S.'s offer of a walk but insisted they avoid the main streets, "so that my father would not see me." As they were promenading through the alleyways behind Oshawa's town hall, Edward pinned Verna down and attempted to rape her.[21] Several other girls ended up spending an evening with their boyfriends (in one case, the couple slept together in an abandoned house) because their parents had locked them out for arriving home late.

Parental protection cut both ways, and some girls paid a double price for defying parental rules. When faced with the choice between taking social risks with a young man versus incurring the wrath of their parents, many girls chose the former, well aware of the unhappy consequences of either option. Many girls chaffed under the rules their parents set for them, but parents, particularly mothers, were also the ones girls turned to first after a sexual assault. Similarly, siblings, especially sisters, could act as a buffer between a frightened, perhaps pregnant girl and her stern parents. But in many instances siblings were also the ones who told on their sisters by reporting gossip or telling secrets to mothers or fathers.

During this period the family's role in regulating morals was changing. Sex education was many years away from being integrated into the school curriculum, so parents were officially responsible for their child's moral and sexual development. American historians have suggested that, until the end of the nineteenth century, the family, far more than church and state, was charged with the task of "creating self-regulating sexual beings."[22] This would change within several decades, and signs of impending changes were already visible. Parents received mixed messages about their ultimate responsibility for a child's welfare. A Canadian moral reform group, the Montreal Society for the Protection of Women and Girls, complained to the Senate in 1890 that too many parents were "foisting their responsibilities on the State" by bringing unruly children forward to be prosecuted as juvenile delinquents. At the same time, however, institutions such as the Children's Aid Society were campaigning for stronger powers, arguing before the federal Justice Department in 1892, for example, that intervention should be allowed when parents were "of reputed bad character, without the onus being imposed upon the rescuers of proving this."[23]

Through encounters with an often hostile legal system, parents learned the price of failure to discharge their duty. Mother blaming was a common response in incest cases, and many more parents (usually mothers) were badgered in court during trials for other sexual offenses. Their own moral behavior (such as their drinking habits or illegitimate children) as well as the amount of privacy and social freedom they allowed their daughters were scrutinized. An errant daughter reflected badly on a parent's reputation as well. But parental control over children was circumscribed by two other institutions wielding moral power in this period, the community and the state.

Community Regulation

Contrary to the fears of the moral reformers of the period, city life did not necessarily bring with it sexual or social anonymity. In New York, for example, a network of informal, reciprocal relations among women neighbors existed, dubbed by Christine Stansell a "moral economy of the tenements," which provided assistance to women in cases of wife abuse.[24] The close quarters of urban life served as a kind of protection, keeping young girls under watchful eyes.

Rural and small-town communities also evolved informal systems of social regulation. Community watchfulness could be helpful at times, freeing a girl from a situation of real sexual danger or catching a rapist as he attempted to escape. At other times, neighbors, friends, or even strangers might thwart a woman's plans to leave town with her lover or report her sexual adventures to her anxious parents. Sometimes too, communities might not report instances of misbehavior but would, much to the displeasure of the legal system, deal with it themselves.

Gossip that reached a parent's ears sometimes acted as a brake on a daughter's romance. In several seduction cases, parents first heard about their daughters' sexual liaisons (including, sometimes, their pregnancies) through rumor. In cases of sexual assault, news traveled fast. Katie G. was assaulted by a neighbor on her way to church one Sunday morning in 1902 but did not immediately tell anyone. By that evening, however, her mother had heard about it from a friend, who told her she had heard the story at church that morning. Similarly, Mary O. heard from "some ladies" that her daughter Elizabeth had gone off with a boy to a berry patch during a church picnic one afternoon, and as she was "apprehensive of evil," she quizzed Elizabeth about it immediately upon her arrival home.[25]

Sometimes rumors were the basis for direct state or institutional entry into private life. When children appeared at risk, neighborhood gossip eventually reached either the police or other authorities. Many of Lettie M.'s schoolmates knew she was being physically abused by her uncle and guardian, and this was passed on to her teacher, who in turn told the Children's Aid Society.[26] While investigating rumors of child neglect, a Children's Aid Society official in Pickering Township warned his superior that "the community is in a ferment" over the gross mistreatment farmer George H. meted out to his children and hinted that if authorities did not act quickly, a lynching might occur.[27] Sometimes neighbors voiced their suspicions of infanticide directly to the police, tipping them off by anonymous letter. Ironically, gossip itself shaped reactions to unwanted pregnancy. Historian René Leboutte's study of infanticide in Belgium reveals that rumor might be the instigator of the crime: "to silence the talk, the accused tried to eliminate her child."[28]

When abuse within families contained a sexual dimension, however, both the state and the community were slower to respond. Silence also allows us to reconstruct sexual standards. The Robinson family scandal was finally brought to light when police acted on numerous rumors and visited the family homestead, but this case developed over a period of several years, so we can only speculate about how long such gossip percolated through the community. Ideas about the privacy and sanctity of the family have long kept hidden sexual and physical abuse, and sometimes acted to deter individuals from taking action against abusive men. Frank S., for example, admitted he had seen his neighbor John A. lying on top of his daughter Mary on the road one evening, but, "I walked away, it was no affair of mine."[29]

Watchfulness was not only the preserve of neighbors and family members. Strangers often noted and acted upon behavior they deemed morally suspect. A hotel proprietor in North Bay alerted police to his suspicions about a couple who had registered as brother and sister. An investigation revealed that the two were lovers on the run; he had a wife and five children in Peterborough, and she was the family domestic servant.[30] A most intriguing story, which reveals how both gossip and community watchfulness might act as forms of regulation, was the relationship between twenty-three-year-old George A. and his fourteen-year-old sister-in-law, Mary R. It appears that George and Mary had been seeing each other surreptitiously for some time. They left their home near Picton together in 1899 and went to Winnipeg for a couple of weeks. Shortly after they returned Mary died, apparently from a botched abortion. No one in Mary's family (including his wife, Mary's sister) was interested in pressing criminal charges against George, but her parents testified at her inquest that they had been subject to extreme community pressure for tolerating Mary's relationship (which they continued to deny). Witness after witness, however, testified to seeing them together around town. The most candid witness was an alert railroad switchman, who saw them in the train station in Trenton, on their way west, laying down together. "We have to keep our eyes open for anything like that . . . to see that nothing improper takes place," he testified; "that's what we are paid for."[31]

Such watchfulness could be a boon to girls in trouble. Joseph G. and Charles C., two employees of the St. Catherines fall fair, noticed a man at the fair surrounded by several young girls, to whom he seemed to be giving money, so they decided to "keep an eye on him." They followed him as he brought eleven-year-old Emily D. behind the grandstand, and stopped him as he attempted to rape her.[32] More than one assault was interrupted by witnesses. Sometimes a rapist was caught when neighborhood men made chase after an assault; in other cases women were able to identify strangers by describing them to others in the community who knew them.

Community regulation thus could impede women and men who transgressed respectable boundaries and help women in times of distress. Sometimes communities could help parents enforce rules of social conduct, and at other times they overrode even parental wishes. Similarly, communities could assist in the legal enforcement of moral standards, letting police or other authorities know about instances of mistreatment or abuse. On other occasions, communities attempted to enforce moral discipline themselves.

Well into the twentieth century, as sexually and morally restrictive laws found increasing favor with legislators, custom continued to be upheld by group action. In Orangeville in 1922, a crowd of two hundred participated in tarring and feathering a man whose affair with a married woman was rumored to be the cause of her husband's recent suicide.[33] Well before the authorities became involved in a notorious case of a 'depraved family,' the D.'s (who were charged with running a brothel and using their daughters as prostitutes), the family had been forced to flee their home in Sault Ste. Marie in 1927, after several crosses had been burned on their lawn.[34]

Organizing charivaris to shame outcasts or extracting financial compensation after a sexual conflict were only a few methods employed by persons or communities to shore up lapses in proper behavior. Sometimes people set pen to paper, sending threatening letters to those deemed guilty of immoral conduct. Others made more open threats. In an unexplained grievance, Robert B. waged a war of words against Helen L. by attaching a notice to the fence outside her home which read, "this way for L. . . . . she charges $1 to $5. . . . . you can come on Wednesday nights, Fred [her husband] will be away." Alice M., a student at Peterborough Business College, received a series of letters from an angry ex-boyfriend who claimed he had seen her flirting with a young man "with a pompador cut of hair"; he also scribbled on the sidewalk outside her school, "A.M. chums with murderers." David A., a doctor in Port Perry, awoke one morning to find notes reading "David A. screws married women" stuck with tar onto the trees outside his home.[35] All of these cases came to light when the recipient of the threats pressed libel charges. Libel cases offer tantalizing evidence of the many creative strategies people employed when sexual reputation was contested; unfortunately, they rarely reveal the relationship between the parties or the source of the conflict.

We see that community regulation might compliment or conflict with the law. Public scrutiny might be experienced as relief from danger or as bothersome meddling. Yet even as small towns and remote regions became 'civilized' through expansion of the legal system, communities continued to exert a significant influence on the social and sexual lives of those in their midst.

Legal Regulation

The regulation of sexuality by the legal system involved more than fixing permissible sexual categories and prosecuting those persons who fell beyond them. Laws defined the appropriate age, status and relationship between persons, but the process of criminal prosecution gave wide latitude to lawyers, police and judges to investigate and make decisions based on the background and character of those suspected of contravening legal standards.

Moral infractions could come under the scrutiny of the legal system indirectly, well before any sexual offense was committed. Criminal charges of various kinds were initiated by police officers who observed couples behaving in what was deemed a morally suspicious manner. In one case an assault charge was laid by a policeman after he spotted a young couple entering an apartment building late one evening, even though the woman involved "seemed as if she did not want to tell her story" in court.[36] Immigrants were particularly vulnerable to unwanted police intervention. Frederick O. was a Ukrainian immigrant in Port Arthur who murdered his estranged wife's lover in 1921. Frederick and his wife, Katy, had an unhappy marriage; the two had separated several times previously. A Port Arthur policeman testified at his trial that this family was well acquainted with the judicial system. The couple had recently been brought to police court because one of their children was persistently truant from school. At this time, according to the officer, the police "brought them together and tried to have them go together but there was no agreement. They went back to their mode of living." He described the numerous legal complaints the two brought against each other, including Fred's attempt to have police intervene when Katy began living with another man. Police investigated Fred's claim that Katy was leading an "immoral life," but stopped short of legal action. As the investigating officer remarked (sadly, one suspects), "we can only go so far in the matter of social relations of people."[37]

Of course not only law pertaining to sex influenced or punished moral infractions. As Valverde and Weir have pointed out, sexuality has tended not to be an "autonomous regulatory site: there never have been ministries of sexuality."[38] Laws that governed everything from alcohol intake to Sunday newspapers were clearly informed by a particular view of the moral universe and acted to encourage others (generally immigrants and the working class) to adopt this perspective as well. Even laws that do not appear to contain a sexual or moral dimension could be applied toward these ends.

Santa T. and her boyfriend, Nicolas P., fled their home in Oshawa together because the girl's parents refused to let her marry. Upon arriving in Guelph in 1916, the first thing they did, after renting a hotel room and buying groceries, was go to the courthouse and register Nicolas's new residency, which as an Austrian 'enemy alien' during World War I he was required to do. Within days, Santa's mother and sister, alerted to her whereabouts by Guelph police, arrived at her hotel room and marched her home.[39]

These years witnessed a flurry of laws that criminalized new sorts of sexual relationships and made illegal (and therefore public) many previously private areas of life. These three institutions—the family, the community and the state—were not alone in their task of moral regulation. Churches, for example, continued to shape notions of morality, and in small towns especially, local factory owners took on the task of 'protecting' the moral life of their employees.[40] Yet despite the state's increasing acceptance (and eventual dominance) as the forum in which to redress sexual grievances and the arbiter of public morality, in this period a more complex and fluid pattern of moral regulation held sway.

We have seen how women and men negotiated the sexual dimensions of their relationship, and how they carved out sites of amusement and privacy, often under the glare of watchful parents, neighbors and authorities. We now turn our sights to the significant sources of social power—gender, class and race—which shaped, limited and gave meaning to nineteenth- and early twentieth-century sexuality.

Sexuality and Power

Gender

Popular cultural assumptions about sexuality set the framework within which personal sexual choices and legal decisions were made. Historians have suggested that, until the 1920s, passionlessness characterized women's relationship to sex. Nancy Cott has used this term to describe "the view that women lacked sexual aggressiveness, that their sexual appetites contributed a very minor part (if any at all) to their motivations, that lustfulness was simply uncharacteristic."[41] Steven Seidman has recently revised this interpretation, suggesting that through most of the nineteenth century, a "spiritualization of love" was the dominant ethos in American culture. Love, he argues, was separated from sex, for both women and men.[42] But as women's sexual possibilities shrank, their capacity for moral purity expanded. Alongside the notion of passionless or spiritual sexuality grew the equally firm idea—brought into mainstream political discourse by the social purity and temperance movements, and embraced enthusiastically by many feminists—that woman's moral nature was supremely passionate.

The down side of passionlessness was that the Victorian sexual ethos required a continuation of the double standard of sexual propriety and the instant condemnation of women who fell outside this overblown standard. But this set of ideas was not foisted upon completely unwilling historical subjects. The positive contribution of the decline in the sexual characterization of women was a corresponding increase in the range of available 'human' pursuits. What women lost in sexual passion, they gained back in moral purity, which had some benefits for some women. American historians have argued that by the end of the century the idea of female passionlessness helped fix into middle-class culture the ideal of marital mutuality and women's right to say no.[43]

The doctrine of female passionlessness represented a significant shift from earlier sexual ideologies. Before the eighteenth century, female sexual pleasure and orgasm were thought to be required for reproduction and thus incorporated as part of the common sense of sexuality. Medical opinion held that ovulation occurred only when enough heat had been produced through vaginal stimulation and orgasm. As historian Thomas Laquer stresses, the evolution of the medical rationale for passionlessness—the discovery of a distinct time of ovulation and the end of associating orgasm with conception—owed more to the political changes of the nineteenth century than to self-propelled scientific advances: "Scientific advances did not . . . banish female orgasm to the physiological periphery. Rather, the political, economic and cultural transformation of the eighteenth century created the context in which the articulation of radical differences between the sexes became culturally imperative."[44]

Social relations between the sexes did not, of course, turn on gender alone. Class and race also shaped the experience of sex and sociability. Cultural respectability came easier to some women; others had to work harder at it. But the double standard of sexual behavior was a social norm of such power it crossed race and class lines. 'Bad girls' came in all classes and colors.

The sexual double standard helped determine the sorts of social, romantic or sexual relationships open to women. Sexual exploitation was not, as the social purity movement might have it, the preserve of mysterious strangers who lurked in big cities. Strangers accounted for a minority of the men who did women sexual harm. Furthermore, the just-off-the-farm (or sometimes, boat) scenario of the innocent rural rube—an image of urban danger promoted by the agricultural press in the hopes of stemming rural depopulation—could apply just as well to a girl arriving in Kirkland Lake or Goderich as Toronto or New York.

It could even work the other way around. Eighteen-year-old Valenda L. was employed as a domestic servant in Ottawa. Because her mother was dead and her father worked out of town, she lived with her brother. On the

street one day she met Frank A. on her way home from work, and he began
to follow her regularly. Frank ran a store in neighboring Hull, but offered
her work in another store he claimed he was about to open in Cochrane.
Within two weeks Valenda was on the train with him to northern Ontario.
Frank changed his mind about their destination, however, and the two of
them ended up in a hotel in Sault Ste. Marie, registered as husband and
wife, where a watchful proprietress 'rescued' Valenda and had Frank arrested on procurement charges.[45] Men could take advantage of women's
sexual innocence, economic vulnerability, or lack of 'protection' by family
members. Men could also easily exploit the double standard of sexual morality and get away with things women could not. But this applied as much
to a man in Cochrane as in Toronto; it stemmed from an unequal distribution of power between the sexes.

The degree of knowledge one possessed about sexuality was very much
informed by gender. Female passionlessness also implied innocence: good
women would confess to very little sexual knowledge. As always, it is difficult to untangle convention from practice. Perhaps shared sleeping accommodations and toilet facilities, home births, and proximity to farm animals
led to sexual knowledge at an early age.[46] Perhaps working-class people had,
as Judith Fingard has suggested, a distinct and more knowledgable approach to sexuality than did the middle class, because of their "early exposure to the realities of life and death."[47] Yet it also seems likely that women
were more sexually ignorant than men. One of the earliest surveys of female
sexual behavior, conducted in the United States by Dr. Celia Mosher between 1892 and 1920, revealed that over half the women surveyed knew
little or nothing about sex until after marriage.[48] Lempi Mansfield, a Finnish
immigrant who grew up in South Porcupine, exemplifies this well. Married
and a mother while still a teenager, she remembered that "for one who knew
nothing about sex, babies or passion at seventeen, I began to learn fast."[49]

Whether or not women were really innocent, sexual modesty was expected in court. Many women of all ages balked at describing the details of
their experiences in a crowded, public courtroom. Crown attorneys bullied
women into telling their tale precisely, and defense lawyers then bullied
them about interpretation and details. The following exchange, between
twelve-year-old Violet M., who claimed that her neighbor assaulted her on
the road one evening, and the crown attorney, is typical.

Q: He stuck something into you—into your private person?
A: I don't understand you.
Q: Where did that something go into you—it wasn't into your
   mouth?
A: No
Q: Where was it placed? Was it on your knee?

A: No
Q: Where was it?
A: Between my legs.

A few moments later, he tried again:

Q: Will you tell us, Violet, where he stuck this thing in you? What do you call it?
A: I don't know what you call it.
Q: What do you call the thing you have?
A: I don't know.
Q: What do you use it for?
A: Well, to make water.
Q: Is that where he stuck it in?
A: Yes.[50]

In another case involving a fifteen-year-old and the hired man, the crown attorney, after relentless questioning, gave up exasperated. "It's the same old story, your honour," he complained, "these witnesses won't talk."[51] But it was not only the young who froze on the witness stand. Hazel B., a married woman who was assaulted by a taxi driver in Fort Frances, was also circumspect about her experience:

Q: What did he do?
A: He did what he wanted to.
Q: Did any part of him touch you?
A: Yes.
Q: What?
A: I don't know how to say that.
Q: If you cannot say it, point to yourself. What part of his body touched any part of your body?[52]

Too much modesty resulted in frustration and badgering by authorities in court, and too little modesty made women morally suspect. Women were also castigated for being too familiar with anatomy and too forthcoming with their stories. After Pansy F. described how her date, Clifford S., attempted to rape her in his car, his lawyer grilled her about her rendering of events. "How," he asked, "did you know it was his private person he had out?" "It felt like it," she answered. "Do you know what it is like to feel one?" "No." "Then how do you know?" he persisted. Pansy held her ground. "I know," she maintained. The defense lawyer tried one more time: "Might it have been his hand?" he asked. "It could have been his hand," she said firmly, "but it was not."[53]

The ultimate contradiction between the prescription for sexual modesty and the reality of heterosexual pursuit was that innocence and trust were often rather misplaced qualities. Women were beaten by their parents and humiliated by the legal system for such indiscretions as accepting a ride, going out for a walk, or paying too much attention to the wrong man. Of course it was difficult to tell wrong men from right men until it was too late. Plenty of women were caught by misplaced trust, but others were not at all naive about the rules. When John S. attempted to assault Lily B., a young domestic servant employed in a hotel in Goderich run by John's parents, she had already been warned by the other servants to be careful of him. Indeed, she didn't bother to tell her employer, John's mother, about her son's harassment because she had heard that another servant had been fired for complaining about John previously. She stayed a few days to collect her pay; then, after telling her mother, she pressed charges. Despite the fact that Florence B., the servant who had been fired, testified on Lily's behalf that she had also been molested by the young man, neither story was believed, and S. was found not guilty.[54]

Women negotiated sexual dangers in a number of ways. They warned each other about troublesome men and potentially dangerous situations; they acted like sexual 'traffic' cops with their boyfriends, struggling to draw sexual boundaries; they tried to avoid known neighborhood menaces.[55] Innocence indeed had its limits and was difficult to maintain in a contested sexual atmosphere.

Naiveté and innocence were qualities expected in respectable girls, but were often unservicable as women went about the daily business of work, romance and play. What happened to women who put up no pretense can be seen in the case of Rosie K. of Sudbury, who broke most of the rules. She had two boyfriends, Peter M. and Fred D., whom she alternated between according to their work schedule (both were loggers and thus away for long periods of time) and her own wishes. While she was living with one she became pregnant by the other; she was never formally married to either. She also had several abortions, and she had had three teenage children with another man, George K., who had left her many years previously. Peter had the most trouble with the situation and often threatened to leave, but Rosie was always able to win him back. Once she was even able to convince him to return from his native Poland, where, he claimed, he fled to escape her. Both Peter and Fred lent her large sums of money, which she used to buy a home she operated as a boardinghouse.

In May 1929 the three were weathering another crisis in their stormy relationship; Rosie and Fred were living together, and Peter was living in another boardinghouse immediately behind Rosie's. Their last parting had not been pleasant. Rosie had attempted to sue Peter for back rent which he successfully disputed, saying he had lived with her as her husband. Fred took Peter to court for stealing his boots. Peter took to staring for hours at

Rosie's house across their backyards and let his desire for revenge be known. He told several of Rosie's other boarders that he intended to kill her and issued the same threat to her in a letter. She received these threats with little fear; she told a mutual friend that Peter was a "damned fool" who could (according to the coy translation of the court clerk) "kiss her backside." She should have paid more attention. One Sunday afternoon Rosie was in her backyard, gathering firewood to begin cooking the evening meal. Peter lowered a gun through his window and shot her; she died almost instantly.[56]

We can do more than conclude glibly that women paid with their lives for stepping out of line as far as Rosie did, although this is, of course, terrifyingly true. What this story illustrates is not only Peter's actions, but his way of rationalizing them—to himself, his friends, and the legal system. Before he shot Rosie, Peter wrote a lengthy letter explaining their relationship and outlining his many grievances against her, which he apparently had intended as a suicide note. At the last minute he "lost his nerve" (according to the judge who reviewed the case for the minister of justice), but the letter was used in court as his confession.

Peter's letter spoke bitterly of Rosie's unfaithfulness, her many abortions, and the money he had spent on her (which he calculated at $2,000). His conscience, he claimed, forced him to "kill my old oppressor and mistress who robbed me of my belongings and destroyed my young life." "She loved me," he acknowledged, "but she played with me like a child." Thus death, he concluded, "is the only payment I am receiving for loving a snake."[57]

Peter's jealousy became the basis of his defense. His lawyer attempted to prove that his client's mind had become "distorted and imbalanced" because of the "treatment he received at the hands of this woman." This theory found some support outside the courtroom as well. The local police reported to the Royal Canadian Mounted Police that Peter "bore a good character amongst other people in the vicinity, all of whom looked on him as being the dupe of this woman." Indeed, over seven hundred of Peter's "countrymen" signed petitions on his behalf, arguing that Rosie "took advantage of the attractions she had for men," "played on their affections," and extorted money from them. Thus Rosie K. was created as one of the classic bad girls of the day, a designing woman who used her allure to secure financial gain and bring about the downfall of unwitting men.

Ultimately it didn't work. Peter M. was found guilty of murder and sentenced to hang; his appeals for clemency were rebuffed. Perhaps racial anxieties eclipsed sexual ones in this instance, since the presiding judge saw this case as yet another example of peasant lawlessness. "I do not know," said Justice Kelly to Peter while sentencing him to hang, "whether in the country from which you come human life is looked upon with less regard than it is here, but . . . you and every other person who comes into the Dominion of Canada is under obligation to drop your past practices and customs and observe the laws of this country."

Peter's attempt to portray himself as the victim of a designing woman was thwarted by the racism of the judicial system—his status as a 'lawless peasant' outweighed any wrongs done to him by a woman, no matter how designing. But his actions also went beyond the permissible range of masculine behavior on other counts. As his lawyer explained, trying to convince the court that Peter was insane at the time of the shooting, "a normal man does not allow things of that kind to upset him as this man was upset." Peter also broke the rules of fair fighting. The judge admonished him that he had done a "cowardly thing," shooting a woman from behind.

It was rare for men to be addressed as men in these proceedings. But there were indeed parameters of appropriate male sexuality, and two important principles by which men were expected to live were chivalry and sexual self-control. Insufficient chivalry was a male moral failing lamented by judges throughout Ontario. The ideology of chivalry, in a sexual context, implied that men were responsible for protecting women. "It should be the pride of every man to show chivalry towards women," stated one judge in Sudbury while sentencing a man on indecent assault charges, for "civilization breaks down when women are not protected."[58] Men who had sex with much younger women, men who were married, and men in positions of relative power (such as employers) were deemed particularly culpable of unchivalrous behavior.

But from what did women need protection? The flip side of chivalry and protection was, of course, control. The actions of Samuel M., a farmer in Perth County, express well this double-sided meaning of chivalry. One afternoon he spied his young domestic servant, Ada F., driving home from her music lessons with a neighbor. He confronted the two and angrily told the neighbor to stay away from the thirteen-year-old girl. Later that day he inquired solicitously of Ada whether the man had "taken advantage of her." (She maintained he had not.) The same evening, after the rest of the household retired, Samuel crept into Ada's bedroom, disrobed and climbed into her bed.[59] In a social context that allowed men the enormous privilege of policing themselves, we can perhaps begin to understand why some nineteenth-century feminists came to look favorably on the state (and each other) for sexual regulation. As the Sudbury WCTU declared in 1916, while lobbying for stronger legal measures against seduction, "if men cannot give both justice and chivalry, let them give justice."[60]

Related to chivalry was men's capacity for sexual self-control. During this period men's sexuality was held to be the reverse of women's; it was lustful, passionate, even "bestial, scarcely capable of containment."[61] This cultur-

ally constructed 'difficulty' men had in controlling their restless and raging
sexual nature could be successfully deployed as a legal defense against sexual crime. The implications of this view were many and continue to rever-
berate through sexual politics. On an individual level, it gave a woman dual
responsibility for sexual behavior, both her own and her boyfriend's. Feminists, however, fashioned an entire movement around this idea, arguing for
the restraining and calming influence of women in campaigns of temperance, social purity, even suffrage. Men's sexual lapses were tolerated by
authorities and accepted as a cultural given, but at a price. Even when men
who had engaged in some type of illicit sex were found legally innocent,
their sexual reputation was dealt a blow, and this in turn cast doubts on their
masculinity. As Ellen Rothman explains, a man soon learned that "the test
of his manliness was the strength of his instincts."[62] Thus men who abandoned their pregnant girlfriends were, according to judges, guilty of "un-
manly conduct." They were "cowardly blackguards," even when they were
found not guilty of seduction. Arthur Brown, the Oshawa relief officer
charged with raping one of his clients, was released after a long and highly
publicized trial, but not before the judge lambasted him for being "weak,
extremely weak, in the woman business." One of four young men accused
of gang rape in Gananoque was set free by the judge with the stern admonition to "go recover your manhood." Manliness was articulated in numerous
contexts historically and was pressed into service to support labor mili-
tancy, military service, or Victorian sexual respectability. But the sexual
side of manliness implied restraint, will power, and the ability to keep one's
sexual nature in check.[63]

Men who made sexual errors learned one set of rules about masculinity
and respectability, yet some of these rules were at odds with lessons they
likely learned as boys about aggressiveness and violence. Mixed messages
about the exact content of respectable masculinity abounded in turn-of-the-
century North America. The middle-class "boy culture," identified by
American historian Anthony Rotundo, thrived in opposition to the domestic female world. Where women's sphere provided morality, gentleness and
nurturing, the world of young boys countered with "energy, self-assertion,
noise and frequent recourse to violence," encouraging competition, mas-
tery, and danger and distaining "weak" emotions. Boys in the new world of
North America were specially encouraged to make the association between
physical aggression and masculinity. Stories of survival in the wild and
woolly west, which often included the killing of hostile native people or animals, enthralled generations of English schoolboys, teaching them, as Canadian historians R. G. Moyles and Doug Owram have argued, that "only
'real' not 'weakling' boys can hope to become heros or Empire men."[64]

Aggressive or morally suspicious men could develop a bad reputation, especially among women. Some women pressing assault charges reported that they had heard stories about their assailant before. Elizabeth W. of Uxbridge, for example, claimed she and "all the other women" in town had long been afraid of the man who attacked her. When Marie O. heard that a woman had been raped on the road near her house, she immediately suspected her neighbor Frank T., who, she said, "did not work much and was a worthless fellow."[65] Having 'a past' did not, however, bring with it the dire consequences that faced insufficiently respectable women. The label 'whore,' a social category that could determine women's economic, family and community standing so completely, really had no male equivalent.

Class: From Sex Pervert to Ladies' Man

Class differences in sexual behavior and meaning are sometimes difficult to grasp historically, but the class basis of sexual regulation is clear. The legal system alone provides voluminous evidence, sometimes in its silence. Instances of middle- and upper-class persons involved in prosecutions for sexual offenses are rare. Rather than assuming that this illustrates the brutishness or immorality of working-class men—as some early feminists concerned about violence against women believed—we see that this phenomenon fits into wider class-based patterns of privacy.

When the occasional upper-class sexual crime came to light, it often generated more than its share of attention, as we have seen. Contrasting the rare prosecution for sexual crime among the upper class with prosecution of 'ordinary' working-class crime reveals how class shaped both sexual experience and regulation. The following two cases also highlight how class helped construct gender, in this case, masculinity.[66]

In 1910 in Goderich, Edward Jardine was convicted of murdering seventeen-year-old Lizzie Anderson. The two met up one evening at the Goderich fall fair, a popular small-town spot for socializing. Lizzie told her brother (with whom she had attended the fair) that Jardine was going to walk her home; then she disappeared. Her body was found several days later in the basement of an abandoned house near the fair ground. She had received a blow to the head, her throat was cut, and her clothing removed. A coroner's jury concluded that "the murderer had evidently been frustrated in the bestial purpose which is supposed to be at the bottom of this crime." After a struggle with her assailant, Anderson had been knocked unconscious and murdered.[67]

After first checking out the possibility that the 'foreigners' who lived in the same building as the Anderson family were responsible, attention then focused on Edward (nicknamed 'Punk') Jardine. Lizzie's mother admitted that Lizzie was "more or less intimate" with Edward and his brothers, and many witnesses reported seeing them leave the fair together. When Edward was arrested, his fate seemed sealed. The Jardines were hardly the best of families. They were poor, fatherless, and two of Edward's brothers had recently served prison terms for sexual assaults against women. The press hinted that this suggested a predisposition to sexual immorality on Edward's part and that murder might have been his attempt to avoid his brothers' fate. Despite her mother's admission of her daughter's relationship with the accused, a parallel construction of Lizzie Anderson as temptress was never suggested. Local consensus indicated that Lizzie was "though rather simple minded, a good girl," who would certainly have "repulsed any advances." Like Jessie Keith and Mary Peake in Stratford, death ensured that Lizze Anderson's reputation remained intact.[68]

It came as no surprise, therefore, when the provincial prison inspector who had visited Jardine in jail reported at his trial that the young man had confessed his guilt to him. The lack of "favourable family surroundings" explained Jardine's downfall. But Dr. Bruce Smith, the prison inspector, also revealed a more sinister problem. Edward Jardine, he concluded, was a "sex pervert," a condition caused by years of masturbation. This immutable physical malfunction had been, according to the doctor, exacerbated by environmental considerations. Jardine's improper family surroundings had ensured that the practice went unchecked. Indeed, Smith claimed that he had been the first person to warn Jardine of the dire consequences of his addiction, too late, as it turned out.[69]

Jardine's lawyer failed in his attempt to argue that sexual perversion was a form of insanity. Despite evidence for the defense from doctors who agreed that sex perverts do not know right from wrong and cannot appreciate the quality of their actions, Jardine was found guilty. His story continued to serve as a warning for errant young men even to the end. His final statement, related to a clergyman, was an earnest plea to other boys. "Go to church," he told them, "and keep good company."

Edward Jardine was the classic working-class boy gone bad. Colonel Samuel Wellington Ray was, in some respects, his upper-class equivalent. Their crimes were quite different, but their contrasting fates and public personalities illustrate well the inextricable ties of sexuality, class and gender.

Colonel Ray was one of Port Arthur's finest citizens. He was related to the local family compact, held a distinguished military title, owned one of the town's first banks, and was a member of the board of Port Arthur's first newspaper. Louise Rose Bathurst also moved in Port Arthur's high society. A middle-class Englishwoman, she had arrived in the district with her husband and two children in the mid-1880s, where her husband, Lancelot, pursued a medical practice. Dr. Bathurst made frequent trips to the mining communities surrounding Port Arthur, and, if his stay was to be lengthy,

Louise and the children checked into a hotel during his absence. On one such occasion in August 1892, Louise was staying at Port Arthur's grand waterfront hotel, the Northern. She attended the Calico Ball at the hotel one evening, where she danced and chatted with Colonel Ray, a man she had known socially for several years. The next day Louise returned to her nearby home for a change of clothing when Ray appeared at the door. Thinking there was no harm in allowing in her house "any man for whom I had respect," Louise invited him in. He then began "mauling" her, confessing his love for her, and pushing up her dress. She promptly fainted (she was "subject to fainting," she explained), thus sparing herself the indignity of describing the details of her experience to the court. But the presence of some "yellow nasty stuff" on her underclothing convinced her she had been assaulted. After "a good cry," she returned to the hotel and told a woman friend there she had been "insulted in her own home." When her husband returned from the mines a couple days later she told him and together they filed a complaint.[70]

The whole story was cloaked in an air of upper-class melodrama. When Dr. Bathurst heard his wife's story he immediately confronted Colonel Ray, who was at that moment observing a large naval exhibition at the waterfront. Thus many of Port Arthur's finest citizens watched as Bathurst, calling Ray a "brute" and accusing him of "seducing an unprotected woman," punched him before setting off to find the police.

This episode had all the elements of a juicy scandal: sex, wealth and power. While stories about the Ray case circulated widely and were reported in newspapers in Toronto, Winnipeg, and Minnesota, scarcely a word was printed in the Port Arthur paper. It would not be overly conspiratorial to suggest that Ray's involvement as shareholder and member of the board of the *Port Arthur Sentinal* might account for this silence.

From the beginning, Colonel Ray was the popular favorite in this story. The *Toronto Daily Mail*, for example, described him as a "great society pet" and "ladies' man," who was "genial, affable, friendly and the best liked citizen of Port Arthur." He maintained his position in the community throughout the scandal and continued his customary high-profile social life. In 1893, between the incident and his trial, he scored first in the Canadian military rifle competitions.[71] There was an unexplained two-year gap between the incident and the trial, an unusual delay even for the relatively primitive justice system in northern Ontario. While it is unclear if any one party initiated this delay, Ray must certainly have been happy to have the gossip die down.

In the face of Ray's popularity and the community's loyalty, Mrs. Bathurst's grasp on respectability began to slip. The *Mail* hinted at the "number of young admirers" who "paid her some attention" during her stay at the Northern. Much less oblique was the allegation, repeated in the *Mail* but denied in the local press, that Louise Bathurst was a designing woman who had actually hired a man to blackmail Colonel Ray.[72] Curiously, the fact that Louise Bathurst was four months pregnant at the time of her assault, which could have embellished her status as a wronged woman, was never exploited. During the trial her character received another pummeling. Ray's lawyer, the famous B. B. Osler, suggested that Louise and "a certain party" had danced, "promenaded," and drunk wine together the evening of the Calico Ball. Whether Osler was refering to Ray or someone else mattered little; the strategy was effective. Ray was found not guilty, even though the jury "strongly disapproved of his conduct."[73]

It is likely that Edward Jardine and Samuel Ray were both guilty. It appears that the juries thought so too; what else would the Thunder Bay jury have "disapproved" of? The two stories with their opposing verdicts certainly illuminate how class might determine the amount of justice one received in court. Ray was able to buy both superior legal assistance and community silence. Yet these stories tell us much more than the accurate but hardly surprising truism that the rich receive better treatment than the poor. What made Jardine's actions those of a sex pervert and Ray's the simple flirtations of a ladies' man?

Murder is of course different than rape, and obviously these two cases were not equally serious. Yet is was not solely the gravity of the crime which accounts for Jardine's conviction and hanging. The apparent ease with which Ray's actions were tolerated—by his community as well as the jury—reveal the brazen double standard of sexual propriety from which many men, but especially economically advantaged men, benefited. Jardine's class background, his distance from wholesome family influences, and his 'unnatural' sexual practices were thus all of a piece. Each played an integral part in constructing the category 'sex pervert,' a term of both explanation and punishment.

Samuel Ray was a product of simultaneous class, gender and sexual privilege. The sudden portrayal of Louise Bathurst as designing woman (despite her years of English Ladies' School and her doctor husband), the continued popularity of Ray throughout the ordeal, and of course the verdict all testify to this. But the subsequent course of Ray's life make these privileges astoundingly clear. Samuel Ray continued to live in Port Arthur as a prominent citizen and accomplished businessman. Seven years after his acquittal, in 1901, Ray was elected alderman. In 1911 he was elected mayor of Port Arthur and served a two-year term. His business continued to flourish, and in 1912 he built Port Arthur's first residential housing subdivision. The community's memory for scandal was, in this instance, remarkably short. In 1913, during Ray's tenure as mayor, the Methodist church conducted a survey of the social and moral life of Port Arthur and was pleased to report that "there have been no charges of graft or malfeasance in the City's history."[74] As he aged, Ray attained revered pioneer status in the community. The *Fort William Times Journal* was happy to report in 1938, for example, that Ray approached his eighty-third birthday "feeling fit and with a glint of humour still shining in his eyes."[75]

Ray's continued success and prominence in northwestern Ontario society did not come after a period of shame or atonement for his past indiscretions. His reputation as a ladies' man was not tainted by sexual scandal. Indeed, one suspects it was enriched. In 1910, as part of an advertising feature for a new real estate development in Fort William, Ray was featured in the Realty Review Hall of Fame as a prominant developer. While his business success and property holdings were mentioned in his biography, far more attention was paid to his social reputation. Ray's "popularity with the fair sex," the "grace of his dancing," his "ravishing beauty," and "brilliant repartee" all contributed to his social esteem. "The Colonel is a carefree bachelor," the story went on, "shame on you, girls."[76] Ray did not have to worry about 'recovering' his good name after the whiff of scandal. As a wealthy single ladies' man, Ray was allowed unparalleled sexual latitude. Even after a rape trial, his good name did not suffer.

Race/Ethnicity

At the turn of the century, Canadians of British descent believed that racial and ethnic minorities in Canada had a distinct set of sexual practices, attitudes, rules and systems of regulation, and that this was a very bad thing indeed. Can we set aside the moral overtones of this question and ask, simply: was this true? It is difficult to separate the question from the various ways perceptions of race and sex combined to mobilize racial prejudice. Racial fears were often sexualized, and Anglo-Saxons, in Canada as elsewhere, used sexuality to maintain racial and ethnic hierarchies. Exactly where distinct cultural practice leaves off and racism begins is hard to determine. For example, did blacks who lived in the southern United States really have looser sexual mores? To what extent was this popular assumption simply an excuse for the racist construction of black men as sexually dangerous (and therefore needing to be controlled) and black women as sexually promiscuous (and therefore available)? Did radical Finns in Canada practice free love, or was this widely held assumption simply the product of Anglo-Saxon worries about immigrant Bolsheviks? The sexual habits of racial and ethnic minorities evolved in a climate of hostility and manipulation. Therefore we should be as suspicious of racial sexual stereotypes as we are of gender stereotypes.

Anxieties about sexuality and ethnicity were promoted in Canada by

popular organizations (trade unions and the women's, social purity, and social gospel movements) as well as by the state (particularly in its immigration and deportation policies).[77] Class and political anxieties were mobilized
by the alleged sexual improprieties of immigrants. Throughout the early
twentieth century in the northern Ontario town of Fort William, for example, a litany of complaints was raised about the apparently rampant alco-
holism, filth, poverty and sexual immorality in immigrant neighborhoods,
especially the coal dock area which housed southern and eastern European
railway workers. According to the *Fort William Daily Times*, the morals in
the coal dock neighborhood were such "as would cause the lower world of
Chicago to stand back and stare."[78] This racial and sexual panic led to the
creation in 1910 of the Fort William Moral Reform League, which represented the town's first official alliance with the Canadian social purity movement. A couple of years later a widespread and violent strike by immigrant
workers in the coal docks seemed to confirm the worst fears of the reformers. Moments of social upheaval such as this helped crystallize race,
gender and class fears. Immediately after the strike, the Methodist church
established a mission in the neighborhood, the Welsely Institute, to better
assimilate immigrants in 'Canadian' culture and mores.[79]

Popular stereotypes attributed various moral failings to particular ethnic
and racial groups. Southern and eastern Europeans, for example, were considered to have spurned the institution of marriage, and Finns in particular
were thought to uphold various immoral practices which came under the
heading free love. Native peoples have historically been characterized by
white colonizers as animalistic, carnal creatures, and in the nineteenth century, Indian reservations were considered sites of notoriously lax morality.
After the rape of a Native woman on Walpole Island in 1882, the Sarnia
press thundered about the number of "young bloods" who "seem possessed
of the idea that young Indian girls are their prey," and insisted that the
white community rally to the protection of Native women, "simple creatures" who could not protect themselves.[80] Chinese men had long been associated with drug smuggling, gambling and prostitution. Legal measures
to ensure the separation of Chinese men and white women, such as the law
passed by the city council in Sudbury in 1926 which prohibited white
women from working in Chinese restaurants, were commonplace.[81]

Part of the reason immigrants were so susceptible to sexual immorality, so
the story went, was that they tended toward criminality in general. As Reverend J. Shaver, a Fort William Methodist minister who worked in the coal
docks in the aftermath of the labor upheavals of 1912 remembered, Canadians formed their opinions of immigrants through the police court column
of the newspaper.[82] And there was certainly a wealth of vituperative commentary on legal proceedings from which to draw. In crime reporting, the

racial or ethnic background of protagonists was made prominent in a manner ranging from the patronizing (women described as "comely, as Galician
women go") to the vicious (the panic about "stiletto wielding Italians"
which followed any news of violent crime among southern Europeans). The
exception to this rule was, of course, when crimes were committed by
Anglo-Saxons.[83]

The view that non-Anglo-Saxons were less 'civilized' and hence more
liable to brutish behavior held wide currency. A double standard stunning
in its hypocrisy was the notion, embraced by feminists and nonfeminists
alike in Canada, that immigrants had far less progressive gender and sexual
politics than the Canadian born. As the *Cobalt Nugget* editorialized in 1914
(at which time Canadian women did not have the right to vote), "among the
foreign born, who in their native land, work their women in the fields, the
old servitude of the weaker sex cannot be abolished." According to Christian missionaries such as Egerton Ryerson Young, Canadian Native people
also behaved like "haughty tyrants" toward their wives, "pictures of abso-
lute serfdom" born down by constant beatings and physical labor.[84]

This view of gender relations among the 'lower orders' was promoted enthusiastically by Canadian feminists. Eager to present themselves as fit candidates for citizenship and suffrage, Canadian feminists attempted to
harness racist stereotypes to their own ends. The resilience of racism in
Canadian political discourse of the period was overwhelming; even the
left wing of the suffrage movement was drawn in. As Flora MacDonald
Denison, one of the more principled suffrage activists, cautioned, Canadians were "welcoming to our shores thousands of immigrants, most of
which are illiterate and often the scum of the earth, and in a few years they
will be empowered to vote and make laws for the women of our land."[85]
Alice Chown, another on the left of the women's movement, also remarked
on the "peasant type" of women, who were "accustomed to being dominated by the men, who would feel that their men did not like them if they
did not boss them."[86]

The leadership of some ethnic groups appears to have accepted some of
these cultural stereotypes and attempted to instill 'proper' Anglo social customs among their community. Religious leaders in the Ukrainian community, for example, attempted to train Ukrainian girls in 'Canadian' courtship
rituals, and the popular sex and deportment manual *What a Young Girl Ought
to Know* was quickly translated and distributed. Immigrant groups, of
course, were not immune to the sexual double standard. For Ukrainians, as
for many others, the survival and prosperity of the community depended
on women's ability to train and raise the 'quality' of the next generation.
Therefore concerns about community morality devolved dispropor-

tionately to women, who were also deemed morally weaker, more emotional, and "more easily swayed than men."[87]

Such were some of the perceptions of non-Anglo-Saxon social mores. Prosecutions for sexual crime suggest that there were indeed some differences between the way immigrants and Anglo-Saxons experienced sexuality. Indications are that immigrant women took more than their share of sexual risks. Rosie K. of Sudbury was one of several immigrant women who lived in a common-law relationship and had more than one lover at a time. Sophia A. of Port Arthur and Annie P. of Sudbury were prosecuted on abortion charges. Both were well known as abortionists by women in their ethnic community. In this study a tiny minority of abortion-related charges involve women, and it is likely not a coincidence that two of the three women charged with abortion offenses served ethnic communities. As we have seen, a high percentage of arrests for abduction, in cases of couples leaving town to escape the disapproval of their parents, involved immigrant girls.

Yet we cannot separate the prospensity of an immigrant woman to risk taking on a second lover, performing an abortion, or leaving town with her boyfriend from the question of state supervision of immigrant morality and the use of sexuality as an instrument of domination. There has been surprisingly little historical research into the differing sexual cultures of racial and ethnic minorities in Canada. Some historians seem bent on rehabilitating 'their' groups' sexual reputation and have argued that the moral panic over immigrant sexuality reflected only prejudice, not practice. Varpu Lindstrom-Best, for example, argues that Finns in Canada rejected not the institution of marriage but its sanctioning by the church and that free love was "more a conversation piece than a practiced reality" among Red Finns.[88]

The question of whether distinct parameters of an immigrant sexual culture existed in Canada is not so simple. Future research must consider the tangled questions of sexuality, the powerful and the powerless, in all their complexity. Recent explorations in lesbian and gay history will be a useful guide in this project. American historian Jennifer Terry uses a medico-scientific study of homosexuality in the late 1930s to investigate what she terms "episodes in the production of deviant subjectivity." Deviant subjectivity is defined by Terry as "the process by which a position or identity space is constructed discursively by sexology and medicine and strategically seized upon by its objects of study." Rather than using this medical study to tell a coherent story about lesbian and gay life in the 1930s, Terry instead locates the sites of conflict, tension and resistance between the doctors and the subjects. Instead of looking for a fully crafted gay identity—an ahistorical project, at best, for the period—Terry suggests that we read accounts like this medical study to find differences within textual operations of elite accounts.[89]

This method could be useful for investigating a range of 'deviant' people historically. In a culture such as turn-of-the-century Canada, in which Anglo hegemony was so strong, anti-immigrant hostility so pervasive, and sexual depravity so much a part of the 'othering' of non-Anglos, we must explore the extent to which we can speak of 'authentic' sexual cultures of nonhegemonic groups. Commenting on John D'Emilio and Estelle Freedman's *Intimate Matters*, Ann duCille castigates them for studying the range of varying histories of sexuality against the backdrop of dominant sexual meanings. She claims that this methodology—filtering a whole spectrum of sexual practices through the lens of white middle-class morality—"automatically abnormalizes all but the beliefs and experiences of the dominant group."[90] One could look at this question another way: Do D'Emilio and Freedman 'abnormalize' non-Anglo sexuality or did history do that?

Immigrant subjectivity has been marginalized for a host of reasons, and sexual 'otherness' has been just one component of this. Yet the connections between the economic, political and sexual marginality of non-Anglo Canadians were powerful indeed. From this perspective, the question of whether immigrants really lived on the sexual fringes is perhaps less important than how regulation, scrutiny and moral condemnation of immigrants contributed to their outcast status.

This chapter has ranged widely, through courtship patterns, the complexities of moral regulation, and the manner in which the large social structures of gender, class and race touched down on the sexual lives of women and men. Sexual meaning cannot be 'read' by gender, race or class, yet social location was instrumental in shaping sexual possibilities and in constructing sexuality as a place of domination and power.

Sexual relations culminating in court battles do not, of course, tell the whole truth. When we learn of people's intimate lives through the prying and hostile eyes of the police, we lose the complexities of personal relations. These stories are often one-sided; there is exasperatingly little exchange between protagonists. We know less than we would like of Marcella C.'s anger toward her authoritarian father or of the way Rosie K. juggled the passion and jealousy of her two lovers. Court records do, however, allow us to reconstruct significant bits of the social and romantic life of persons who passed through history—when they have been recognized at all—as builders of railroads, organizers of strikes, and settlers of new lands. In turn-of-the-century Ontario, power and domination took many forms.

CHAPTER SIX

Sex and the Single-Industry Community: The Social and Moral Reputation of Rural and Northern Ontario

IN DECEMBER 1989, A JUDGE IN THE Northwest Territories created a furor (and subsequently found himself the subject of a judicial inquiry) when he told the press that he treated sexual assault cases in the North with more lenience than those he heard as a judge in the southern Ontario university town of Kingston. "The majority of rapes in the Northwest Territories occur when the woman is drunk and passed out. A man comes along and sees a pair of hips and helps himself," explained Michael Bourassa. "That contrasts sharply to the cases I dealt with before, of the dainty co-ed who gets jumped from behind."[1]

These comments illuminate dramatically the continuing relationship between region and reputation. The story is an oddity only in its historical setting; Bourassa would not have made national headlines or been reprimanded in the 1920s. Region, in this story, is in part a code word for class and race. Bourassa's "dainty co-ed" is a young, white, middle-class university student, while the drunken "pair of hips" is a Native or Inuit woman. At times race, class and gender combine in particular spatial ways to create powerful perceptions of entire regions, which in turn influence the social and economic development of these areas. In this chapter I look at the historical roots of this phenomenon.

The period between 1880 and 1930 saw profound changes in Canadian social and economic life. Three themes—industrialization, immigration, and urbanization—have become the historians' shorthand to express the complex processes that irrevocably altered the working, social and family lives of women and men. Both Ontario regions—north and south—were affected by turn-of-the-century economic upheavals in particular ways. By the early twentieth century, the economic and social decline of rural southern Ontario had earned the sober label 'rural problem,' the contours of which politicians, church leaders and, later, historians debated for some time. The 'rural problem' was defined in a number of ways: as a crisis of depopulation, a question of inadequate political representation, a problem of agricultural economic decline, or of farmers' adverse reactions to World War I and to conscription in particular.[2]

Northern Ontario also was changing. By the 1890s the 25 percent success rate of farm settlements in the north suggested that the potential of this region as an agricultural mecca had been overstated. In its place, however, stood the hope, nurtured by business interests and government alike, that the seemingly boundless natural resources of the area suited it well for industrial development. As H. V. Nelles, one of the few historians who has studied northern Ontario's economic development, explains, the region "needed capital more than farmers; it was more of an industrial than an agricultural frontier."[3] Abundant minerals, forests and rivers do not, however, make a community. By the early twentieth century, what began as small, hastily constructed outposts populated by young male, often immigrant, laborers were starting to establish themselves as villages, towns and cities.[4]

In a sense both regions were experiencing the problems of nation building, albeit in different directions. The rural south was a community in decline, desperately attempting to maintain its population and its economic equilibrium. The north was a community in creation; it too needed people and economic growth to fulfill its promise as a new place of prosperity. Yet to define the rural problem or the development of northern Ontario solely in terms of political economy is to ignore the moral and sexual dimensions of the issue. The historical process of nation building required more than the formation of political and economic infrastructures. In the "human nation," the proper sort of citizens, subjects with 'character,' was necessary.[5] As studies in immigration policy document, the Canadian government has historically used moral as well as political and racial criteria to select suitable candidates for entry to (or exit from) the country.[6] Similar concerns about the character and morality of citizens obtained at the regional and community levels.

Commentators on the 'rural problem' and the boosters of New Ontario indeed put their case in political and economic terms. But they also spoke of morality, sexuality and character. An appreciation of the symbolic meaning of sexuality allows us to make sense of this discourse. As historian Carol Smith-Rosenburg has argued, in the nineteenth century, "different social and economic groups, experiencing economic and demographic change differently, having different degrees of power with which to respond to the alterations that affected their lives, created disparate fantasies, debated with one another, condemned one another—all in the language of sexuality."[7] Today we tend to think of people, not regions, in sexual terms. Yet in the past, both areas of the province bore distinct moral reputations. Rural Ontario attempted to exploit the widely held association of country living and moral purity to its advantage. Promoters warned of the inherent dangers of city life for restless rural youth and at the same time tried to bolster the sagging social fortunes of the area by encouraging progressive farming practices and healthy recreation. Those attempting to fashion mining settlements and logging enclaves into towns and cities in the north had continually to deflect and reshape criticism of the region as a wild and immoral netherland.

In this chapter I step far beyond the courtroom to investigate how sexual and moral questions became part of the discourse of economic decline, development and nation building. Discursive formulations of national development do not exist apart from those of traditionally conceived questions of political economy. The moral reputation of northern Ontario took a downward turn in the early twentieth century precisely because of massive immigration to the region of ethnic, politically radical male workers. A full social and economic history of northern Ontario has yet to be written, however, and no such attempt is ventured here. My task is to emphasize an often-neglected dimension of the complex and multifaceted process of nation building: changes, both real and imagined, in gender and sexual relations.

Sites, of course, are never simply locations; the spatial, too, is socially constructed. Social divisions are often spatialized; as geographer Rob Shields argues, places become labeled, much like deviant individuals. This combination of social divisions and spatial metaphors (such as the 'wrong side of the tracks') become incorporated into what Sheilds calls "imaginary geographies," so much so that certain sites become associated with "particular values, historical events and feelings."[8]

This association of space and values or feelings helps explain the relationship between region and sexual danger, a phenomenon that has become obvious through this study but which is certainly not unique to northern Ontario. In Russia, for example, physicians defined syphilis in sexual terms when it occurred in cities, but in terms of peasant ignorance of sanitation and cleanliness in the countryside.[9] Like sexual disease, sexual crime was also a socially constructed and constantly shifting phenomenon, which took its shape primarily from the dominant social structures of gender, race and class. But region too influenced the social perceptions of sexuality. According to Russian historian Laura Engelstein, it was conflicting views of gender, particularly the contrast between the asexual, virtuous peasant woman and the pathologically sexual urban prostitute, which help account for changing interpretations of the source of sexual disease in Russia.[10] We have seen that incest could be diagnosed differently depending on where it occurred; it was a problem of working-class congestion in cities and rural isolation in the country. Region weighed heavily on the minds of turn-of-the-century social reformers and medical and legal commentators, providing simple answers to what were complicated political questions.

Times of great social and economic change also involve challenges to the moral and sexual order of life, challenges which are felt by those involved in them as deeply as economic or political upheavals. Thus we must broaden our understanding of the sexual, the political and the economic. Sexuality and sexual politics can serve in such periods as reservoirs of imagery, through which people express their experience of and feelings toward change.[11]

THE MANLY NORTH

Before widespread settlement by whites, northern Ontario was, according to Nelles, a "land of mystery, a silent kingdom of fur-trading companies and Indians, a massive indistinct blur on the maps marked "Immense Forests."[12] This mysterious quality of the north was reflected in nineteenth and early twentieth-century literary depictions and travelers' guides, creating an image of a land to be "feared, avoided, and on occasion, exploited."[13] Travelers delighted in visiting the romantic and primitive wilds of northern Ontario, turning the resident voyageur into a tourist attraction in his own right.[14]

The forbidding image of northern Ontario cast the region in decidedly masculine terms. A travelers' guide described Lake Superior as "a man's lake." According to T. M. Langstreth, it was "the most dangerous body of water in the world. It takes a man to master it."[15] Danger, fear and mystery have dominated the often awe-struck portrayals of the north in the imaginations of observers. The region was sexualized, but not, initially, negatively.

Indeed, a popular early conceptualization of northern Ontario's social life was an enthusiastic approval of the region's hearty stock and rough and ready democracy. One English traveler was not impressed with the early physical settlement at Port Arthur and Fort William, but the quality of its people more than compensated for the rough surroundings:

> There is nothing picturesque in these twin towns. . . . There
> are not made-roads. The weather decides whether you travel
> over dry earth or through slush. The houses are of wood, some
> with an endeavour after pretension, but mostly of rough-hewn
> logs. There is plenty of land round each; but there are no grass
> plats or flower beds. There are decrepit fences and wild vegeta-

tion, and refuse pitched anywhere. Neither Port Arthur nor
Fort William has had time to beautify itself.
But mark the contrast between the men and the women. The
women are gentle-featured, and as well-dressed as their sisters
of the settled east. . . . The men are of a different stamp. They
are slim and loose-limbed, and have the stride of men well
pleased with themselves. They are broad-shouldered. They
have strong, clean-cut, clean-shaven countenances; steely eyes,
straight lips. They wear broad-brimmed slough hats with impudent dents in the side. Their language is blunt, decisive, full
of character.

In the north, he concluded, visitors will find "men who may not be cul-
tured . . . but they are the real metal with no tinsel."[16]
These themes were echoed in other travelers' accounts of the regions.
T. M. Langstreth spoke admiringly of the "wholeness" of life in the north.
"I like the idea of your financiers stepping outside the door to hunt, or your
hunters buying poetry, and your poets erecting cabins with their hands."
Where else, he wondered, "could one find a more satisfactory combination
of forest and fireside?"[17] A later visitor drew an explicit parallel between the
pioneer personality and the democracy of the frontier:

The North is a county with a personality. It is composed of opti-
mism, fortitude, and a gay willingness to take a chance. It is reflected in its people and it breeds a hardy race. The North
country opens its arms to men and women of like character. It
offers nothing to the weakling or the failure from a softer way of
life. . . . Rich or poor, the Northland asks only of its people that
they be resolute and steadfast.[18]

Both the natural beauty and the 'hearty stock' in the north became important selling points for the early tourist industry in the area. Middle-class
urbanites enjoyed the rest cure in a canoe that northern Ontario promised.
Since the 1850s, tourists had boarded steamers to seek miracle cures in the
Lake Superior air. Wilfred William Campbell, a clergyman turned poet and
travel writer, in 1910 rhapsodized about all of Canada's Great Lakes, regarding them as "not mere bodies of water . . . but as vast influences,
powers, consolers and sources of infinite wisdom, comfort and rest." Lake
Superior, he wrote, combined "sublimity, mystery . . . and vast loneli-
ness." Even into the 1930s, government-issued tourist literature invited visitors to "come north for health," for "invigorating atmosphere, cool nights
for refreshing slumber, and abundance of pure and wholesome food and
fine drinking water all contributed to a healthy, hard race." Yet as one traveler reminded potential tourists, camping and canoeing in the north "is
man's work . . . not to be taken lightly."[19] Nineteenth-century cultural de-

pictions of the 'true north' combined geographical location and climatic condition to mold both racial and gender character. The north has always been 'man's country'—tough, rugged, with just enough danger to make it exciting. As Ian Radforth pointed out, such bluntly masculine images of the north made Canadians "into a hardy, ruddy-cheeked people made of sterner stuff than our effeminate neighbours to the south."[20]

Travelers were not the only ones to comment on the region's superior physical environment. Publications issued by the federal and provincial governments from the 1880s through the 1920s promoted the region as an agricultural area. Skeptical Canadians in other regions, as well as immigrants, were told repeated tales by enthusiastic northern pioneers of the "healthy climate," "clear, bracing air," the abundance of "pure water," even the "healthy looking trees." One pioneer who had left Toronto with his ailing wife to homestead in the north wrote, in a publication titled *A Plain Tale of Plain People,* "looking at my wife I was glad I had decided to come north. No one would recognize in the robust and rosy cheeked woman the frail invalid of a year ago."[21] To drive home the point, the provincial government sponsored touring agricultural exhibits of the products of northern farms and greenhouses. One such greenhouse exhibit was photographed for the *Toronto Globe* in 1916 and bore the headline, "This is Not in Rosedale" (an upper-class residential neighborhood of Toronto).[22]

When observers addressed themselves to the women of the region, it was often in the same breathless rhetoric they used for the men. Langstreth described a boating excursion he took down the Kaministiqua River in northwestern Ontario with several local women and men, and was amazed to discover that "the women in our party were so able for adventure." Normally, he went on,

> one must accept women as one accepts the weather: when she is fine she is heaven's blue itself; when she storms she is of a sprightly active interest to a student of the race; it is useless to storm in return and unwise to argue. But now and then happens a woman whose plane of life lies above the superficial squall, one equipped with a humour to gild any cloud, whose temper is as serene, as refreshing and as sweepingly powerful, too, as the prevailing westerlies. They can usually cook well also.[23]

Women themselves were often less sanguine about life in the north. Ellen Knox, in her survey of employment and living options for young post–World War I females 'of the new day,' remarked that "you cannot help thinking as you stand at the rear of a car speeding east or west in northern Ontario along one of the three railroad lines . . . that you are at the end of civilization."[24] Aili Schneider remembers her mother sitting down and weeping upon her arrival in Timmins. The houses, she thought, had been built for "not too fussy chickens."[25] Belle Kettridge, who worked in Port Arthur as a stenographer in the 1890s, dreamed the universal small-town girl's dream of escape to New York City, which would take her "out of the narrowing process of a life in which one never hears anything discussed beyond one's neighbours."[26]

Isolation, particularly from female company, was high on the list of northern women's grievances. Elizabeth MacEwan remembers arriving to join her husband at the railway station in Cobalt and gazing at "the biggest crowd of all men I had ever seen in my life." After spending a winter with her husband in a shack outside Cobalt, she visited friends in New Liskeard and on the way was thrilled to see another woman: "I had not spoken to a woman since coming to the country, and when I saw one on the train I stopped and asked her to say hello to me."[27]

Women in the north were aware of potential sexual dangers. MacEwan spoke of one incident in which she and her husband trudged the one and a half miles from their home to the post office in town, only to discover halfway through their journey they had forgotten their letters. Her husband insisted she stay in the bush and wait for him to retrieve the letters and, giving her a gun, admonished her to "shoot anything that comes along." She described standing, "pitch dark among the trees . . . picturing all kinds of wild animals and most dreaded of all, a man."[28]

But while sexual danger was recognized by women who lived there, many claimed that the camaraderie and pioneer spirit of the community included them and protected them from harm. Both women and men in Radforth's study of northern Ontario logging camps insisted that there was "never any shenanigans" among the female cooks and male loggers. As one logger explained, a woman's "brothers, cousins etc. might be in camp, you didn't know."[29] Aili Schneider claimed that local loggers "never used foul language as they teased me about boyfriends and dates," and Elizabeth MacEwan defended Cobalt as "probably the most law-abiding town of its kind in history." "I do not mean," she went on, "that Cobalt was not a roaring rowdy mining camp, it was and roared with the best of them—but it was a nice kind of roar." Indeed, the overwhelming male-to-female ratio was often enjoyed by women, since it vastly increased their dating possibilities. Schneider, for example, reported happily that there were at least thirty men to each woman in Timmins.[30]

There was no need to apologize for living in the north throughout most of the nineteenth and early twentieth century. As Carl Berger has argued, Canada's intemperate climate and rugged geography were thought to provide a number of advantages. Nineteenth-century political commentators considered that the geographic climate would pay important social dividends: the nation would not be plagued by 'Negro problems' or other racial unpleasantness, French/English conflicts would be subsumed under a common northern heritage, and the vigor produced by living with bracing weather would foster a superior political and economic system.[31] Changing class, race and political relations in the twentieth century, however, created a very different perception of life in the north.

THE CHASTE SOUTH

Perceptions of rural life in southern Ontario seem the reverse of those of the north. Social assumptions about life on the farm made it appear extremely pleasant. And rural life has long been associated with sexual purity, naturalness and simplicity.

Raymond Williams, in his study of several centuries of English literary depictions of rural and urban life, notes that there appears to be a timeless, transcendent quality to the wistful longing for rural innocence and virtue. Since at least the seventeenth century, English writers have regularly lamented the passing of the golden age of harmonious rural life. This sentimentalized view is not, he suggests, a historical error, but rather a question of historical perspective. Periods of rural dissatisfaction, in which return to an idyllic past is explicitly invoked, correspond to times of change and disruption in the rural economy.

> People have often said 'the city' when they meant capitalism or bureaucracy or centralised power, while 'the country' . . . has at times meant everything from independence to deprivation. . . . Most obviously since the Industrial Revolution, but in my view also since the beginning of the capitalist agrarian mode of production, our powerful images of country and city have been ways of responding to a whole social development.[32]

Williams points toward the changing social relations of industrial capitalism in order to comprehend the fervent declarations of nostalgia which accompanied periods of rural economic decline. Yet the language of sexuality and morality was chosen by Canadians to express concerns about rural economic decline. The western Canadian agricultural press, for example, constantly reminded its readers of the host of moral and sexual dangers which might beset young men and women foolish enough to leave the farm for the city. The ever-colorful writings of Canadian feminist Nellie McClung capture well the sexual contrast between city and country:

> The city offers so many dazzling, easy ways to wealth. It is so rich in promise, so treacherous in fulfillment. The city is a lenient, unfaithful nurse, pampering and pandering the child in her care not for his own good, but for her gain, soothing him

with promises she never means to keep, a waster of time, a de-
stroyer of ambition, a creator of envy, but dazzling gay with tinsel and redolent with perfume, covering poverty with cheap lace
and showy ribbons, a hole in her stocking but a rose in her hair!
The country is a stern nurse, hard but just, making large demands on the child in her care, but giving great rewards. She
tells the truth, demands obedience, and does better than she
promises. Though she sends her child on long cold journeys,
and makes him face the bitter winds of winter, she rewards him
with ruddy health, high purpose and clear vision. Though she
makes him work till every muscle aches she rewards him with a
contented mind, an appetite that makes his life a joy, and though
the midday sun may blaze on him with burning heat, at evening
time comes rosy slumber.[33]

McClung's choice of metaphors is revealing. 'City' and 'country' are in-
terchangable with 'good' and 'bad,' and the gender is obvious. Central to the
definition of each was sex, and the choice was clear: one had it, one did not.
In this schema, sex and cities were linked as inherently dangerous, draining
energy from the more important matters of hard work, health and content-
ment.

The preceding pages of this book have documented that sex, in both its
dangerous and pleasurable forms, could be found as often in rural roads and
berry patches as in urban streets and dance halls. Why then did the image of
rural Ontario as a place of moral purity and innocence persist, indeed,
gather increasing momentum, in this period? Why were sexual dangers in
rural areas so often overlooked?

English historians Leonore Davidoff, Jean L'Esperance and Howard
Newby have provided part of the answer to this question. Their analysis of
home and community in English history combines gender with Raymond
Williams's reflections on the ideas of country and city, and adds a spatial
dimension to feminist interpretations of the Victorian domestic ideal. The
middle-class idealization of women as 'angels in the house' merged, they
argue, with notions of rural purity, creating a very specific idea of women's
proper place. "The very core of the ideal," they suggest, "was home in a
rural village community."[34]

Home and community share similar social relations. Both are hierarchical institutions, but authority in each case is so hegemonic it appears as 'natural,' as though it had always been so. Thus both the home and the village
were "the spatial framework within which deference operated." Even as increasing numbers of rural dwellers voted with their feet and left the countryside, the traditional power of male authority continued to hold sway in
domestic ideology. Family and household became "countries of the mind."[35]

This parallel between family and rural community helps us understand nineteenth-century conceptualizations of and responses to sexual danger. Both rural communities and families were understood to be zones of moral safety, 'havens' ruled by benevolent but unquestioned patriarchs. To suggest that sexual abuse or domination could exist within the borders of home or rural community would be to defy the power of traditional authority and would also call into question two mainstays of civilization.

THE BINARY LOGIC OF NORTH AND SOUTH

The moral and sexual images of northern and rural Ontario underwent a change in the early twentieth century. In the south, religious commentators, the press, temperance advocates and other molders of public opinion marshaled traditional notions of rural innocence and began a sustained campaign to protect and expand the moral virtue of country life. They were assisted by the social purity and urban reform movements, which advanced a massive critique of the moral hazards, particularly for women, of city life.

Northern Ontario was tarred with the same brush as the cities. From a dangerously exciting, healthy place of adventure, the north became, at the hands of its southern detractors, a dangerously immoral, uncivilized place of vice. A chorus of defensive voices in the north rose to protest this new characterization, thus infusing the attempt to boost the economic and social development of the region with a strongly moral element.

These changes occurred simultaneously and were not coincidental. The changing moral images of north and south were inextricably related. Historically, changing moral conceptions of north and south illustrate what Mary Poovey calls the "binary logic that governed the Victorian symbolic economy."[36] Similarly, Rob Sheilds suggests that binary oppositions between high and low culture, a staple of European civilization, have sometimes been spatialized geographically as the "central/marginal" dualism.[37] The 'civilized' rural south could only assert its moral superiority by contrasting it to something else, by creating an immoral adversary in the cities and the north. Thus as the rural south got 'cleaner,' the north became 'dirtier.'

That the rural crisis was, in large measure, a moral crisis was a pronounced theme in the arguments of observers. John MacDougall, commissioned by the Presbyterian church in 1913 to study the 'rural problem,' stated his case bluntly. After an exhaustive statistical analysis of the extent of population decline in parts of rural Canada, combined with a study of some of the economic causes of agricultural decline, MacDougall pronounced that the real crisis was moral. "The abandoned dwelling," he argued, "is a lesser social evil than the weakened household."[38] Rural households were weakening, MacDougall was surprised to learn, because women were leaving the farm at a faster rate than men. He cited a number of reasons for this trend. Like Edward Amey, who surveyed "servant girls' grievances" before him, as well as newly organized rural women themselves, MacDougall suggested that the long and arduous hours of toil endured by rural women accounted for their desire to leave the farm. But he also posed the problem in terms of sexual politics, stating that "the longing to escape from country to town is being taken advantage of by designing men to lure girls to their ruin."[39]

Whatever the cause of women's flight from the farm, the results, for the moral tone of rural life, were clear. According to MacDougall,

> the chief factor in the moral strain [of rural life] is the fact that moral enthusiasms are lacking in the country owing to the present trend. Where people are discontent with their lot and seek to escape it, with no fine aspirations leading them to any other walk in life, there is an absence in moral incentives which made rural morality so splendid a thing in the past.[40]

Two strategies emerged from this analysis of the rural problem. One involved reasserting rural virtue by encouraging persons to stay or return to the farm. At the same time, immoral straw men were created in those places where rural dwellers were seeking new opportunities: the cities and the north.

That there was a perceived healing or corrective power of rural life was evident in many turn-of-the-century social reform schemes. The Children's Aid Society, for example, preferred to place errant children in farm households rather than in cities, since the "wholesomeness and honest toil of farm life would develop moral and industrious habits." The same logic dictated that farm boys be given priority over city boys in winning early release from reformatories and led medical experts of the period to champion the healing power of rural life.[41] Ellen Knox saw country living as a solution to the rural problem, the city problem and the race problem at once. In the 1920s she advised young women to band together and move back to the farm. "A colony of capable women," she argued, "will give a different aspect to the countryside, and if they marry, they will make royal farmer's wives. Out-of-door women of this description, of good stock, Canadian, Scotch and English, are exactly what are wanted, exactly what will bring fresh vitality into places run down and discouraged by unscientific farming and intermarriage."[42]

Knox's formula indicates a second major thrust of the campaign to assert the virtue of rural life, that is, to attend to its flagging social and recreational aspects. MacDougall lamented that farmers "accept [their] recreation from town" and pressed the case for "healthy" rural social amusements. Sports, regulated playgrounds in the schools, and improved neighborly contact through telephones and mail delivery would assist in fostering a spirit of "community ideals," which he found sadly lacking in rural areas.[43] The investigation into rural social life undertaken by the Methodist and Presbyterian churches in 1913 came to the same conclusion. "The place for leisure and recreation is simply not recognized by most farmers," stated the report of the social survey of Huron County. "It is not surprising that, failing to get leisure, income or property, the young people quietly slip off to the city or the West."[44] Farmers also heard this message at the meetings of the Farmers' Institute. In 1895 the North Perth Institute, for example, heard a series of lectures, titled "Home Life on the Farm," from the director of the Teachers' Institute for Ontario. He told farmers that the physical drudgery and social isolation of farm work was what was driving young people away, but this could easily be remedied by use of labor-saving machinery, stronger rural social networks, and closer attention to the physical surroundings of the farm household. "A nicely kept lawn with trees and flowers," he suggested, "has its civilizing effect and invariably wields an influence for good."[45]

If community socials and attractive flower beds did not convince rural youth to stay home, perhaps stern warnings about the dangers of urban life might. The core imperative governing rural thinking in early twentieth-century Canada was that "people born on the land should stay on the land." The rural press duly warned its readers of the dire consequences of ignoring this maxim.[46] Transplanted rural men could expect a life of poverty, loafing and, likely, crime. Rural women would suffer an even worse fate. As an editorial in the *New York Tribune*, featured in the *Woodstock Sentinal Review*, explained, the yearning for adventure and a love of finery which drew girls toward the city had a brutal underside: moral corruption. City girls were noted for

> the vulgar insolence of their talk; their swagger, their inane, giggling efforts to attract the notice of men passing by; the vacuity, the incipient depravity. . . . There is no sight more tragic on earth than that of one of these women, meant by God to be a pure wife and mother, frisking jauntily down her way to ruin. The temptation to ruin does not come to the native American girl through any natural proclivity to vice, but through her vanity, her intense desire to be noticed, her nervous craving for excitement.[47]

"Happy home ties and home influence," claimed the *Goderich Signal*, "cannot be severed without pain." In order to resist the "great temptations which lie in wait" for girls who leave the country, farmers were encouraged to allow their daughters to make their own income on the farm, by keeping poultry, marketing vegetables, even haying and harvesting.[48] The moral reputation of northern Ontario became linked with this characterization of city life in various ways. The religious reformers who surveyed the social life of rural Ontario wondered where persons leaving the farm had gone. In response to the reformers' questions, those remaining in the area stated that the others had gone West and to New Ontario, which ranked before the cities as the perceived new world beckoning rural youths.[49] The dangers that northern Ontario held were even more complex than those of the city, however. In the north one found not just sex but race and political radicalism as well.

Some historians have reproduced the historical perception that the absence of women in logging and mining camps explained their reputation for rowdiness and lawlessness. Michael Cross, for example, suggests that the "long, lonely and womanless winter in the woods" was responsible for the raucous behavior of lumbermen who invaded Ottawa each spring. Terry Chapman, studying western Canada, concurs. "The very nature of the frontier experience," she argues, "with its preponderance of single males, was not conducive to moderation in its social activities."[50] It was such perceptions of northern Ontario which encouraged female teachers to refuse jobs in particularly isolated parts of the region and caused the WCTU to establish missions in northern logging camps, to warn inhabitants of the dangers of drink and prostitution. Logging and mining camps bore the brunt of moral anxieties about the region. Social purity crusaders reported that logging camps were where white slavers in the cities deposited their conquests, and the National Council of Women lamented that this practice was "more or less openly tolerated" by local authorities. The socialist press was of the opinion that Indian women had their skin bleached to pass as white and were bought and sold as slaves by bush workers.[51]

To accept that by itself the presence of large numbers of men explained (and justified) fears of immorality in northern Ontario is to miss two other key factors—ethnicity and politics. The men of the north were of a particular type: immigrants, prone to political radicalism. The harsh conditions in northern Ontario lumber and mining camps produced periodic but dramatic upsurges in organized working-class discontent. Ethnic solidarity, particularly among Finns and eastern Europeans, made for a political cohesiveness rare among urban workers. This cohesiveness, combined with prevailing assumptions about the criminality and sexual immorality of immigrants, made the region look extremely frightening to the 'civilized' world. Northern Ontario became a lightning rod, touching multiple fears of class, gender, race and politics. Radforth quotes an alarmed logging company editorial, which brings these anxieties into sharp relief: "From the top to the bottom, Bolshevism is composed chiefly of featherless buzzards and moral hyenas. Its instincts are a cross between those of Jack-the-Ripper and Lucretia Borga. . . . Its idea of Heaven is a defenseless woman. Its chief God is a rape fiend."[52]

The logging industry had an obvious and self-serving motive; after all, it wanted to protect its profits from the growing strength of organized labor and the Left. But this passage indicates larger social fears. In the early twentieth century, the strands of political radicalism, gender relations and racism converged, creating a moral panic about life in the north.

Early attempts at boosting settlement in the region reveal the genesis of this panic. Agricultural promotional literature was initially silent about the sorts of people required to inhabit the north, but by the 1890s the pitch was made to "solid Ontario farmers' sons." By the turn of the century, concerns about the changing ethnic complexion of the region were obvious. A correspondent for the *Toronto Mail and Empire*, who accompanied a trainload of pioneers north in 1901, commented on the "advantages of settling among educated intelligent people as compared to settling in the districts partly alloted to foreigners who do not understand the language, laws or customs of the country." The settlement of the north, he went on, "is yet one of those events which awakens in the heart of the Briton that feeling of . . . the colonizing spirit which has caused English to be spoken in every part of the globe.[53] Another newspaper correspondent, writing two years later, declared proudly that the settlers he met were "Anglo Saxon Canadians, just the men and women who have made Old Ontario what it is, wholesome citizens with the same ideals and the same mother tongue." Even as late as 1913, settlers' testimonials continued to speak of their pride and "British pluck" in clearing new lands.[54]

Individual instances of "British pluck" could, however, do little to halt the changing demographics of the region. Like many other parts of the country, northern Ontario experienced a massive change in its ethnic makeup in a relatively short period of time: in 1871 the population of the north was 50 percent Native, 32 percent British and 15 percent French; by 1911 this had changed to 5 percent Native, 50 percent British, 21 percent French and 23 percent other, mainly Finns, Ukrainians and Italians. That immigration by Britons had actually increased seemed lost in a sea of new and 'othered' faces.[55]

The religious wing of the social purity movement eagerly fueled this panic. A survey of rural Huron County undertaken by the Methodist and Presbyterian churches studied the religious, educational and economic life of the community and, as we have seen, made various recommendations aimed at improving the social life and community spirit of the area. By contrast, the surveys undertaken of Port Arthur and Fort William made the cities appear swamped with vice. Surveyors cataloged the number of pool rooms, moving picture shows, dance halls, houses of prostitution and bars; provided a list of arrest statistics; counted and analyzed the mortality rate and hospital services; and, in the various ethnic neighborhoods, literally counted the number of people living (and sleeping) in each household. Predictably, investigators found in each city, especially in the immigrant sections, a "wear and tear upon the nervous system of individuals by enforced close contact with others" and "the loss of the quality of delicacy," all of which culminated in "the production of petty crime."[56] The Methodist and Presbyterian churches also tried to interest the provincial attorney general's office in the claim that police officers and local magistrates in northern Ontario were lax in enforcing prostitution laws. Even into the 1930s, some eugenics advocates singled out northern Ontario as a place where the 'feeble-minded' could breed without restriction.[57]

A temperance novel, *Pine Lake: A Story of Northern Ontario*, published in 1901, also voiced the sexual dangers of life in the north. Its protagonist, Miss Daisy Murphy, was a young schoolteacher who secured her first job in a northern town near a lumber mill. Her near 'fall' was slightly more subtle than other dangers feared by social purity crusaders. Daisy's story is about her victory over the evils of dancing, which to her dismay was "the most popular amusement in Pine Lake." However benign they may appear, the temptations of dancing were expressed in much the same language as other bodily perils. Daisy describes watching a square dance while an "almost irresistible something" took hold of her, causing her feet to tap, her brain to reel, and her heart to thump. "Was this," she wondered, "the oft talked about ruinous fascination of the dance?" Despite such moments of weakness and curiosity, Daisy stays true to her promise to her parents that she would never dance. Indeed, her resolve is strengthened when a "Pine Lake dude" laughingly tells her that "her father won't know" if she has an "innocent bit of fun." Vowing never to "prove herself false against her home, training, mother's prayers and own honor," Daisy switches gears, becoming an opponent of drink, dancing, and public houses and organizing Pine Lake's first Women's Christian Temperance Union chapter. Thus both Pine Lake and Daisy herself are redeemed, and perhaps even more so when Daisy returns, with her new husband, the reformed Pine Lake dude, to her home in southern Ontario.[58]

Community leaders in the north were defensive about the area's reputation for immorality and took pains to challenge it. In Cobalt, for example, a spirited "Go to Church" campaign was waged in 1914. As the *Cobalt Nugget* explained, "in older communities, where social and church activities are interwoven, there is not the same need for a novel suggestion in order to obtain a larger percentage of the population in church. But there is a disregard of some of the conventions in a mining town and a new country that also cuts the ties of Sunday observance."⁵⁹ In nearby Haileybury, the town council, fearing that the "morals of the town were not what they should be," hired a private detective to investigate a series of gambling rumors. Citizens of North Bay were stung by the "strong adverse comments" about northern juries made by the crown attorney after one such jury found a lumber worker not guilty of murdering a prostitute, and in Sudbury the press reacted angrily to the suggestion made by some "Toronto women" that James Robinson, the man who raped and impregnated several of his daughters, be lynched. "Even if we do live in New Ontario," declared the *Sudbury Journal*, "we are just as law abiding as they are in Toronto."⁶⁰

Gender and sexual relations were central to the changes in the social fortunes of northern and rural southern Ontario and key components in campaigns to win back moral legitimacy. Perhaps the moral boosters of each region were correct in their estimation of their area's woes. Was the link between all-male work enclaves, Bolshevism, and Jack the Ripper simply the political paranoia of those who stood to gain the most by economic development in the region? In deconstructing the moral panic over the decline of rural southern Ontario and the development of the north, we must not lose sight of how geographic dimensions of sexual morality influence the social definitions of sexual crime.

REGION, REPUTATION AND MORAL BOOSTERISM

I have sought to disprove the nineteenth-century belief that sexual danger, abuse and exploitation (or, for that matter, sexual pleasure) were solely features of urban life. It is social power, generally parceled out in different packages according to race, gender and class, which shapes experiences of sexual danger. We have also learned, however, that geographic isolation contributed to women's sense of fear and heightened women's vulnerability. Women such as Tockha K., who was stuck until spring thaw in a lumber camp with an abusive boss, or Mary S., whose boyfriend threatened to let her freeze in the bush while they were out dog sledding if she did not give in to his demand for sex, obviously faced an added level of insecurity.⁶¹

Region could also influence the perception of sexual crime in the eyes of the public and the law. We have seen this happen once already. One of Annie Robinson's clerical supporters suggested that the unfortunate fate of the Robinson family could be accounted for by their move to New Ontario and the consequent absence of "elevating influences" in their lives. Evelyn E., a traveling chewing-gum salesman, tried (successfully) a similar defense. His response to a charge of exposure and indecent assault of a ten-year-old girl and her infant sister in Sault Ste. Marie was that the "lonesomeness of travelling in this North Country" caused him to come under a "foolish spell."[62] In these examples we can see where differing material realities of life in the north (isolation, vulnerability, even climate) leave off and social prejudice begins.

It was sometimes suggested that those from 'primitive' regions deserved leniency in sentencing for sexual crime. The defense lawyers for Isaac W. and his two sons, who lived in Thessalon and were convicted of regularly having sex with their young ward, appealed to the judge for clemency on the grounds that the family was raised "in a primitive section of the country and have not had the benefit of the refining influence of education." Similarly, the lawyer for Telesphore B., found guilty of raping a twelve-year-old girl on her way home from school outside Sault Ste. Marie, suggested that his client "has had no education and was raised in a primitive region."[63] Judges were not always moved by this argument; in both these cases the men received stiff jail sentences. But these stories do indicate another bit of social construction: how questions of gender relations might be reinterpreted as questions of poverty, education and environment.

'Northern' was a frame of mind as much as a distinct geographic entity; even isolated regions in southern Ontario were morally suspect. A judge sentencing a Dufferin County man on seduction charges complained that "parents are too careless of the well being of their girls, and also boys, in outlying places." Lovinca T., a woman from the northern reaches of Frontenac County convicted of murdering her illegitimate infant was described by federal Justice Department officials as living in "a section of the county where immorality was notorious."[64]

Two counties were singled out for particular scrutiny. In 1916 Reverend A. H. Tyrer used the pages of the Toronto press to sound the alarm about "poverty, mental breakdown and moral degeneration" in the "remote parts of the backwoods" of Muskoka County. His aim in exposing such conditions, he explained, was to raise funds for what he called his "people of the woods." Economic problems, he thought, were at the root of the region's woes; parts of the area were "totally unfit" for agriculture and thus "poverty and isolation, with too frequent maternity and insufficient nourishment," contributed to moral breakdown. Readers of the *Toronto World*, *Star*, and *Evening News* were asked to send money to alleviate the "misery and wretchedness" in Muskoka.[65]

Tyrer was an Anglican church minister who lived in the region. His concerns about 'moral degeneration' launched him, several years later, into the leadership of the Canadian birth control and eugenics movement. In the 1930s he opened a birth control clinic in the slums of Toronto, and he published a number of birth control and marriage manuals.[66] His first excursion into public life, however, created a minor furor in the Toronto press and a major one in Muskoka. He was initially circumspect about the region's problems, claiming he could not "state publicly the details of the awfulness of things," but invited readers to write him to learn the "facts of the case." (He even claimed to have pictures.) When the *Toronto World* took up his appeal, chastizing the churches, local officials and the provincial government for their "conspiracy of silence," it filled in some of the missing details. "Incest and adultery," claimed the paper, caused "physical deformity and disease" in the region. The citizens of Muskoka were outraged.[67]

Tyrer repeated his charges in Muskoka, this time claiming that cases of "idiocy, incest, adultery, frightful deformities, insanity and abject poverty" could all be found within five miles of Huntsville, The *Huntsville Forrester* vehemently disagreed. A quick check with the township clerk revealed that a mere three or four of the last eighty births registered in the region were illegitimate, a record that was, according to the press, nothing to be ashamed of, especially when compared to other communities.[68]

Local citizens were especially concerned that Tyrer's charges created an "unfavourable opinion from the outside," serving to "stigmatize the District as a hive of poverty and incest." A couple of weeks later these fears seemed to come true. A local farmer, by all accounts a "responsible citizen," was about to sell his farm when the buyer read Tyrer's story in the Toronto press. The farmer was "humiliated" when the buyer asked him indignantly what kind of district he was inviting him to be a resident of; the deal fell through. Thus local efforts to "strengthen individual and commercial interest in Muskoka, and to induce settlers to take up vacant farms" were jeopardized by Tyrer's campaign, which "broadcast that immorality, degeneracy, incest and poverty are rampant in the District." Regional boosters no doubt also attempted to maintain an attractive image given the importance, since the 1890s, of tourism to the area.[69]

A similar story unfolded the same year in Peterborough, when a string of particularly lurid sexual crimes prompted an assize court judge to direct the sitting grand jury to investigate the moral conditions in the northern reaches of the county, an area popularly known as the badlands. The grand jury's report contained a familiar litany of charges. Poverty, illiteracy and isolation caused a host of moral catastrophes: incest, adultery, marriage of the feeble-minded, even murder. While the jury was quick to point out that "there are slum conditions in every urban municipality, so there are similar conditions in the rural district," they called for a number of changes, including hiring of more police, legislation providing for separate bedrooms for female children, and, significantly, removal of the truly destitute to farms in New Ontario.[70]

These stories highlight a number of themes we have previously addressed. The equation between isolation and incest stands in direct contradiction to the more typical association of incest with the overcrowding of urban tenements. It is not as though one diagnosis of the problem was 'wrong.' Rather, as Engelstein has suggested with respect to sexual disease, definitions of sexual crime could readily "adapt to the cultural environment."[71] Both diagnoses of incest, of course, leave unexplored the question of private, patriarchal family structures.

The presumed common denominator between rural and urban definitions of incest was poverty. Thus we can also see how quickly economic issues could become sexualized. The easy association of poverty with immorality provided state officials and reformers with a strong rationale for intervention in the intimate lives of the poor. But this association also reveals something of early twentieth-century bourgeois thinking about poverty, class and nation. To the middle class, poverty was not objectionable in and of itself. Poverty was problematic because of the moral baggage thought to accompany it, and these problems cast neighborhoods, regions, even entire countries, in a negative light. The point, then, of middle-class concerns about poverty and vice among the working class and immigrants was more than a simple imposition of middle-class values onto the poor. As Valverde has argued, social reformers did want their charges to "embrace the culture and values of Anglosaxon, Protestant, middle-class urban Canadians: but this was to ensure that the power of the WASP bourgeoisie would appear as legitimate, not to democratize society."[72]

Local reaction to Reverend Tyrer's comments about Muskoka reveals the bedrock upon which regional reputation rested: bad sexuality made for bad business. Local industrialists waged campaigns, termed 'economic boosterism' by urban historians, to create the necessary capital to turn rural towns into urban commercial districts.[73] Similarly, women's organizations appealed to the 'boosterish' impulses of local politicians and businessmen in order to attain funding for women's services. The YWCA, for example, asked businessmen to consider "what would happen to their reputations and to the reputation of their community should they fail to support the YWCA."[74] This convergence of discourses—of national economic and social development, gender relations, sexual morality, and crime—forms what I have called moral boosterism. The perceived need for economic growth and the desire to cleanse one's community of vice thus arose from the same impulse and often from the same people. Upstanding, moral citizens were crucial to regional growth and prosperity. Those waging campaigns against immorality in the north were the elite, and their explicit targets were the ethnic working class. As German historian George Mosse has argued, nationalism enlarges the parameters of respectability by sanctioning middle-class morality and "spreading respectability to all classes of the population."[75]

Moral boosterism regularly accompanied the opening of the criminal court. A judge in Oxford County opened his court in 1909 with a few words of congratulations to the citizens for a relatively clear criminal docket, using this fact to show that the county was home to "a fine, industrious class of people." Conversely, the spring 1894 assize court in Perth County opened with the stern judicial admonition that there appeared a "carnival of crime" against women in the area, and a sober editorial in the press stated that the assizes "disclosed a state of immorality in the city and county shockingly disgraceful."[76]

It was the presence or absence of specifically sexual crimes which was noticed and duly commented upon by legal and community authorities. Thus prosecutions for sexual crime became a sort of moral pulse-taking through which the social health of the community could be gauged. Instances of sexual conflict and crime effected not only those who had the misfortune to appear before the courts, but the reputation, well-being and prosperity of the community as well. Gender identities and notions of appropriate moral conduct, then, extended far beyond the relations of individual men to individual women.

CONCLUSION:

The Double Standard, Twice Over

Acording to Alice Chown, an early twentieth-century Canadian feminist writer, "once we are willing to be frank and truthful, we shall find our way out of this morass of falsehood, hypocrisy, and illicit relations, with their heart-breaking results. Henceforth I hope I shall be brave and not try to cover over my own or any other person's sex experience with moral platitudes."[1] Alice Chown was an optimist. Most women in turn-of-the-century Ontario did not find their way out of the morass of patriarchal definitions of sexuality, either individually or collectively. Indeed, an obvious conclusion of this study is the awful sameness of sexual abuse and danger in both the 'bad old days' and our own.

This book confirms several central contemporary feminist conclusions about sexual violence. Rape and related crimes are not acts of individual pathology but rather expressions of asymmetrical relations of power between women and men. Yet women who take their complaints to the courts face a barrage of prejudices concerning their past morality and sexual conduct. These judgments scrutinize the actions of 'bad' or 'designing' women more severely than the court scrutinizes men who breach either the desires of individual women or the criminal law.

I have conceptualized sexual violence as a component of patriarchal domination. Yet male power does not rest on coercion alone. Acts of rape, the unmet promises of 'rakish' men to their pregnant girlfriends, the distinction between 'maidenly girls' and 'designing women,' and the legal system's disbelief of women who attempt to punish an assailant are all of a piece. Their common denominators are suspicion and hostility toward the ex-

pression of autonomy, especially sexual autonomy, by women. Their persistence reflects the multiple ways in which sexuality fits into the panoply of
patriarchal power.

These are a few of the many threads which link past experiences of sexual
danger to those of the present. I have also pointed to the historically specific
nature of sexual crime. The fifty years this study has examined were considered, by contemporaries, times of immense sexual peril. The several
hundred women who make up this case study would certainly have agreed.
Yet in many ways the most dangerous villain facing the women I studied
was shame. The potent weapon of humiliation touched all those who went
public with their stories of sexual conflict, even when they were believed
in the courtroom. Too many questions lurked unanswered: What was a
woman really doing on that street, at that time? How could she not know
that the hired man had his eye on her? Could a father really do that to his
daughter? Shame, of course, has not completely disappeared from contemporary discourses of female sexuality. At the turn of the century, however,
there were no shades of gray: good women were not associated with such
sordid matters as forced sex. Bad women, the kind who got caught, were
liable to scrutiny, suspicion and disbelief.

To argue that gender and gendered standards of sexual conduct matter in
sexual conflicts is hardly contentious. More controversial, perhaps, is to
suggest that race, ethnicity and class matter as well. Yet just as sexuality
forms part of the arsenal of patriarchal control, so too has sexual domination
sustained racial and class hierarchies. The concept of 'character,' so crucial
in determining the credibility of a rape victim, was invested with various
social meanings generally assigned to persons on the basis of their sex, class
and race. Class helped determine a woman's level of vulnerability to sexual
danger, for example, whether she was alone and poor in a new community
and forced to rely on the kindness (or brutality) of strangers. Class also
shaped the experiences of men accused of sexual crimes. The difference between a 'sex pervert' and a 'society pet' was determined largely by the economic and social advantages of class. Race also determined whether a
person's sexual conduct would be more stringently policed and tended to
have pernicious effects on non-WASP immigrant men as well as women.
Just as the moral virtue of working-class or immigrant women was suspect, immigrant men also faced a set of assumptions about "animalistic
foreigners" or "Bolshevik moral hyenas." The popular notion of the "fascination of the foreign races for Canadian girls" contributed to a dispropor-
tionate level of scrutiny of and judgment against immigrant men and their
sexuality.[2]

I have argued that beyond the courtroom, there were indeed elaborate
'discourses of sexual danger' which developed in turn-of-the-century On-

tario, few of which bore any relationship to women's actual experience of abuse. The moral silences of the period have been interrogated as well as the moral panics, confirming historically another contention of contemporary feminist analysis: women in fact faced considerable harm from men who were their nearest and dearest—boyfriends, neighbors and family members. An examination of the social and spatial settings of assault reveal that two of the most hallowed and morally revered locations historically—the rural village and the family—were sites of sexual exploitation. The outcry, in the early twentieth century, over the sins of city life obscured sexual danger in rural areas, turning the matter into a question of geography rather than gender. Similarly, the privacy of the 'antisocial' family or household has long kept hidden sexual abuse of daughters, nieces, sisters and domestic servants. Two-thirds of the women in this study were assaulted by men they knew.

I have also argued that coercive sexual relations were not a mere reflection of 'normal' heterosexuality. If this were so, how are we to understand the multitudes of women in the past, only a few of whom emerge in this book, who recognized and resisted unwanted male incursions on their bodies by taking their cases to court? That most of these women were disbelieved was, I suggest, because they found themselves in situations that fell beyond the tightly drawn boundaries of permissable 'victimhood.' When women were acquainted with their assailants, the conviction rate varied between 33 percent for work-related assaults, to 42 percent for date rape, to 49 percent for assault by family members. If a woman was assaulted by a stranger, however, her chances of finding support in the courtroom were vastly improved. In over 70 percent of such situations the defendants were judged guilty. The story these numbers tell is amplified many times over by the qualitative experience of women on the witness stand. "I screamed and cried," said one woman in court, recounting her story. "With joy?" asked the defense lawyer.[3]

Relations between the sexes were and are complicated. I have also used stories of sexual conflict to explore pleasure, and I have argued for the possibility for a noncoercive heterosexuality. In the records of prosecutions for voluntary sexual liaisons, seduction and abduction specifically, we can trace the often tortured path of courtship. How did it happen that some couples ended up in church, happily reciting pledges of lifetime commitment, while others found themselves in court, bitterly disputing each other's promises and betrayals? Laws governing voluntary sexual relationships had a number of possible effects on these scenarios. Such laws were used by women whose boyfriends reneged on romantic promises and by parents to shore up familial control over impudent daughters. These laws rarely worked, as their legislative proponents had hoped, to rescue maidenly girls from wiley men, because few girls fit the standards of virtue demanded by the courts. The 'soft cops' of patriarchal sexual regulation, laws governing voluntary liaisons, helped entrench one-dimensional ideas about female desire, autonomy and self-assertion.

Historically, the law has not been the only source of redress in cases of sexual conflict. Through examining the theater of the court, and several criminal cases which became, for a variety of reasons, highly publicized sexual scandals, I have documented the slow and uneven pace of development of legal hegemony. Sexual crimes provide a distinctive forum for studying the development of legal authority, for in this period, in these regions, legal structures were often rudimentary and communities continued to play an active role in moral regulation and punishment. The change in moral regulation from community scrutiny to community participation in the legal system to the final 'triumph' of legal hegemony did not occur in a straightforward or linear manner, for all three were evident in this period.

I have also discussed what could be called the background scenery of case files and court transcripts: the history of heterosexual courtship, the complexities of moral regulation, and the relationship between regional economic growth or decline and moral citizenship. All of these issues set the context for individual sexual liaisons. Courtship has been conceptualized without ignoring the power dynamics between women and men, or parents and children, but also in a way that respects women's attempts to carve out social and sexual territory for themselves. Previous works in the history of courtship have tended to individualize too much; I have attempted to understand the social forces that shaped, limited or made possible relations between individual women and men.

Finally, I have explored the geographic location of this study, northern and rural southern Ontario. Both settings have received scant attention from Canadian social historians, and our knowledge of the social, recreational and romantic lives of people in these places has tended to rely on cardboard regional stereotypes.[4] This book sheds light on the recreational lives of people presumed to have had few amusements (in the rural and small-town south) or excessive pleasure (as in the north). Studying these regions at this pivotal moment in their tumultuous economic history has allowed me to appreciate the symbolic power of sexuality and morality in shaping perceptions of place and development. Sexuality looms larger than individual instances of courtship or conflict. It has also been incorporated into national development and identity. Northern communities waging defensive campaigns to attract the 'proper' sort of settler and those lamenting the decline of the pastoral, virtuous rural way of life knew very well the powerful association of morality, gender and citizenship.

A lot happened in Canada between 1880 and 1930. A new stage of capitalist industrialization took hold, an international war was fought, and women emerged as an important political force, winning, among other social reforms, the right to vote. The lives of all Canadians were altered by these experiences, and I do not suggest that women stood apart from these historical times. Yet in studying some of the most hidden and personal experiences in people's lives, we see an uncomfortable disjuncture between standard notions of historical periodization and change, and the things a great many Canadians had on their minds. Passion, love, sex, violence, reputation and revenge: all of these are difficult to map historically and more difficult still to incorporate into the wider fabric of social life, politics and power.

Historians have started to rewrite the history of Canada as though women and workers mattered. We must now also begin to rethink Canadian history as though sexuality mattered. At this point a national synthesis of the history of sexuality in Canada is difficult to imagine but delightful to speculate about. This book points toward many questions we need answers to. The sexual politics of Canadian feminists deserve careful consideration. We have seen that labor feminists such as Katie McVicar were firm proponents of legislation to protect women from unsavory employers. Reversing this same formula, which explains sexual conflict primarily in terms of class, white middle-class feminists were equally concerned about the sexual exploitation of women within the working class and immigrant and Native groups, and apparently silent about its occurrence within their own class and ethnic group. Surely there is more to this story. Mariana Valverde's recent exploration of how race, reproduction and sexuality were understood by the Women's Christian Temperance Union in Canada raises important questions about the sexual politics of some first-wave Canadian feminists; these questions deserve further research.[5] Feminist historians in Canada have charted important differences in political strategy and philosophy among the first wave, but one wonders about debate, difference and disagreement within the movement on topics of sexuality.

This study discusses the question of racially or ethnically distinct sexual cultures in Canada and has much to say about how the private lives of immigrants, both male and female, received more than their share of policing and scrutiny. Recent studies of the social purity movement in Canada also help round out the story of the relationship between sexuality and race/ethnicity in the early twentieth century. Less is known in Canadian history about the specific content of ethnically distinct sexual behavior, mores and customs. Emerging insights from other branches of the history of sexuality could be valuable tools to help Canadian immigration historians deconstruct the

Anglo-Saxon panic about sexuality and morality and to understand more about the conquest of Canadian Native people and successive waves of non-Anglo immigrants.

That I have framed this study from the perspective of women reflects my training and interests as a women's historian as well as my sympathies. I have argued that men were not immune from prevailing behavioral codes, systems of moral regulation, and indeed punishment for transgressing them, however disproportionately this punishment was meted out. I have not, however, problematized or examined empirically men as much as I have women. The stunning insight that maleness, too, is socially constructed has eluded social historians for too long, and the growing interest among scholars about the history and changing contours of masculinity promises to provide a more thorough and complete version of the past. I look forward to the time that unproblematized masculinity is relegated to the dustbin of historiography, and perhaps this study will encourage others to take a more complete and critical look at the construction of masculine sexuality, morality and power in Canada.

This study has also contributed to the history of heterosexuality. While in many ways it is premature in Canadian historiography to call for an end to 'heterosexual hegemony,' since so few studies have problematized male/female coupling against the full range of sexual possibilities, the story of that range of possibilities has yet to be fully told. How ironic that while speculation about the sexual lives of a great many important figures in Canadian history—leading feminists, the architects of our social welfare system, even a prime minister or two—have entertained historians in private for some time, a serious commitment to lesbian and gay scholarship is still in its infancy. What will the emerging pattern of lesbian and gay history yield in Canada, and how will it force us to change 'common-sense' notions of heterosexual norms?

There are other questions facing historians of sexuality in all national contexts. A few historians, such as Judith Allen in Australia and Steven Seidman in the United States, have suggested inventive periodizations of different past sexual moments.[6] In Canada, Carolyn Strange's work suggests a useful framework for understanding how the turn-of-the-century 'problem' of the single girl in the city changed from the morally and spiritually 'adrift' woman fresh from the farm and in need of protection to a more coercive response to the 'good times girl' of the 1920s.[7] How were these different sexual moments arrived at? In the history of sexual relations, what forces determine change? Using a case study of a 'family protection' institution, U.S. historian Linda Gordon has traced how the social problem of family violence was conceptualized and processed by different generations of social reformers.[8] Gordon's work points us in the direction of the reform and sexual politics of the day to appreciate the changing social definitions of 'private' conflict, but where does that leave some of the other big questions? How can we uncover more about the relationship between gender, sexuality and political economy in order to appreciate regional and geographic variations?

Interpreting the world, of course, is one thing; changing it is quite another. A thorough examination of the history of sexuality in Canada holds promise for both important tasks.

APPENDIX

The court cases upon which this study is based were tried between 1880 and 1929 in the criminal assize and county or district court judges' criminal court, the top two levels of the criminal court system in Ontario at the time. I studied all cases of sexual crime in these jurisdictions, selecting all districts in northern Ontario and half (randomly selected) of the counties in southern Ontario. After finding the cases, I then matched them with local newspaper reports of the crimes and the trials.

Table 1. Countries/Districts Surveyed and Their Court Jurisdictions, 1880–1929

Counties/Districts	Court Jurisdictions	Counties/Districts	Court Jurisdictions
Algoma	CAI	Muskoka	CAI
	DCJCC	Nipissing	CAI
Carleton	CAI	Norfolk	CAI
	CCJCC	Ontario	CAI
Cochrane	CAI		CCJCC
Dufferin	CAI	Oxford	CAI
Elgin	CAI	Parry Sound	CAI
	CCJCC	Perth	CAI
Frontenac	CAI		CCJCC
Huron	CAI	Peterborough	CAI
	CCJCC	Prince Edward	CAI
Kenora	CAI	Rainy River	CAI
Lambton	CAI	Stormont,	CAI
	CCJCC	Dundas and	CCJCC
Leeds and Grenville	CAI	Glengarry	
	CCJCC	Sudbury	CAI
Lincoln	CAI	Temiskaming	CAI
	CCJCC	Thunder Bay	CAI

Notes: CAI = Criminal Assize Indictment; DCJCC = District Court Judges' Criminal Court; CCJCC = County Court Judges' Criminal Court.

Table 2. Types and Numbers of Sex-Related Crimes in the Survey

Type/Crime	Number
Sexual violence Rape, attempted rape, indecent assault, carnal knowledge	446
Consensual crimes	70
Seduction	53
Abduction	17
Incest[a]	18
Infanticide[b]	31
Abortion[b]	16
Libel[b]	22
Bestiality	9
Sex-related murder/attempted murder	18
Homosexual-related (men only)	20
Miscellaneous	15
TOTAL	665

a. Incest cases were sometimes prosecuted as rape.
b. These numbers reflect only cases whose facts indicate a sex-related conflict.

Table 3. Sexual Violence Scenarios and Conviction Rates

	Total Number	Guilty	Not Guilty	No Record	Conviction Rate (percentage)
By strangers	51	35	9	7	56%
Street/bush	38	27	8	3	71
Travel	4	3	0	1	100
Break-in	9	5	1	3	50
By gang	30	17	9	4	56
Against children (under age twelve, not by family member)	39	23	13	3	59
By household member	66	33	28	3	50
Family member	47	23	21	1	49
Farmhand	12	6	5	1	50
Boarder	7	4	2	1	57
By date	40	17	18	5	42
By pickup	14	4	7	3	28
By neighbor	46	21	22	3	45
By friend of family	23	7	15	1	30

(*continued*)

Appendix

Table 3. (*Continued*)

	Total Number	Guilty	Not Guilty	No Record	Conviction Rate (percentage)
Work-related	30	10	17	2	33
By acquaintance (unclear)	9	3	6	0	33
TOTAL	348	170	144	31	49%

Note: This table includes the crimes of rape, attempted rape, carnal knowledge, and indecent assault.

Table 4. Verdicts for Crimes of Sexual Violence, 1880–1929

	Guilty	Not Guilty	Disposition Unclear
1880s	38%	51%	11%
1890s	45	48	7
1900s	48	42	10
1910s	56	35	9
1920s	54	27	19

NOTES

INTRODUCTION

1. *Toronto Globe and Mail*, 27 November 1989, 28 April 1990, 25 July 1990.
2. *Ottawa Citizen*, 7, 9, 15, 16, 17, and 18 January 1986.
3. Andrea Dworkin, "Why So-Called Radical Men Love and Need Pornography," in Laura Lederer, ed., *Take Back the Night: Women on Pornography* (New York: William Morrow, 1980), p. 152. For accounts of sexual politics in the early days of the women's movement in Canada, see Becki Ross, "The House That Jill Built: Reconstructing the Lesbian Organization of Toronto, 1976–1980," Ph.D. diss., University of Toronto, 1992. Internationally, see Sheila Rowbotham, *The Past Is Before Us* (London: Pandora, 1989), pp. 59–120, and Alice Echols, *Daring to Be Bad* (Minneapolis: University of Minnesota Press, 1989).
4. Southern Women's Writing Collective, "Sex Resistance in Heterosexual Arrangements," and Sheila Jeffreys, "Eroticizing Women's Subordination," in Dorchen Leidholdt and Janice Raymond, eds., *The Sexual Liberals and the Attack on Feminism* (New York: Pergamon, 1990), pp. 134, 143.
5. Ann Snitow, "Retrenchment vs. Transformation: The Politics of the Antipornography Movement," in Varda Burstyn, ed., *Women against Censorship* (Toronto: Douglas and McIntyre, 1985), p. 112. For a critique of what is known as essentialist feminist sexual politics, see also Alice Echols, "The New Feminism of Yin and Yang," and Joan Nestle, "My Mother Liked to Fuck," in Ann Snitow, Christine Stansell, and Sharon Thompson, eds., *Powers of Desire: The Politics of Sexuality* (New York: Monthly Review Press, 1983), pp. 439–60, 468–70; and Lynne Segal, *Is the Future Female? Troubled Thoughts on Contemporary Feminism* (London: Virago, 1987), pp. 70–116.
6. Carol Vance, "Pleasure and Danger: Toward a Politics of Sexuality," in Carol

Vance, ed., *Pleasure and Danger: Exploring Female Sexuality* (Boston: Routledge and Kegan Paul, 1986), p. 7.

7. Mary MacLeod and Ester Saraga, "Challenging the Orthodoxy: Towards a Feminist Theory and Practice," *Feminist Review*, no. 28 (January 1988): 40.

8. Joan Nestle, *A Restricted Country* (Ithaca, N.Y.: Firebrand Books, 1987), pp. 100–109.

9. Anne Phillips, *Divided Loyalties: Dilemmas of Sex and Class* (London: Virago, 1987), p. 78. On the middle-class social reform movement in Canada, see Carol Bacchi, *Liberation Deferred?* (Toronto: University of Toronto Press, 1983); Linda Kealey, ed., *A Not Unreasonable Claim* (Toronto: Women's Press, 1979); Veronica Strong-Boag, "Setting the Stage: National Organization and the Women's Movement in the Late Nineteenth Century," in Susan Trofimenkoff and Alison Prentice, eds., *The Neglected Majority* (Toronto: McClelland and Stewart, 1977), pp. 87–103; and idem, *The Parliament of Women: The National Council of Women of Canada, 1893–1929*, Mercury Series, History Division Paper No. 18 (Ottawa: National Museum of Man, National Museums of Canada, 1976).

10. On the Canadian social purity movement, see Mariana Valverde, *The Age of Light, Soap and Water: Moral Reform in English Canada, 1885–1920* (Toronto: McClelland and Stewart, 1991).

11. Karl Marx and Friedrich Engels, *The Communist Manifesto* (1888; reprint, Harmondsworth, England: Penguin, 1975). An excellent study of changes in workers' lives as a result of industrial capitalism remains E. P. Thompson, "Time, Work-Discipline and Industrial Capitalism," *Past and Present* 38 (December 1967): 56–96.

12. Joan Kelly, "The Doubled Vision of Feminist Theory," in Judith Newton, Mary Ryan, and Judith Walkowitz, eds., *Sex and Class in Women's History* (London: Routledge and Kegan Paul, 1983), pp. 259–70.

13. Gayle Rubin, "Thinking Sex: Notes for a Radical Theory of the Politics of Sexuality," in Vance, *Pleasure and Danger*, p. 300.

14. Recent Canadian works on contemporary sexual politics include Laurie Bell, ed., *Good Girls/Bad Girls: Sex Trade Workers and Feminists Face to Face* (Toronto: Women's Press, 1987); Burstyn, *Women against Censorship;* Susan G. Cole, *Pornography and the Sex Crisis* (Toronto: Amanita, 1989); Gary Kinsman, *The Regulation of Desire* (Montreal: Black Rose Press, 1987); and Mariana Valverde, *Sex, Power and Pleasure* (Toronto: Women's Press, 1985).

15. Michael Bliss, "Pure Books on Avoided Subjects: Pre-Freudian Sexual Ideas in Canada," in Michiel Horn and Ronald Sabourin, eds., *Studies in Canadian Social History* (Toronto: McClelland and Stewart, 1974), pp. 326–46.

16. Beth MacAuley has made this point about Canadian historiography in her fine M. A. thesis, "Beyond the Boundaries of Respectability: Women's Experience of Violence in the Newcastle District of Upper Canada, 1803–1839," University of Toronto, 1986, pp. 8–14. See Kenneth McNaught, "Violence in Canadian History," in Horn and Sabourin, *Canadian Social History*, pp. 377–89; Desmond Morton, "Aid to the Civil Power: Canadian Military in Support of Social Order," *Canadian Historical Review* 51 (1970): 407–27; Michael Cross, "Violence and Author-

ity: The Case of Bytown," in David J. Bercuson and Louis Knafla, eds., *Law and Society in Canada in Historical Perspective* (Calgary: University of Calgary, 1979), pp. 23–49; and idem, "The Shiners' War: Social Violence in the Ottawa Valley in the 1830s," *Canadian Historical Review* 59 (1973): 1–26.

17. Peter Ward, *Courtship, Love and Marriage in Nineteenth-Century English Canada* (Montreal: McGill-Queen's University Press, 1990). Several recent Canadian studies treat the history of sexuality in a more thoughtful way and have been useful to my work. See, for example, Bruce Curtis, "Illicit Sex and Public Education in Ontario, 1840–1907," *Historical Studies in Education* 1, no. 1 (Spring 1989): 73–94; Judith Fingard, *The Dark Side of Life in Victorian Halifax* (Porter's Lake, Nova Scotia: Pottersfield Press, 1989); Angus McLaren and Arlene Tigar McLaren, *The Bedroom and the State* (Toronto: McClelland and Stewart, 1986); Angus McLaren, *Our Own Master Race* (Toronto: McClelland and Stewart, 1990); and idem, "Sex Radicalism in the Canadian Pacific Northwest, 1890–1920," *Journal of the History of Sexuality* 2, no. 4 (April 1992): 527–46; Carolyn Strange, "From Modern Babylon to a City upon a Hill: The Toronto Social Survey Commission of 1915 and the Search for Sexual Order in the City," in Roger Hall, William Westfall, and Laurel Sefton MacDowell, eds., *Patterns of the Past: Interpreting Ontario's History* (Toronto: Dundern, 1988), pp. 255–78; and idem, "The Perils and Pleasures of the City: Single, Wage-Earning Women in Toronto, 1880–1930," Ph.D. diss., Rutgers University, 1991; and Valverde, *Age of Light, Soap and Water.*

18. Linda Gordon, *Heroes of Their Own Lives: The Politics and History of Family Violence* (New York: Viking, 1988), pp. 3–6; and idem, "The Politics of Child Sexual Abuse: Notes from American History," *Feminist Review*, no. 28 (January 1988): 88–102.

CHAPTER ONE

1. Guido Ruggiero, *The Boundaries of Eros: Sex Crime and Sexuality in Renaissance Venice* (New York: Oxford University Press, 1985), p. 101. See also Barbara Lindemann, "To Ravish and Carnally Know: Rape in Eighteenth-Century Massachusetts," *Signs* 10, no. 1 (Autumn 1984): 81; and Anna Clark, *Women's Silence, Men's Violence: Sexual Assault in England, 1770–1845* (London: Pandora, 1987).

2. Ellen DuBois and Linda Gordon, "Seeking Ecstasy on the Battlefield: Danger and Pleasure in Nineteenth-Century Feminist Sexual Thought," in Carol Vance, ed., *Pleasure and Danger: Exploring Female Sexuality* (Boston: Routledge and Kegan Paul, 1984), pp. 32–33.

3. See, for example, the argument advanced by the London Rape Crisis Centre, that rape is the "extreme and logical conclusion of the ways in which men relate to women." London Rape Crisis Centre, *Sexual Violence: The Reality for Women* (London: Women's Press, 1984), p. 5.

4. *Toronto Star*, 10 October 1991.

5. Roy Porter, "Rape—Does It Have a Historical Meaning?" in Sylvana Tomaselli and Roy Porter, eds., *Rape: An Historical and Social Enquiry* (London: Basil Blackwell, 1986), pp. 216–36.

6. In discussing these cases I have used the first initial of the last name of both

parties, with the exception of some well-publicized cases detailed in chapters 2 and 4. Provincial Archives of Ontario, RG 22, Criminal Assize Indictments (hereafter cited as CAI), S., Ontario County, 1919.

7. CAI, R., Prince Edward County, 1892.

8. CAI, M., Elgin County, 1921.

9. CAI, S., Algoma District, 1916.

10. CAI, J., Huron County, 1912.

11. See, for example, CAI, D., Carleton County, 1916; and CAI, B., Leeds and Grenville County, 1902.

12. Lyndal Roper, "Will and Honor: Sex, Words and Power in Augsburg Criminal Trials," *Radical History Review* 43 (Winter 1989): 45–71.

13. E. P. Thompson, *The Making of the English Working Class* (Harmondsworth, England: Penguin, 1963), p. 13.

14. On feminist responses to wife and child abuse in the United States, see Elizabeth Pleck, "Feminist Responses to 'Crimes against Women,'" *Signs* 8, no. 3 (Spring 1983): 451–70; and Linda Gordon, *Heroes of Their Own Lives* (New York: Viking, 1988), pp. 253–57. On Britain, see Carol Bauer and Lawrence Ritt, "A Husband Is a Wife-Beating Animal: Francis Power Cobbe Confronts the Wife Abuse Problem in Victorian England," *International Journal of Women's Studies* 6, no. 2 (March–April 1983): 99–118; Sheila Jeffreys, ed., *The Sexuality Debates* (London: Routledge and Kegan Paul, 1987), pp. 219–83. For an examination of the racist dimension of early feminist campaigns around sexual and domestic violence in Canada, see Mariana Valverde, "When the Mother of the Race Is Free: Race, Reproduction and Sexuality in First-Wave Feminism," in Franca Iacovetta and Mariana Valverde, eds., *Gender Conflicts: Essays in Women's History* (Toronto: University of Toronto Press, 1992).

15. DuBois and Gordon, "Seeking Ecstasy on the Battlefield," p. 32.

16. Mariana Valverde, *The Age of Light, Soap, and Water: Moral Reform in English Canada, 1885–1920* (Toronto: McClelland and Stewart, 1991).

17. Valverde, "Mother of the Race." See also Lucy Bland, "Marriage Laid Bare: Middle Class Women and Marital Sex, 1880–1914," in Jane Lewis, eds., *Labour and Love: Women's Experience of Home and Family* (Oxford: Basil Blackwell, 1986), pp. 123–46.

18. The best overview of maternal feminist organizing in Canada remains Linda Kealey, ed., *A Not Unreasonable Claim: Women and Reform in Canada, 1880s–1920s* (Toronto: Women's Press, 1979). On the sexual politics of Canadian feminists in this period, see also Carol Lee Bacchi, *Liberation Deferred? The Ideas of the English-Canadian Suffragists, 1877–1918* (Toronto: University of Toronto Press, 1983), pp. 104–16; and Veronica Strong-Boag, *The Parliament of Women: The National Council of Women of Canada, 1893–1929*, National Museum of Man Mercury Series, History Division Paper No. 18 (Ottawa: National Museum of Man, National Museums of Canada, 1976), pp. 269–75. For an assessment of the legacy of British feminism's alliance with the social purity movement, see Judith Walkowitz, "Male Vice and Female Virtue: Feminism and the Politics of Prostitution in Nineteenth-Century Britain," in Ann Snitow, Christine Stansell, and Sharon Thompson, eds., *Powers of Desire: The Politics of Sexuality* (New York: Monthly Review, 1983), pp. 419–38.

19. An excellent historical study of women's resistance to sexual assault is Marybeth Hamilton Arnold, "The Life of a Citizen in the Hands of a Woman: Sexual Assault in New York City, 1790–1820," in Kathy Peiss and Christina Simmons, eds., *Passion and Power: Sexuality in History* (Philadelphia: Temple University Press, 1989), pp. 35–57.

20. CAI, K., Leeds and Grenville County, 1899.

21. CAI, M., Thunder Bay District, 1910; and *Fort William Times Journal*, 17 and 22 February and 20 April 1910.

22. CAI, S., Carleton County, 1892; and *Ottawa Citizen*, 28 August and 10 October 1892.

23. *Stratford Daily Herald*, 26 July, 19 August, and 27 October 1921.

24. Carolyn Strange, "Wounded Womanhood and Dead Men: Chivalry and the Trials of Clara Ford and Carrie Davies," in Iacovetta and Valverde, *Gender Conflicts*, pp. 149–188. See also Ruth Harris, "Melodrama, Hysteria and Feminine Crimes of Passion in the Fin-de-Siecle," *History Workshop Journal* 25 (Spring 1988): 31–63.

25. Terry Chapman, "Sex Crimes in Western Canada, 1890–1920, Ph.D. diss., University of Alberta, 1984, p. 81.

26. On infanticide in Canada, see Constance Backhouse, "Desperate Women and Compassionate Courts: Infanticide in Nineteenth-Century Canada," *University of Toronto Law Journal* 34 (1984): 447–78. See also William Langer, "Infanticide: A Historical Survey," *History of Childhood Quarterly* 1, no. 3 (Winter 1974): 353–66.

27. On the history of abortion in Canada, see Angus McLaren and Arlene Tigar McLaren, *The Bedroom and the State* (Toronto: McClelland and Stewart, 1986).

28. CAI, M., Elgin County, 1894.

29. CAI, P., Dufferin County, 1896.

30. *Sarnia Observer*, 15 October 1897.

31. *Woodstock Sentinal Review*, 25 March 1897.

32. For an explanation of the Ontario court system in this period, see Margaret A. Banks, "The Evolution of the Ontario Courts, 1788–1981," in David Flaherty, ed., *Essays in the History of Canadian Law* (Toronto: University of Toronto Press, 1982), vol. 2, pp. 418–91. On the legal processes pertaining to sexual crime specifically, see Chapman, "Sex Crimes in Western Canada," pp. 27–30.

33. Details of the evolution of the laws on sexual crime can be found in Constance Backhouse, "Nineteenth-Century Canadian Rape Law, 1800–1892," in Flaherty, *Essays in the History of Canadian Law*, vol. 2, pp. 200–247; idem, "Nineteenth-Century Canadian Prostitution Law: Reflection of a Discriminating Society," *Histoire Sociale/Social History* 18, no. 36 (November 1985): 387–423; Chapman, "Sex Crimes in Western Canada"; John McClaren, "Chasing the Social Evil: Moral Fervour and the Evolution of Canada's Prostitution Laws, 1867–1917," *Canadian Journal of Law and Society* 1 (1986): 125–65; idem, "White Slavers: The Reform of Canada's Prostitution Laws and Patterns of Enforcement, 1900–1920," *Criminal Justice History* 8 (1987): 53–119; Graham Parker, "The Origins of the Canadian Criminal Code," in David Flaherty, ed., *Essays in the History of Canadian Law* (Toronto: University of Toronto Press, 1981), vol. 1, pp. 249–81; idem, "The Legal Regulation of Sexual Activity and the Protection of Females," *Osgoode Hall Law Journal* 21, no. 2 (June 1983): 187–224; and James Snell, "The 'White Life for Two': The

Defence of Marriage and Sexual Morality in Canada, 1890–1914," *Histoire Sociale/ Social History* 16, no. 31 (May 1983): 111–28.

34. Parker, "Origins of Canadian Criminal Code," p. 268.

35. *Huron Signal*, 5 April 1881. Chapman, "Sex Crimes in Western Canada," pp. 85–86 and 128.

36. Chapman, "Sex Crimes in Western Canada," pp. 77–79; Lindemann, "To Ravish," p. 86.

37. Ruggiero, *Sex Crime*, p. 93; Nazife Bashar, "Rape in England between 1550–1700," in London Feminist History Workshop, *The Sexual Dynamics of History* (London: Pluto Press, 1983), p. 40.

38. Carolyn Strange, "The Perils and Pleasures of the City: Single, Wage-Earning Women in Toronto, 1880–1930," Ph.D. diss., Rutgers University, 1991.

39. Ellen Ross, among other labor historians, has documented how working men and women incorporated elements of bourgeois social norms for their own purposes. Within the working class, the quest for respectability extended beyond the size of one's paycheck to include an array of cultural codes of behavior, dress and manners. See Ellen Ross, "Not the Sort That Would Sit on the Doorstep: Respectability in Pre–World War One London Neighbourhoods," *International Labour and Working-Class History* 27 (Spring 1985): 39–59. See also Robert Gray, *The Labour Aristocracy in Victorian Edinburgh* (Oxford: Clarendon Press, 1976); and Patrick Joyce, *Work, Society and Politics: The Culture of the Factory in Later Victorian England* (Brighton, England: Harvester, 1980).

40. CAI, B., Ontario, 1910.

41. Ross, "Not the Sort," p. 39.

42. Anna Clark, "Whores and Gossips: Sexual Reputation in London, 1770–1825," in Arina Angerman et al. eds., *Current Issues in Women's History* (London: Routledge and Kegan Paul, 1989), pp. 231–48.

43. Bruce Curtis, "Illicit Sex and Public Education in Ontario, 1840–1907," *Historical Studies in Education* 1, no. 1 (Spring 1989): 81.

44. John D'Emillio and Estelle Freedman, *Intimate Matters: A History of Sexuality in America* (New York: Harper and Row, 1988), p. 70.

45. CAI, W., Frontenac County, 1881.

46. CAI, H., Lambton County, 1881.

47. CAI, M., Elgin County, 1894.

48. District Court Judges' Criminal Court (hereafter cited as DCJCC), H., Algoma District, 1927.

49. CAI, G., Stormont, Dundas and Glengarry District, 1902; and *Cornwall Standard*, 21 March 1902.

50. Elizabeth Mills, "One Hundred Years of Fear: Rape and the Medical Profession," in Nicole Hahn Rafter and Elizabeth Stanko, eds., *Judge, Lawyer, Victim, Thief: Women, Gender Roles and Criminal Justice* (Boston: Northeastern University Press, 1982), p. 45.

51. CAI, S., Elgin County, 1900.

52. *Huron Signal*, 15 April 1881.

53. *Gananoque Reporter*, 22 April 1882.

54. *Cornwall Freeholder*, 10 October 1895.

55. *Parry Sound Star*, 29 October 1903.

56. CAI, J., Huron County, 1912; CAI, C., Ontario County, 1896.

57. CAI, M., Peterborough County, 1908.

58. CAI, W., Frontenac County, 1917.

59. See, for example, County Court Judges' Criminal Court (hereafter cited as CCJCC), P., Ontario County, 1914; CAI, P., Oxford County, 1908.

60. CAI, V., Lambton County, 1913.

61. CAI, S., Thunder Bay District, 1914.

62. CAI, H., Rainy River District, 1927; CAI, W., Ontario County, 1929.

63. CAI, W., Stormont, Dundas and Glengarry County, 1902.

64. CAI, D., Algoma District, 1921; and *Sault Ste. Marie Star*, 10 April 1921.

65. CAI, K., Ontario County, 1910; CAI, M., Carleton County, 1910.

66. *Kingston British Whig*, 22 October 1880.

67. Major radical feminist antipornography works include Andrea Dworkin, *Pornography: Men Possessing Women* (New York: Perigree Books, 1979); Laura Lederer, ed., *Take Back the Night: Women on Pornography* (New York: William Morrow, 1980); Susan G. Cole, *Pornography and the Sex Crisis* (Toronto: Amanita, 1989); and Dorchen Leidholdt and Janice G. Raymond, eds., *The Sexual Liberals and the Attack on Feminism* (New York: Pergamon Press, 1990).

68. Hester Eisenstein, *Contemporary Feminist Thought* (Boston: G. K. Hall, 1983), p. 27. Brownmiller herself has backed away from this formulation, acknowledging in an interview in 1984 that this sentence was "carelessly written." See Steven Pistono, "Susan Brownmiller and the History of Rape," *Women's Studies* 14 (1988): 273. See also a compelling critique of Brownmiller by Angela Davis, *Women, Race and Class* (New York: Random House, 1981), p. 182.

69. Susan Brownmiller, *Against Our Will* (New York: Bantam, 1975), pp. 4–6.

70. Lynne Segal, *Is the Future Female? Troubled Thoughts on Contemporary Feminism* (London: Virago, 1987), p. 73.

71. Sheila Rowbotham, "The Trouble with 'Patriarchy,'" and Sally Alexander and Barbara Taylor, "In Defence of 'Patriarchy,'" both in Raphael Samuel, ed., *People's History and Socialist Theory* (London: Routledge and Kegan Paul, 1981), pp. 364–69 and 370–74.

72. Zillah Eisenstein, "Developing a Theory of Capitalist Patriarchy and Socialist Feminism," in Zillah Eisenstein, ed., *Capitalist Patriarchy and the Case for Socialist Feminism* (New York: Monthly Review, 1979), pp. 5–40; Varda Burstyn, "Masculine Dominance and the State," in Varda Burstyn and Dorothy Smith, *Women, Class, Family and the State* (Toronto: Garamond, 1985), pp. 45–89. A recent review of feminist theorizing on patriarchy is Bonnie Fox, "Conceptualizing 'Patriarchy,'" *Canadian Review of Sociology and Anthropology* 25, no. 2 (May 1988): 163–82.

73. See, for example, Michèle Barrett, *Women's Oppression Today* (London: Verso, 1980); Varda Burstyn, "Economy, Sexuality, Politics: Engels and the Sexual Division of Labour," *Socialist Studies: A Canadian Annual* (1983): 19–39; Bonnie Fox, ed., *Hidden in the Household* (Toronto: Women's Press, 1980); Roberta Hamilton, *The Liberation of Women* (London: George Allen and Unwin, 1978); Heidi Hartmann, "Capitalism, Patriarchy, and Job Segregation by Sex," in Eisenstein, ed., *Capitalist Patriarchy*, pp. 206–48; Meg Luxton, *More Than a Labour of Love* (Toronto: Women's

Press, 1980); Heather Jon Maroney and Meg Luxton, eds., *Feminism and Political Economy* (Toronto: Metheun, 1987); and Lydia Sargent, ed., *Women and Revolution* (Boston: South End Press, 1981).

74. Lorna Weir, "Socialist Feminism and the Politics of Sexuality," in Maroney and Luxton, eds., *Feminism and Political Economy,* pp. 70–71.

75. Burstyn, "Masculine Dominance," p. 54.

76. Lorene Clark and Debra Lewis, *Rape: The Price of Coercive Sexuality* (Toronto: Women's Press, 1977), p. 28.

77. Ibid., p. 124.

78. Ibid., p. 130.

79. Lynne Segal, *Slow Motion: Changing Masculinities, Changing Men* (London: Virago, 1990), p. 245.

80. Another attempt to understand sexual violence in a materialist framework, Julia Schwendinger and Herman Schwendinger, *Rape and Inequality* (Beverly Hills, Calif.: Sage, 1983), also tends to obscure specifically sexual dimensions.

81. Edward Shorter, "On Writing the History of Rape," *Signs* 3, no. 2 (1977): 474. See also the response by Heidi Hartmann and Ellen Ross, "Comment on 'On Writing the History of Rape,'" *Signs* 3, no. 4 (1978): 931–35.

82. Sylvana Tomaselli, "Introduction," in Tomaselli and Porter, *Rape,* p. 11. For an explanation of the psychic traumas of sexual assault, see John Forrester, "Rape, Seduction and Psychoanalysis," in Tomaselli and Porter, *Rape,* pp. 57–83.

CHAPTER TWO

1. Jeffrey Weeks, *Sex, Politics and Society* (London: Longmans, 1981), p. 14.

2. Of the many authors who are attempting to understand the contemporary 'sex panic,' those I find the most helpful are: on AIDS, Dennis Altman, *AIDS in the Mind of America* (Garden City, N.Y.: Anchor Press, 1986); Douglas Crimp, eds., *AIDS: Cultural Analysis Cultural Activism* (Cambridge, Mass.: MIT Press, 1988); Robert Padgug, "Gay Villain, Gay Hero: Homosexuality and the Social Construction of AIDS," in Kathy Peiss and Christina Simmons, eds., *Passion and Power: Sexuality in History* (Philadelphia: Temple University Press, 1989), pp. 293–313; and Cindy Patton, *Sex and Germs: The Politics of AIDS* (Boston: South End Press, 1985). On pornography and prostitution see Laurie Bell, ed., *Good Girls/Bad Girls: Sex Trade Workers and Feminists Face to Face* (Toronto: Women's Press, 1987); Varda Burstyn, "Anatomy of a Moral Panic," *Fuse,* Summer 1984, pp. 30–37; idem, "The Left and the Porn Wars," in Howard Buchbinder, Varda Burstyn, Dinah Forbes, and Mercedes Steedman, eds., *Who's on Top? The Politics of Heterosexuality* (Toronto: Garamond, 1987), pp. 13–46; idem, ed., *Women against Censorship* (Toronto: Douglas and McIntyre, 1985). On the antiabortion and antifeminist movement, see Barbara Ehrenreich, "The Women's Movement—Feminist and Anti Feminist," in *Radical America* 15, nos. 1 and 2 (Spring 1981): 93–101; and Rosalind Pollack Petchesky, *Abortion and Women's Choice* (Boston: Northeastern University Press, 1984), esp. pp. 241–85. Good general overviews of the contemporary sex crisis are John D'Emilio and Estelle Freedman, *Intimate Matters: A History of Sexuality in America* (New York: Harper and Row, 1988), pp. 344–60; and Jeffrey Weeks, *Sexuality and Its Discontents* (London: Routledge and Kegan Paul, 1985), pp. 3–61.

3. John D'Emilio, "The Homosexual Menace: The Politics of Sexuality in Cold War America," in Peiss and Simmons, *Passim and Power*, pp. 226–40; Geoffrey Smith, "National Security and Personal Isolation: Sex, Gender and Disease in Cold-War United States," *International History Review* 14, no. 2 (May 1992): 307–37; and Gary Kinsman, *The Regulation of Desire: Sexuality in Canada* (Montreal: Black Rose Press, 1987), esp. pp. 109–38.

4. Michel Foucault, *The History of Sexuality: An Introduction* (New York: Vintage, 1978), p. 31.

5. Virtually every contemporary feminist analysis of rape makes this point. The studies I have found most useful for this project are Susan Brownmiller, *Against Our Will* (New York: Bantam, 1975); Lorenne Clark and Debra Lewis, *Rape: The Price of Coercive Sexuality* (Toronto: Women's Press, 1977); Connie Guberman and Margie Wolfe, eds., *No Safe Place* (Toronto: Women's Press, 1985); London Rape Crisis Centre, *Sexual Violence* (London: Women's Press, 1984); and Elizabeth Stanko, *Intimate Intrusions* (London: Routledge and Kegan Paul, 1985).

6. Provincial Archives of Ontario, RG 22, Criminal Assize Indictments (hereafter cited as CAI), S., Muskoka District, 1905.

7. CAI, C., Algoma District, 1913.

8. CAI, M., Lambton County, 1882.

9. Ellen Knox, *The Girl of the New Day* (Toronto: McClelland and Stewart, 1919), p. 57; Marjorie Cohen, *Women's Work, Markets and Economic Development in Nineteenth-Century Ontario* (Toronto: University of Toronto Press, 1988), p. 91.

10. *Belleville Times*, 21 September 1909. On the social fears about tramps in this period, see James Pitsula, "The Treatment of Tramps in Late Nineteenth-Century Toronto," *Historical Papers* (1980): 116–32. We will explore the moral panic over tramps in more detail in chapter 5.

11. *Sault Ste. Marie Star*, 8 October 1924.

12. CAI, W., Algoma District, 1924.

13. Kathy Peiss, *Cheap Amusements* (Philadelphia: Temple University Press, 1986), p. 156.

14. Karen Dubinsky, "The Modern Chivalry: Women and the Knights of Labor in Ontario, 1880–1891," M. A. thesis, Carleton University, 1985, pp. 189–90. Peter McGahan also comments on an outcry against street harassment in St. John during World War I; this time it was soldiers apparently harassing women. The St. John press attempted to use patriotism to quell this behavior: "This," they claimed, "is the sort of thing we despise the Germans for; let us not act like them." McGahan, *Crime and Policing in Maritime Canada* (Fredericton, New Brunswick: Goose Lane Editions, 1988), p. 101.

15. Lynne Marks, "Ladies, Loafers, Knights and 'Lasses': The Social Dimensions of Religion and Leisure in Late Nineteenth-Century Small-Town Ontario," Ph.D. diss., York University, 1992, pp. 185–253.

16. CAI, H., Perth County, 1919; *Cobalt Nugget*, 22 May 1914.

17. On the moral concerns about women and children on city streets in this period, see Rebekah Coulter, "The Young of Edmonton, 1921–1931," and Susan Houston, "The 'Waifs' and 'Strays' of a Late Victorian City: Juvenile Delinquents in Toronto," both in Joy Parr, ed., *Childhood and Family in Canadian History* (Toronto:

McClelland and Stewart, 1982), pp. 143–59 and 129–42; and Carolyn Strange, "From Modern Babylon to a City upon a Hill: The Toronto Social Survey Commission of 1915 and the Search for Sexual Order in the City," in Roger Hall, William Westfall, and Laurel Sefton MacDowell, eds., *Patterns of the Past: Interpreting Ontario's History* (Toronto: Dundern: 1988), pp. 255–78. U.S. studies on women and street life are Joanne Meyerowitz, *Women Adrift: Independent Wage Earners in Chicago, 1880–1930* (Chicago: University of Chicago Press, 1988); Peiss, *Cheap Amusements;* and Christine Stansell, *City of Women: Sex and Class in New York, 1789–1860* (New York: Alfred A. Knopf, 1986).

18. Christopher Frayling, "The House That Jack Built: Some Stereotypes of the Rapist in the History of Popular Culture," in Sylvana Tomaselli and Roy Porter, eds., *Rape: An Historical and Social Enquiry* (London: Basil Blackwell, 1986), p. 214. See also Judith Walkowitz, "Jack the Ripper and the Myth of Male Violence," *Feminist Studies* 8, no. 3 (1982): 542–72.

19. *Stratford Evening Beacon*, 3 February 1894; *Peterborough Examiner*, 26 September 1894; *Woodstock Sentinal Review*, 30 March 1897.

20. Marvin MacDonald, "Protestant Reaction to Non-English Immigration in Port Arthur and Fort William, 1903–1914," M.A. thesis, Lakehead University, 1976, p. 22; CAI, E., Algoma District, 1916.

21. *Stratford Evening Beacon*, 3 February 1894; *Cobalt Nugget*, 22 May 1914.

22. On the growth and regulation of working-class male culture, see, for example, Bryan D. Palmer, *A Culture in Conflict: Skilled Workers and Industrial Capitalism in Hamilton, Ontario, 1860–1914* (Montreal: McGill-Queen's University Press, 1979), pp. 35–70; Peter DeLottinville, "Joe Beef of Montreal: Working Class Culture and the Tavern, 1869–1889," *Labour/Le Travailleur* 8–9 (Autumn–Spring 1981–82): 9–40; and Marks, "Ladies, Loafers." An important U.S. study on the regulation of workingmen off the job is Roy Rosenzweig, *Eight Hours for What We Will* (Cambridge: Cambridge University Press, 1983).

23. *Stratford Evening Beacon*, 20 October 1894.

24. Marks, "Ladies, Loafers," p. 488.

25. CAI, L., Leeds and Grenville County, 1880.

26. *Hamilton Palladium of Labor*, 26 January 1884.

27. Ibid., 21 June 1884.

28. Emily Murphy, *The Black Candle* (Toronto: Thomas Allen, 1922; reprint, Toronto: Coles, 1973), p. 134. Rebekah Coulter also describes a lurid story which rocked Calgary in 1929 of a "poor and lonely" girl who "fell in" with a taxi driver, in "The Young of Edmonton," p. 143.

29. CAI, H., Rainy River District, 1927; *Stratford Evening Beacon*, 25 January 1895.

30. Diana Pederson, "Keeping Our Good Girls Good: The YWCA and the 'Girl Problem,' 1870–1930," *Canadian Women's Studies* 7, no. 4 (Winter 1986): 20–24; Barbara Roberts, *Whence They Came* (Ottawa: University of Ottawa Press, 1988), pp. 110–14. Ernest A. Bell, *War on the White Slave Trade* (original, n.d.; reprint, Toronto: Coles, 1980), includes an illustration of a young female immigrant who, on arriving at the dock, is greeted by 'friends' waiting to snatch her into white slavery.

31. CAI, L., Algoma District, 1903.

32. CAI, R., Norfolk County, 1893.

33. CAI, C., Frontenac County, 1908; and *Kingston British Whig*, 17 February 1908.

34. CAI, R., Lambton County, 1927. Carolyn Strange, in her study of sexual danger in Toronto during this period, discovered a case quite similar to this one in which a young woman, parked with her boyfriend in a secluded area, was raped by two men posing as police officers. See Strange, "The Perils and Pleasures of the City: Single, Wage-Earning Women in Toronto, 1880–1930," Ph.D. diss., Rutgers University, 1991, p. 266.

35. CAI, R., Leeds and Grenville County, 1882; and *Gananoque Reporter*, 5 November 1881; CAI, C., Thunder Bay District, 1927.

36. *Brockville Recorder*, 27 April 1882.

37. CAI, M., Peterborough County, 1908.

38. CAI, B., Carlton County, 1904; and *Ottawa Journal*, 30 March 1904.

39. *Sudbury Star*, 11 March 1911.

40. Stansell, *City of Women*, p. 97.

41. Lyndal Roper, "Will and Honor: Sex, Words and Power in Augsburg Criminal Trials," *Radical History Review* 43 (Winter 1989): 45–71.

42. CAI, K., Sudbury District, 1929.

43. On the mores of Finnish immigrants in this period, see Varpu Lindstrom-Best, *Defiant Sisters: A Social History of Finnish Immigrant Women in Canada* (Toronto: Multicultural History Society of Ontario, 1988), p. 46. CAI, K., Sudbury District, 1929; and *Sudbury Star*, 3 August and 21 September 1929.

44. CAI, B., Dufferin County, 1927; and *Orangeville Sun*, 20 October 1927.

45. Francoise Barret-Ducrocq, *Love in the Time of Victoria* (London: Verso, 1991), p. 110.

46. CAI, B., Stormont, Dundas and Glengarry County, 1896; CAI, M., Leeds and Grenville County, 1923.

47. CAI, A., Stormont, Dundas and Glengarry County, 1918.

48. CAI, B., Ontario County, 1896; and *Whitby Gazette and Chronicle*, 20 November 1896; CAI, A., Stormont, Dundas and Glengarry County, 1900.

49. CAI, T., Carleton County, 1915.

50. *Hamilton Palladium of Labor*, 10 October 1885.

51. Dubinsky, "Modern Chivalry," pp. 181–93; Janice Newton, "From Wage Slave to White Slave: The Prostitution Controversy and the Early Canadian Left," in Linda Kealey and Joan Sangster, eds., *Beyond the Vote: Canadian Women and Politics* (Toronto: University of Toronto Press, 1989), pp. 217–39.

52. On the sex and gender concerns of the Royal Commission, see Susan Trofimenkoff, "One Hundred and Two Muffled Voices: Canada's Industrial Women in the 1880s," *Atlantis* 3, no. 1 (1977): 67–82.

53. Frank Mort, *Dangerous Sexualities: Medico-Moral Politics in England since 1830* (London: Routledge and Kegan Paul, 1987), pp. 44 and 47–53.

54. Genevieve Leslie, "Domestic Service in Canada," in Janice Acton, Penny Goldsmith, and Bonnie Shepard, eds., *Women at Work, 1850–1930* (Toronto: Women's Press, 1974), p. 83. See also B. Roberts, *Whence They Came*, pp. 56–57; Wayne Roberts and Alice Klein, "Beseiged Innocence: The 'Problem' and Problems

of Working Women, Toronto, 1896–1914," in Acton, Goldsmith, and Shepard, *Women at Work*, pp. 211–60; Marilyn Barber, "The Women Ontario Welcomed: Immigrant Domestics for Ontario Homes, 1870–1930," in Alison Prentice and Susan Trofimenkoff, eds., *The Neglected Majority* (Toronto: McClelland and Stewart, 1985), pp. 102–21; and Varpu Lindstrom-Best, "I Won't Be a Slave! Finnish Domestics in Canada, 1911–30," in Jean Burnet, ed., *Looking into My Sister's Eyes: An Exploration in Women's History* (Toronto: Multicultural History Society of Ontario, 1986), pp. 33–54.

55. Alan A. Brookes and Catherine Wilson, "Working Away from the Farm: The Young Women of North Huron, 1910–1930," *Ontario History* 77, no. 4 (December 1985): 290. See also Edward Amey, *Farm Life as It Should Be and Farm Labourers' and Servant Girls' Grievances* (Toronto: Ellis and Moore, 1885).

56. On the British experience, see Anna Clark, *Women's Silence, Men's Violence: Sexual Assault in England, 1770–1845* (London: Pandora, 1987), p. 107; and John Gillis, "Servants, Sexual Relations and the Risks of Illegitimacy in London, 1801–1900," in Judith Newton, Mary P. Ryan, and Judith R. Walkowitz, eds., *Sex and Class in Women's History* (London: Routledge and Kegan Paul, 1983), pp. 114–45. Constance Backhouse found that most of the women charged with infanticide in nineteenth-century Canada were young, single domestic servants. Backhouse, "Desperate Women and Compassionate Courts: Infanticide in Nineteenth-Century Canada," *University of Toronto Law Journal* 34 (1984): 447–78.

57. CAI, M., Perth County, 1894.

58. CAI, S., Thunder Bay District, 1914.

59. As well as the literature cited in note 54 above, see Wayne Roberts, *Honest Womanhood: Feminism, Femininity and Class Consciousness among Toronto Working Women, 1893–1914* (Toronto: New Hogtown Press, 1976); Joan Sangster, "Finnish Women in Ontario, 1890–1930," *Polyphony* 3, no. 2 (Fall 1981): 46–54. On the problems of organizing domestic workers in the contemporary period, see Makeda Silvera, *Silenced* (Toronto: Williams Wallace, 1983).

60. Jan Lambertz, "Sexual Harassment in the Nineteenth-Century English Cotton Industry," *History Workshop Journal* 19 (Spring 1985): 29–61.

61. Philippe Ariès, *Centuries of Childhood* (New York: Alfred A. Knopf, 1962), p. 119.

62. Foucault, *History of Sexuality*, pp. 27–30.

63. Houston, "'Waifs' and 'Strays,'" p. 134; Neil Sutherland, *Children in English Canadian Society* (Toronto: University of Toronto Press, 1976), pp. 128–32; Mary Odem, "Bad Girls on Trial: Female Juvenile Court Hearings in Early Twentieth-Century Los Angeles," paper presented at the Eighth Berkshire Conference on the History of Women, June 1990.

64. Linda Gordon, *Heroes of Their Own Lives* (New York: Viking, 1988), p. 295; and Mary Odem, "Single Mothers, Delinquent Daughters, and the Juvenile Court in Early 20th Century Los Angeles," *Journal of Social History* 25, no. 1 (Fall 1991): 27–43.

65. CAI, O., Stormont, Dundas and Glengarry County, 1915; CAI, S., Algoma District, 1926; and *Sault Ste. Marie Star*, 8 October 1926.

66. CAI, M., Ontario County, 1929.

67. CAI, R., Peterborough County, 1894; CAI, L., Perth County, 1895; CAI, T., Algoma District, 1919.

68. Susanna Moodie, *Roughing It in the Bush* (London: Richard Bently, 1852; reprint, London: Virago, 1986), p. 139. On misogynist attitudes toward female children in England during this period, see Sheila Jeffreys, *The Spinster and Her Enemies: Female Sexuality in Britain, 1880–1930* (London: Pandora Press, 1985), pp. 54–71.

69. Sutherland, *Childhood in Canada;* Joy Parr, *Labouring Children: British Immigrant Apprentices to Canada, 1869–1924* (Montreal: McGill-Queens University Press, 1980); Bettina Bradbury, "Pigs, Cows and Boarders: Non-Wage Forms of Survival among Montreal Families, 1861–1891," *Labour/Le Travail* 14 (Fall 1984): 9–48; and John Bullen, "Hidden Workers: Child Labour and the Family Economy in Late Nineteenth-Century Urban Ontario," *Labour/Le Travail* 18 (Fall 1986): 163–88.

70. CAI, W., Cochrane District, 1929; and *North Bay Nugget*, 29 January 1929.

71. Anthony Wohl, "Sex and The Single Room: Incest among the Victorian Working Class," in Anthony Wohl, ed., *The Victorian Family: Structure and Stress* (New York: St. Martin's Press, 1978), pp. 197–216.

72. This allegation could very well have been true. Margaret Little has discovered several instances of political favoritism and moral threats in the disbursement of Mothers' Allowance benefits by local authorities in this period. See Margaret Little, "No Car, No Radio, No Liquor Permit: The Moral Regulation of Single Mothers in Ontario, 1922–1991," Ph.D. diss., York University, in progress.

73. CAI, B., Algoma District, 1919; CAI, W., Rainy River District, 1929.

74. CAI, S., Elgin County, 1900.

75. Gordon, *Heroes*, p. 96; Margaret Little, "Mothers First and Foremost," paper presented at the Canadian Political Science Association Annual Meeting, June 1990. On the economic importance of boarders to working-class households, see Bradbury, "Pigs, Cows."

76. CAI, M., Temiskaming District, 1920; CAI, B., Algoma District, 1911.

77. Gordon, *Heroes*, p. 205.

78. CAI, E., Carlton County, 1891.

79. Gordon, *Heroes*, p. 209.

80. CAI, S., Peterborough County, 1913; CAI, P., Lincoln County, 1896; CAI, F., Perth County 1929.

81. CAI, F., Stormont, Dundas and Glengarry County, 1890; CAI, V., Muskoka District, 1899.

82. CAI, B., Perth County, 1894; and *Stratford Evening Beacon*, 31 March and 24 April 1894.

83. For an analysis of the phenomenon of mother blaming in incest today, see Janet Liebman Jacobs, "Reassessing Mother Blame in Incest," *Signs* 15, no. 3 (1990): 499–515; and Mary MacLeod and Esther Saraga, "Challenging the Orthodoxy: Toward a Feminist Theory and Practice," *Feminist Review*, no. 28 (January 1988): 40–65.

84. CAI, Robinson, Sudbury District, 1909; National Archives of Canada, RG 13, Capital Case File 49, vol. 1,484; *Sudbury Journal*, 12 and 19 August, 16, 23, and 30 September, 7, 14, 21 October, 4 and 11 November 1914, 25 March 1915.

85. CAI, Robinson, Sudbury District, 1909; National Archives of Canada, RG 13, Capital Case File 49, vol. 1,484.

86. CAI, W., Algoma District, 1919; CAI, D., Algoma District, 1927; CAI, W., Parry Sound District, 1900.

87. NAC, RG 13, Capital Case File 49, vol. 1,484.

88. Mariana Valverde, "The Rhetoric of Reform: Tropes and the Moral Subject," *International Journal of the Sociology of Law* 18, no. 1 (1990): 63; Linda Gordon, "The Politics of Child Sexual Abuse: Notes from American History," *Feminist Review*, no. 28 (January 1988): 88–102.

89. Stansell, *City of Women*, pp. 55–61; Ellen Ross, "Fierce Questions and Taunts: Married Life in Working-Class London, 1870–1914," *Feminist Studies* 8 (Fall 1982): 575–602; Nancy Tomes, "A 'Torrent of Abuse': Crimes of Violence between Working Class Men and Women in London, 1840–1875," *Journal of Social History* 11, no. 3 (Spring 1978): 329–45; Katherine Harvey, "To Love, Honour and Obey: Wife Battering in Working-Class Montreal, 1869–1879," *Urban History Review* 19, no. 2 (October 1990): 128–40.

90. The best contemporary feminist critique of the patriarchal family is, in my view, Michèle Barrett and Mary McIntosh, *The Anti-Social Family* (London: Verso, 1982). See also Linda Gordon's insightful analysis of the political climate and family conditions which tend to keep cases of incest hidden, in "Politics of Child Sexual Abuse."

CHAPTER THREE

1. This is one of the central principles of John D'Emilio and Estelle Freedman's overview, *Intimate Matters: A History of Sexuality in America* (New York: Harper and Row, 1988).

2. Rosalind Coward, *Female Desires* (New York: Grove Press, 1985), p. 42.

3. Mary Poovey, among others, argues that differences in sexual desire were a key component of the Victorian construction of gender difference. See Poovey, *Uneven Developments: The Ideological Work of Gender in Mid-Victorian England* (Chicago: University of Chicago Press, 1988), p. 6.

4. John Charlton, "My Autobiography and Recollections, from 1829 to 1907," University of Toronto Rare Books Library, no date, unpublished, p. 802.

5. John Charlton, *Speeches and Addresses: Political, Literary and Religious* (Toronto: Morang and Co., 1905), pp. x–xi.

6. Canada, House of Commons *Debates*, 15 March 1883, p. 220.

7. Charlton, *Speeches*, p. 277.

8. Canada, House of Commons *Debates*, 1 April 1886, p. 442.

9. The classic statement of this position is Carol Lee Bacchi, *Liberation Deferred?* (Toronto: University of Toronto Press, 1983).

10. Mariana Valverde and Lorna Weir, "The Struggles of the Immoral: Preliminary Remarks on Moral Regulation," *Resources for Feminist Research* 17, no. 3 (September 1988): 31–34.

11. John Charlton, unpublished diary, vol. 5, 1891.

12. Charlton, "Autobiography," p. 407.

13. Charlton, *Speeches*, p. 281. The concept of regional 'moral boosterism' is explored in chapter 6.

14. The features of the seduction law are detailed in Constance Backhouse, "Nineteenth-Century Canadian Rape Law, 1800–1892," in David Flaherty, ed., *Essays in the History of Canadian Law* (Toronto: University of Toronto Press, 1983), vol. 2, pp. 200–247; and idem, *Petticoats and Prejudice: Women and Law in Nineteenth-Century Canada* (Toronto: Women's Press, 1991); John McLaren, "Chasing the Social Evil: Moral Fervour and the Evolution of Canada's Prostitution Laws, 1867–1917," *Canadian Journal of Law and Society* 1 (1986): 125–65; and idem, "White Slavers: The Reform of Canada's Prostitution Laws and Patterns of Enforcement, 1900–1920," *Criminal Justice History* 8 (1987): 53–119; Graham Parker, "The Legal Regulation of Sexual Activity and the Protection of Females," *Osgoode Hall Law Journal* 21, no. 2 (June 1983): 187–224; and James Snell, "The 'White Life for Two': The Defence of Marriage and Sexual Morality in Canada, 1890–1914," *Histoire Sociale/Social History* 16, no. 31 (May 1983): 111–28.

15. Canada, House of Commons *Debates*, 10 and 16 April 1890, pp. 3166–68 and 3441. See also *Debates* on the bill in 1882 (20 February and 13 March); 1883 (6, 12, 20, and 28 March); 1885 (18 March and 22 June); 1886 (1, 8, and 14 April); and 1887 (25 April and 4 and 6 May).

16. National Archives of Canada (hereafter NAC), RG 13, Department of Justice, File 63/1894, Letters and Submissions to the Department of Justice re: 1892 Criminal Code; R. C. Smith to John Thompson, 6 May 1892. On Watt see Parker, "Legal Regulation"; and Henry Morgan, ed., *The Canadian Men and Women of the Times* (Toronto: William Briggs, 1912), p. 1149.

17. Joy Parr, *The Gender of Breadwinners* (Toronto: University of Toronto Press, 1990), p. 35.

18. *Hamilton Palladium of Labor*, 10 November 1883. On Maria McCabe, see NAC, RG 13, Capital Case File 174A, vol. 1,419, 1883–89.

19. *Hamilton Palladium of Labor*, 18 July 1885. The best account of the Maiden Tribute story is Deborah Gorham, "The 'Maiden Tribute of Modern Babylon' Re-Examined: Child Prostitution and the Idea of Childhood in Late Victorian England," *Victorian Studies* 21, no. 3 (Spring 1978): 353–79.

20. *Hamilton Palladium of Labor*, 18 July 1885.

21. Ibid., 10 April 1886, 12 April 1884, and 31 July 1886. As well as constructing an alternative discourse of upper-class immorality, the charge was, in this instance, prophetic. One of the most outspoken participants in the discussions of the seduction law in the House of Commons was Malcolm Cameron, M.P. from Huron. Sometime after arguing against the bill in Parliament, he was the subject of an enormous scandal in Goderich for allegedly seducing his orphaned servant, who died giving birth. I explore the Cameron scandal in chapter 5.

22. Barbara Taylor, "The Men Are as Bad as Their Masters . . .": Socialism, Feminism and Sexual Antagonism in the London Tailoring Trade in the 1830's," in Judith L. Newton, Mary P. Ryan, and Judith R. Walkowtiz, eds., *Sex and Class in Women's History* (London: Routledge and Kegan Paul, 1983), pp. 187–220. An account of how the British labor movement constructed the class dynamics of sexual assault is Anna Clark, *Women's Silence, Men's Violence: Sexual Assault in England, 1770–1845* (London: Pandora Press, 1987), pp. 90–110.

23. McLaren, "Chasing the Social Evil," and "White Slavers."

24. Backhouse, "Nineteenth-Century Canadian Rape Law."

25. Parker, "Legal Regulation," p. 187.

26. American historian Mary Odem has reached similar conclusions about the operation of the law pertaining to statutory rape, noting that while men were subject to criminal prosecution, women were usually also incarcerated in juvenile detention centers. It does not appear that Canadian women involved in seduction charges were treated similarly; however, women involved in abduction incidents were often detained in children's shelters. See Odem, "Statutory Rape Prosecutions in Alameda County, California, 1910–1920," paper presented at the Organization of American Historians Annual Meeting, April 1989. Thanks to Christina Simmons for providing me with this paper. See also Anna Clark, "Rape or Seduction? A Controversy over Sexual Violence in the Nineteenth Century," in London Feminist History Workshop, *The Sexual Dynamics of History* (London: Pluto Press, 1983), pp. 13–27.

27. Christine Stansell, *City of Women: Sex and Class in New York, 1789–1860* (New York: Alfred A. Knopf, 1986), p. 87. See also Francoise Barret-Ducrocq's insightful analysis of the sexual barter system in nineteenth-century London, *Love in the Time of Victoria* (London: Verso, 1991), pp. 98–108.

28. Provincial Archives of Ontario, RG 22, Criminal Assize Indictments (hereafter cited as CAI), S., Carleton County, 1891.

29. Odem, "Statutory Rape Prosecutions," p. 2.

30. CAI, J., Parry Sound District, 1897.

31. County Court Judges' Criminal Court (hereafter cited as CCJCC), C., Ontario, 1917.

32. Cited in Mary Bularzik, "Sexual Harassment at the Workplace: Historical Notes," *Radical America* 12, no. 4 (Fall 1978): 35.

33. On nineteenth-century sexual harassment in the workplace, see Constance Backhouse and Leah Cohen, *The Secret Oppression: Sexual Harassment of Working Women* (Toronto: Macmillan, 1978), pp. 53–72; and Jan Lambertz, "Sexual Harassment in the Nineteenth-Century English Cotton Industry," *History Workshop Journal* 19 (Spring 1985): 29–61.

34. CAI, D., Elgin County, 1894; and *St. Thomas Daily Times*, 9 March 1894.

35. CCJCC, C., Ontario County, 1903.

36. CAI, M., Oxford County, 1895; and *Woodstock Sentinal Review*, 10 January and 22 March 1895.

37. John Gillis, "Servants, Sexual Relations and the Risks of Illegitimacy in London, 1801–1900," in Newton, Ryan, and Walkowitz, *Sex and Class*, pp. 114–45. On illegitimacy in Canada in a later period, see Andrée Levesque, "Deviants Anonymous: Single Mothers at the Hôpital de la Misericorde in Montreal, 1929–1939," *Historical Papers* (1984): 168–83.

38. Peter Ward, "Unwed Motherhood in Nineteenth-Century English Canada," *Historical Papers* (1981): 34–56.

39. District Court Judges' Criminal Court (hereafter cited as DCJCC), L., Algoma District, 1917; and CAI, L., Algoma District, 1922.

40. Parker, "Legal Regulation," p. 236.

41. CAI, W., Dufferin County, 1922; and *Orangeville Sun*, 8 June 1922.

42. Quoted in Backhouse, *Petticoats and Prejudice*, pp. 75–76.

43. CCJCC, H., Perth County, 1896.

44. DCJCC, C., Algoma District, 1918.

45. CAI, T., Perth County, 1892; and *Stratford Evening Beacon*, 5 and 6 October 1892.

46. CAI, H., Perth County, 1896.

47. CCJCC, M., Lambton County, 1917.

48. Kathy Peiss, "Charity Girls and City Pleasures: Historical Notes on Working-Class Sexuality, 1880–1920," in Ann Snitow, Christine Stansell, and Sharon Thompson, eds., *Powers of Desire* (New York: Monthly Review Press, (1983), pp. 74–87.

49. DCJCC, C., Algoma District, 1896; CAI, C., Dufferin County, 1927.

50. CAI, T., Perth County, 1892; CAI, F., Dufferin County, 1896.

51. Rosemary J. Coombe, "'The Most Disgusting, Disgraceful and Inequitous Proceeding in our Law': The Action for Breach of Promise of Marriage in Nineteenth-Century Ontario," *University of Toronto Law Journal* 38 (1988): 80.

52. Constance Backhouse, "The Tort of Seduction: Fathers and Daughters in Nineteenth Century Canada," *Dalhousie Law Journal* 10, no. 1 (June 1986): 45–80.

53. McLaren, "Chasing the Social Evil," p. 150.

54. Backhouse, "Tort of Seduction," p. 77.

55. Backhouse, *Petticoats and Prejudice*, p. 61.

56. Parker, "Legal Regulation," pp. 211–13 and 217–26; Backhouse, "Nineteenth-Century Canadian Rape Law," pp. 203–4.

57. DCJCC, W., Algoma District, 1928.

58. CAI, G., Carleton County, 1912; CCJCC, Y., Ontario County, 1910; CC-JCC, P., Ontario County, 1916.

59. *Orangeville Sun*, 31 March and 20 October 1927.

60. Unidentified newspaper clipping found in CCJCC, Y., Ontario County, 1910.

61. *Parry Sound Star*, 13 October 1904.

62. *Sudbury Star*, 25 March 1916.

63. DCJCC, W., Algoma District, 1928.

64. Lykke de la Cour, "'Tis Not as It Should Be: The Regulation of Unwed Motherhood in Ontario, 1870s–1920s," manuscript, York University, January 1990. On the continued moral regulation of unwed mothers through state welfare policies, see Veronica Strong-Boag, "Wages for Housework: Mothers' Allowance and the Beginnings of Social Security in Canada," *Journal of Canadian Studies* 14, no. 1 (May 1979): 24–34; and Margaret Little, "Mothers First and Foremost," paper presented at the Canadian Political Science Association Annual Meeting, 1990.

Chapter Four

1. This account is drawn from Provincial Archives of Ontario, RG 22, Criminal Assize Indictments (hereafter cited as CAI), O'Brien, Carleton County, 1881; and *Ottawa Citizen*, 12, 15, and 17 August 1881.

2. Douglas Hay, "Property, Authority and the Criminal Law," in Douglas Hay et

al., eds., *Albion's Fatal Tree: Crime and Society in Eighteenth-Century England* (New York: Pantheon, 1975), p. 25.

3. *Ottawa Citizen*, 12 August 1881.

4. Quoted in *Ottawa Citizen*, 17 August 1881.

5. Ibid., 15 August 1881.

6. Ibid.

7. Lynne Marks, "The Knights of Labor and the Salvation Army: Religion and Working-Class Culture in Ontario, 1882–1890," *Labour/Le Travail* 28 (1991): 89–128; and idem, "The 'Hallelujah Lasses': Women and the Salvation Army in English Canada, 1882–1892," in Franca Iacovetta and Mariana Valverde, eds., *Gender Conflicts: Essays in Women's History* (Toronto: University of Toronto Press, 1992). On charivaris in Canada, see Bryan Palmer, "Discordant Music: Charivaris and White-capping in Nineteenth Century North America," *Labour/Le Travailler* 3 (1978): 5–62.

8. Aili Schneider, *The Finnish Baker's Daughter* (Toronto: Multicultural History Society of Ontario, 1986), p. 56; *Fort William Times Journal*, 19 April 1910; *Rat Portage Souvenir Diamond Jubilee Guide* (Toronto: Hunter Rose, 1897).

9. Alfred Soman, "Deviance and Criminal Justice in Western Europe, 1300–1800: An Essay in Structure," *Criminal Justice History* 1 (1980): 4; John Beattie, "Judicial Records and the Measurement of Crime in Eighteenth-Century England," in Louis A. Knafla, ed., *Crime and Criminal Justice in Europe and North America* (Waterloo, Ont.: Wilfrid Laurier University Press, 1981), p. 134. Neil Sutherland has advanced a similar argument about the juvenile court system in Canada, claiming that the lack of legal resources in rural areas delayed the establishment of the full range of supervisory and rehabilitative mechanisms advocated by the child rescue movement and implemented in urban areas. Sutherland, *Children in English Canadian Society* (Toronto: University of Toronto Press, 1976), p. 129.

10. County Court Judges' Criminal Court (hereafter cited as CCJCC), H., Ontario County, 1917; CAI, C., Parry Sound District, 1901.

11. W. D. Logan, *Report of the Stipendiary Magistrates with Respect to the Northerly and Westerly Parts of the Province of Ontario* (Toronto: C. B. Robinson, 1882), p. 89.

12. CAI, McGrath, Nipissing District, 1913. Several years later another OPP constable in Temiskaming was charged with extorting money from a prostitute, and in 1921 police were charged with attempting to extort an Italian storekeeper who dabbled in illegal liquor. See CAI, Meredith, Temiskaming District, 1915; and District Court Judges' Criminal Court (hereafter cited as DCJCC), Ewan, Algoma District, 1921.

13. Edwin Bradwin, *The Bunkhouse Man: A Study of the Work and Pay in the Camps of Canada, 1903–1914* (New York: Columbia University Press, 1928; reprint, Toronto: University of Toronto Press, 1972), p. 218.

14. Crown Attorney Letterbooks, Ontario County, 1878–1882, Letterbook 2.

15. Hay, "Property," p. 27.

16. Paul Craven, "Law and Ideology: The Toronto Police Court, 1850–1880," in David Flaherty, ed., *Essays in the History of Canadian Law* (Toronto: University of Toronto Press, 1983), vol. 2, p. 288.

17. Ruth Harris, "Melodrama, Hysteria and Feminine Crimes of Passion in the Fin-de-Siecle," *History Workshop Journal* 25 (Spring 1988): 31–63. See also Carolyn Strange, "Wounded Womanhood and Dead Men: Chivalry and the Trials of Carrie Davis and Clara Ford," in Iacovetta and Valverde, *Gender Conflicts*.

18. See, for example, *Huntsville Forrester*, 15 May 1913, and *Sarnia Observer*, 29 March 1895. Rosemary Coombe suggests that civil actions for actual breach-of-promise cases were also popular and well attended by the community. See Coombe, "The Most Disgusting, Disgraceful and Inequitous Proceeding in Our Law: The Action for Breach of Promise of Marriage in Nineteenth-Century Ontario," *University of Toronto Law Review* 38 (1988): 64–108.

19. CAI, L., Carleton County, 1898; CAI, B., Frontenac County, 1908; CCJCC, P., Ontario County, 1909.

20. On McVicar, see Bryan Palmer and Gregory Kealey, *Dreaming of What Might Be: The Knights of Labor in Ontario, 1880–1900* (Toronto: New Hogtown Press, 1987), pp. 143–44; Karen Dubinsky, "The Modern Chivalry: Women and the Knights of Labor in Ontario, 1880–1891," M.A. thesis, Carleton University, 1985, pp. 47–53; on Amelia Turner, see Patricia Roome, "Amelia Turner and Calgary Labour Women, 1919–1935," in Linda Kealey and Joan Sangster, eds., *Beyond the Vote: Canadian Women and Politics* (Toronto: University of Toronto Press, 1989), p. 94.

21. *Gananoque Reporter*, 19 August 1882; *Brockville Recorder*, 2 November 1894.

22. *Woodstock Sentinal Review*, 15 November 1889.

23. *Ottawa Journal*, 26 October 1898.

24. National Archives of Canada (hereafter NAC), Department of Justice correspondence, Toronto Children's Aid Society to Minister of Justice, 7 March 1893 and 24 January 1895. The Children's Aid Socity enclosed a story from the *Toronto Globe*, which detailed the story of two girls forced to describe to "an audience of men" their "shame and ruin" at the hands of their father, and an editorial which urged the government to pass legislation outlawing spectators in court. Judith Fingard's research on sexual crime in Nova Scotia indicates that, as early as the 1860s, courthouses were cleared in "salacious" cases. Fingard, *The Dark Side of Life in Victorian Halifax* (Porter's Lake, Nova Scotia: Pottersfield Press, 1989), p. 109.

25. *Sault Ste. Marie Star*, 20 January 1928; *Goderich Star*, 13 April 1911.

26. *Sault Ste. Marie Star*, 7 February 1925. On how contemporary press reporting affects rape victims, see Carol Smart and Barry Smart, "Accounting for Rape: Reality and Myth in Press Reporting," in Carol Smart and Barry Smart, eds., *Women, Sexuality and Social Control* (London: Routledge and Kegan Paul, 1978), pp. 87–103. See also Keith Soothill and Sylvia Walby, *Sex Crime in the News* (London: Routledge, 1991).

27. On the historical concept of forbidden regions of social life, see Christine Stansell, "Pornography and Eros," lecture delivered at the University of Western Ontario, April 1990.

28. Guido Ruggiero, *The Boundaries of Eros: Sex Crime and Sexuality in Renaissance Venice* (New York: Oxford University Press, 1985), p. 147.

29. Simon Watney, "The Spectacle of AIDS," in Douglas Crimp, ed., *AIDS: Cultural Analysis, Cultural Activism* (Cambridge, Mass.: MIT Press, 1988), p. 80.

30. Throughout this section I use the full names of both parties in these cases, in part because of the overwhelming publicity the cases received and in part because some have been written about elsewhere.

31. Hay "Property," p. 39.

32. Wendy Holloway, "I Just Wanted to Kill a Woman: Why? The Ripper and Male Sexuality," in Feminist Review Collective, *Sexuality: A Reader* (London: Virago, 1987), p. 124.

33. Donald Swainson, "Schuyler Shibley and the Underside of Victorian Ontario," *Ontario History* 65, no. 1 (March 1973): 51–60; and A. J. Birrell, "D. I. K. Rine and the Gospel Temperance Movement in Canada," *Canadian Historical Review* 58, no. 1 (March 1977): 23–42. Judith Fingard also recounts the story of Isaac Sallis, a 'career criminal' in Halifax who was able, by the end of his life, to fashion a respectable reputation for himself. Many of his earlier troubles with the law had been for abusing women. Fingard, *Dark Side*, pp. 61–76.

34. *Whitby Gazette and Chronicle*, 1 and 6 May 1913.

35. Quoted in *Goderich Signal*, 28 July 1892. On the Cameron scandal, see CAI, William, Huron County, 1892; CAI, Mitchell, Huron County, 1892; and CAI, Gore, Huron County, 1892.

36. *Goderich Signal*, 29 September 1892.

37. Ibid., 23 March 1893.

38. *Oshawa Daily Reformer*, 26 and 27 November 1926.

39. CAI, Chattelle, Perth County, 1895; and NAC, RG 13, Capital Case File 1,832, CC 273, 1895.

40. CAI, Roughmond, Perth County, 1909.

41. *Stratford Evening Beacon*, 20 October 1894; *Listowel Banner*, 26 October and 2 November 1894; *Stratford Evening Beacon*, 22 October 1894; *Stratford Daily Herald*, 1 October 1908.

42. *Listowel Banner*, 10 August 1967. I am grateful to Franca Iacovetta for passing this information on to me.

43. *Stratford Daily Herald*, 1 October 1908.

44. Du Vernet would, several years later, go on to further legal fame as the prosecutor in the Carrie Davis case. See Strange, "Wounded Womanhood."

45. His description was sent by local police to Scotland Yard. *Stratford Evening Beacon*, 25 October 1894.

46. Ibid., 20 October 1894.

47. George Mosse, *Nationalism and Sexuality: Respectability and Abnormal Sexuality in Modern Europe* (New York: Howard Fertig, 1985), p. 32.

48. *Stratford Evening Beacon*, 23 October 1894.

49. Ibid., 29 October 1894.

50. Ibid., 28 March 1895.

51. Estelle Freedman, "Uncontrolled Desires: The Response to the Sexual Psychopath, 1920–1960," *Journal of American History* 74, no. 1 (June 1987): 83–106.

52. *Stratford Evening Beacon*, 29 March 1895.

53. *Stratford Daily Herald*, 1 October 1908 and 5 May 1909.

54. Freedman, "Uncontrolled Desires," p. 209.

55. *Stratford Daily Herald*, 5 May and 28 June 1909.

56. Address delivered by William Algie of Alton, Ontario, at the unveiling of the monument to Jessie Keith in Fairview Cemetery, Listowel, 24 May 1896 (text in author's possession).

57. *Stratford Evening Beacon*, 20 and 29 October 1894; *Stratford Daily Herald*, 3 October 1908.

58. *Stratford Daily Herald*, 6 May 1909.

59. *Stratford Evening Beacon*, 3 April 1895.

60. Judith Walkowitz, "Jack the Ripper and the Myth of Male Violence," *Feminist Studies* 8, no. 3 (1982): 542–72.

61. I would like to acknowledge the assistance, in both research and analysis, of Franca Iacovetta on the Napolitano case. See Karen Dubinsky and Franca Iacovetta, "Murder, Womanly Virtue and Motherhood: The Case of Angelina Napolitano," *Canadian Historical Review*, December 1991, pp. 505–31.

62. CAI, Napolitano, Algoma District, 1911; and NAC, RG 13, Capital Case File 1,476A, CC 22, pts. 1–5, 1911–22.

63. NAC, RG 13, Capital Case File 1,476A, CC 22, pts. 1–5, 1911–22.

64. CAI, Robinson, Sudbury District, 1909; and NAC, RG 13, Capital Case File, vol. 1, 484, CC49, pts. 1–3.

65. NAC, Napolitano Capital Case File correspondence, Brown, 12 May 1911, and Mort, no date.

66. *Sault Ste. Marie Star*, 3 June and 6 July 1911. On the racism of the Sault Ste. Marie press, see John Abbott, "Ethnicity as a Dynamic Factor in the Education of an Industrializing Town: The Case of Sault Ste. Marie, 1895–1914," *Ontario History* 79, no. 4 (December 1987): 327–52.

67. NAC, Napolitano Capital Case File correspondence, Bloor Street Baptist Church, 31 May 1911.

68. Ibid., unsigned, 14 July 1911.

69. Ibid., *Common Cause*, 17 August 1911, and *Votes for Women*, 21 July 1911.

70. Ibid., Hurtubis, 18 July 1911.

71. Ibid., Bittner, 15 July 1911.

72. Ibid., Sommerville, 21 July 1911.

73. Ibid., Denison, 20 March 1914; MacMurchy, 29 May and 30 June 1911; NAC, MG 28, vol. 22, file 1, National Council of Women, Minutes of Annual Meeting, June 1911.

74. NAC, Napolitano Capital Case File correspondence, Toronto Suffrage Association, 17 May 1911 and no date.

75. Ibid., Mills, n.d.

76. Ibid., No Tax No Vote League, n.d.

77. Ibid., Villeneuve, 6 July 1911; Boyce, 6 June 1911.

78. Ibid., group of women teachers, December 1911; Hochelaga WCTU, 19 May 1911.

79. Ibid., *Grand Rapids Evening Press*, 26 June 1911.

80. Provincial Archives of Ontario, MU 6363, Toronto Local Council of Women, Minutes, 10 April and 8 May 1912.

81. NAC, Robinson Capital Case File correspondence, Florence Huestis, 10 December 1909; Stevens, November 1909; Savage, 5 October 1909.

82. Quoted in *Sudbury Journal*, 14 October 1909.

83. NAC, Robinson Capital Case File correspondence, MacMurchy, 26 October 1909.

84. NAC, Napolitano Capital Case File correspondence, Aylesworth to Geldhof, 30 June 1911.

85. NAC, Robinson Capital Case File correspondence, Blakely, January 1910.

86. NAC, Napolitano Capital Case File correspondence, Governor General to Napolitano, 25 April 1924.

87. Of all the "Bambi" books, the most reliable is her own: Lawrencia Bembenek, *Woman on Trial* (Toronto: Harper Collins, 1992).

CHAPTER FIVE

1. Jonathan Ned Katz, "The Invention of Heterosexuality," *Socialist Review* 20, no. 1 (March 1990): 8.

2. Peter Ward, *Courtship, Love and Marriage in Nineteenth-Century English Canada* (Montreal: McGill-Queen's University Press, 1990); and idem, "Courtship and Social Space in Nineteenth-Century English Canada," *Canadian Historical Review* 68, no. 1 (1987): 35–62; Ellen Rothman, *Hands and Hearts: A History of Courtship in America* (New York: Basic Books, 1984); Beth Bailey, *From Front Porch to Back Seat: Courtship in Twentieth-Century America* (Baltimore: Johns Hopkins University Press, 1988). On courtship in Canada see also Joy Parr and Beth Light, eds., *Canadian Women on the Move, 1867–1920* (Toronto: New Hogtown Press, 1983), pp. 109–31; and Veronica Strong-Boag, *The New Day Recalled: Lives of Girls and Women in English Canada, 1919–1939* (Toronto: Copp-Clark Pitman, 1988), pp. 81–112.

3. The phrase 'compulsory heterosexuality,' and indeed, the first careful probing of the institution of heterosexuality, comes from Adrienne Rich, "Compulsory Heterosexuality and Lesbian Existence," *Signs* 5, no. 4 (1980): 631–60. For an analysis of how "heterosexual hegemony" shapes contemporary masculinity, see Blye Frank, "Hegemonic Heterosexual Masculinity," *Studies in Political Economy* 24 (Autumn 1987): 159–69. See also Gary Kinsman, *The Regulation of Desire: Sexuality in Canada* (Montreal: Black Rose Press, 1987).

4. Kathy Peiss, *Cheap Amusements: Working Women and Leisure in Turn-of-the-Century New York* (Philadelphia: Temple University Press, 1986); Christine Stansell, *City of Women: Sex and Class in New York, 1789–1860* (New York: Alfred A. Knopf, 1986).

5. Malcolm Graham Decarie, "The Prohibition Movement in Ontario, 1894–1916," Ph.D. diss., Queen's University, 1972, p. 54.

6. Roy Rosenzweig, *Eight Hours for What We Will: Workers and Leisure in an Industrial City, 1870–1920* (Cambridge: Cambridge University Press, 1983), p. 225.

7. See, for example, Peiss, *Cheap Amusements*, pp. 163–84; and Joanne Meyerowitz, *Woman Adrift: Independent Wage Earners in Chicago, 1880–1930* (Chicago: University of Chicago Press, 1988), pp. 43–68 and 92–116. On Canada see Diana Pederson, "Keeping Our Good Girls Good: The YWCA and the 'Girl Problem,' 1870–1930," *Canadian Women's Studies* 7, no. 4 (Winter 1986): 20–24; and Carolyn Strange, "The Perils and Pleasures of the City: Single, Wage-Earning Women in Toronto, 1880–1930," Ph.D. diss., Rutgers University, 1991.

8. Lynne Marks, "Ladies, Loafers, Knights and 'Lasses': The Social Demsions of Religion and Leisure in Late Nineteenth Century Small Town Ontario," Ph.D. diss., York University, 1992.

9. Rothman, *Hands and Hearts*, pp. 207–8; Ward, *Courtship*, pp. 64–89.

10. John D'Emilio and Estelle Freedman, *Intimate Matters: A History of Sexuality in America* (New York: Harper and Row, 1988), p. 73.

11. Provincial Archives of Ontario, RG 22, Criminal Assize Indictments (hereafter cited as CAI), M., Lambton County, 1917.

12. Peiss, *Cheap Amusements*, p. 106. Stansell concurs, in *City of Women*, p. 86.

13. CAI, S., Perth County, 1894; Percy Beale, unpublished diary, 21 August 1887, Baldwin Room, Metropolitan Toronto Reference Library.

14. John Abbott, "Accomplishing a Man's Task: Rural Women Teachers, Male Culture and the School Inspectorate in Turn-of-the-Century Ontario," *Ontario History* 78, no. 4 (December 1986): 313–30.

15. *Simcoe British Canadian*, 5 May 1880.

16. Quoted in Varpu Lindstrom-Best, *Defiant Sisters: A Social History of Finnish Immigrant Women in Canada* (Toronto: Multicultural History Society of Ontario, 1988), p. 62. See also Aili Schneider, *The Finnish Baker's Daughter* (Toronto: Multicultural History Society of Ontario, 1986).

17. Alan A. Brookes and Catherine Wilson, "Working Away from the Farm: The Young Women of North Huron, 1910–1930," *Ontario History* 77, no. 4 (December 1985): 281–300. On rural women's employment, see also Marjorie Cohen, *Women's Work, Markets and Economic Development in Nineteenth-Century Ontario* (Toronto: University of Toronto Press, 1988); Joy Parr, *The Gender of Breadwinners* (Toronto: University of Toronto Press, 1990); Sara Brooks Sundburg, "Farm Women on the Canadian Prairie Frontier: The Helpmate Image," in Veronica Strong-Boag and Anita Clair Fellman, eds., *Rethinking Canada* (Toronto: Copp-Clark Pitman, 1986), pp. 95–106; and Mary Kinnear, "Do You Want Your Daughter to Marry a Farmer? Women's Work on the Farm, 1922," *Papers in Rural History* 6 (1986): 137–53.

18. CAI, S., Algoma District, 1917; CAI, W., Lincoln County, 1925.

19. Peiss, *Cheap Amusements*, p. 69.

20. County Court Judges' Criminal Court (hereafter cited as CCJCC), C., Ontario County, 1911.

21. CAI, S., Ontario County, 1919.

22. D'Emilio and Freedman, *Intimate Matters*, p. xvii.

23. D. A. Watt, *Moral Legislation* (Montreal: Gazette Printing, 1890), p. 31; National Archives of Canada (hereafter NAC), RG 13 File 63/1894, Submissions to the Department of Justice re: 1892 Criminal code. Toronto C.A.S. submission, 29 March 1892. See also Andrew Jones and Leonard Rutman, *In the Children's Aid* (Toronto: University of Toronto Press, 1981).

24. Stansell, *City of Women*, pp. 41–63.

25. CAI, W., Stormont, Dundas and Glengarry County, 1902; CAI, P., Peterborough County, 1884.

26. CCJCC, D., Ontario County, 1915.

27. CCJCC, H., Ontario County, 1907.

28. René Leboutte, "Offences against Family Order: Infanticide in Belgium from

the Fifteenth through the Early Twentieth Centuries," *Journal of the History of Sexuality* 2, no. 2 (October 1991): 177. See, for example, CAI, B., Carleton County, 1916; *Ottawa Journal*, 23 March 1916; and CJCC, H., Ontario County, 1895. In both Puritan New England and turn-of-the-century working-class London, historians have noted the same willingness of neighbors to intervene—either directly or indirectly, through the state—in cases of physical abuse or child neglect. See Elizabeth Pleck, *Domestic Tyranny: The Making of American Social Policy against Family Violence from Colonial Times to the Present* (New York: Oxford University Press, 1987), p. 18; and Ellen Ross, "Labour and Love: Rediscovering London's Working-Class Mothers, 1870–1918," in Jane Lewis, ed., *Labour and Love: Women's Experience of Home and Family, 1850–1940* (Oxford: Basil Blackwell, 1986), pp. 73–98.

29. CAI, A., Carleton County, 1882.

30. *North Bay Nugget*, 13 April 1926.

31. CAI, A., Prince Edward County, 1899.

32. CAI, A., Lincoln County, 1901.

33. *Orangeville Sun*, 18 May and 1 June 1922. Josephine Phalen has written about a case of tarring and feathering in an earlier period in which adultery was also the issue. See "The Tar and Feather Case, Gore Assizes, August 1827," *Ontario History* 68, no. 1 (March 1976): 17–23.

34. District Court Judges' Criminal Court (hereafter cited as DCJCC), D., Algoma District, 1927. This family was white. On the Ku Klux Klan's efforts to punish wife beaters in the southern United States, see Elizabeth Pleck, "Wife Beating in Nineteenth-Century America," *Victimology* 4, no. 1 (Fall 1979): 70–71.

35. CAI, B., Lambton County, 1921; CAI, T., Peterborough County, 1899; CAI, J., Peterborough County, 1923.

36. *Orangeville Sun*, 31 January and 7 February 1895.

37. CAI, O., Thunder Bay District, 1921.

38. Mariana Valverde and Lorna Weir, "The Struggles of the Immoral: Preliminary Remarks on Moral Regulation," *Resources for Feminist Research* 17, no. 3 (September 1988): 31–34.

39. CCJCC, P., Ontario County, 1916.

40. On religious teaching regarding courtship and marriage, see Ward, *Courtship*, pp. 15–31. On moral supervision by factory owners, see Parr, *Gender of Breadwinners*, pp. 34–58.

41. Nancy F. Cott, "Passionlessness: An Interpretation of Victorian Sexual Ideology, 1790–1850," *Signs* 4 (1978): 219–36; reprinted in Thomas Altherr, ed., *Procreation or Pleasure? Sexual Attitudes in American History* (Malabar, Fl.: Robert E. Kriefer Publishing Co., 1983), p. 18. See also Christina Simmons, "Modern Sexuality and the Myth of Victorian Repression," in Kathy Peiss and Christina Simmons, eds., *Passion and Power: Sexuality in History* (Philadelphia: Temple University Press, 1989), pp. 157–77.

42. Steven Seidman, *Romantic Longings: Love in America, 1830–1980* (New York: Routledge, Chapman and Hall, 1991).

43. Ellen DuBois and Linda Gordon, "Seeking Ecstacy on the Battlefield: Danger and Pleasure in Nineteenth-Century Feminist Sexual Thought," in Carol

Vance, ed., *Pleasure and Danger: Exploring Female Sexuality* (Boston: Routledge and Kegan Paul, 1984), p. 37.

44. Thomas Laquer, "Orgasm, Generation and the Politics of Reproductive Biology," in Catherine Gallagher and Thomas Laquer, eds., *The Making of the Modern Body: Sexuality and Society in the Nineteenth Century* (Berkeley: University of California press, 1987), p. 35.

45. DCJCC, A., Algoma District, 1920.

46. Bruce Curtis, "Illicit Sex and Public Education in Ontario, 1840–1907," *Historical Studies in Education* 1, no. 1 (Spring 1989): 78.

47. Judith Fingard, *The Dark Side of Life in Victorian Halifax* (Porter's Lake, Nova Scotia: Pottersfield Press, 1989), p. 105.

48. Rothman, *Hands and Hearts*, p. 257. See also Christine Ball, "Female Sexual Ideologies in Mid to Late Nineteenth-Century Canada," *Canadian Journal of Women and the Law* 1, no. 2 (1983): 324–38; Angus McLaren, *Our Own Master Race* (Toronto: McClelland and Stewart, 1990), pp. 68–88; and Strong-Boag, *New Day Recalled*, pp. 81–112.

49. NAC, MG 31, H 95, file 51, Lempi Mansfield, "Aim for the Broom," manuscript, 1976, p. 10.

50. CAI, H., Peterborough County, 1927.

51. CAI, V., Rainy River District, 1929.

52. CAI, H., Rainy River District, 1927.

53. CAI, S., Lambton County, 1927.

54. CAI, S., Huron County, 1915.

55. Rothman, *Hands and Hearts*, p. 235.

56. CAI, M., Sudbury District, 1929; NAC, RG 13, Capital Case File, 1929, vol. 1,555; *Sudbury Journal*, 29 May, 1 June, 18 September, 21 September and 11 December 1929.

57. NAC, RG 13, Capital Case File, 1929, vol. 1, 555. The quotations in the following three paragraphs are also found in this case file.

58. *Sudbury Star*, 3 August 1929.

59. CAI, M., Perth County, 1925.

60. *Sudbury Journal*, 26 October 1916. On the campaign by British feminists in support of state regulation of sex and female police, see Lucy Bland, "In the Name of Protection: The Policing of Women in the First World War," in Julia Brophy and Carol Smart, eds., *Women-in-Law: Explorations in Law, Family and Sexuality* (London: Routledge and Kegan Paul, 1985), pp. 23–49.

61. D'Emilio and Freedman, *Intimate Matters*, p. 179. See also G. J. Barker-Benfield, "The Spermatic Economy: A Nineteenth-Century View of Sexuality," in Altherr, *Procreation or Pleasure?* pp. 47–70.

62. Rothman, *Hands and Hearts*, p. 231.

63. *Oshawa Daily Reformer*, 27 November 1926; *Kingston Daily British Whig*, 1 April 1908. For historical perspectives on working-class conceptions of masculinity in Canada, see Mark Rosenfeld, "It Was a Hard Life: Class and Gender in the Work and Family Rhythms of a Railway Town, 1920–1950," *Historical Papers* (1988): 237–79; Steven Maynard, "Rough Work and Rugged Men: The Social Construction of

Masculinity in Working-Class History," *Labour/Le Travail* 23 (Spring 1989): 159–70; and Parr, *Gender of Breadwinners*.

64. E. Anthony Rotundo, "Boy Culture: Middle-Class Boyhood in Nineteenth-Century America," in Mark C. Carnes and Clyde Griffen, eds., *Meanings for Manhood: Constructions of Masculinity in Victorian America* (Chicago: University of Chicago Press, 1990), p. 19; R. G. Moyles and Doug Owram, *Imperial Dreams and Colonial Realities: British Views of Canada, 1880–1914* (Toronto: University of Toronto Press, 1988), p. 47.

65. CAI, C., Ontario County, 1896; CAI, T., Ontario County, 1900.

66. Again, because of the highly public nature of these two cases, I use the full names of the parties involved.

67. CAI, Jardine, Huron County, 1911.

68. Ibid.; and *Goderich Star*, 29 September, 6 October 1910, and 6 and 13 April, 15 June 1911. The information on Jardine in the following three paragraphs is also found in these sources.

On the history of the insanity defense in criminal trials, see Simon Verdun-Jones, "The Historical Roots of the Canadian Insanity Defence, 1843–1920," in Louis Knafla, ed., *Crime and Criminal Justice in Europe and North America* (Waterloo, Ont.: Wilfred Laurier University Press, 1981), pp. 179–218; and Estelle Freedman, "Uncontrolled Desires: The Response to the Sexual Psychopath, 1920–1960," *Journal of American History* 74, no. 1 (June 1987): 83–106. On the creation of psychological categories to deal with 'deviant' women, see Elizabeth Lunbeck, "A New Generation of Women: Progressive Psychiatrists and the Hypersexual Female," *Feminist Studies* 13, no. 3 (Fall 1987): 513–43.

69. On attitudes to masturbation in this period, see Michael Bliss, "Pure Books on Avoided Subjects: Pre-Freudian Sexual Ideas in Canada," in Michiel Horn and Ronald Sabourin, eds., *Studies in Canadian Social History* (Toronto: McClelland and Stewart, 1974), pp. 327–28.

70. CAI, Ray, Thunder Bay District, 1892. Biographical information on Ray is from George B. Macgillivray, *A History of Fort William and Port Arthur Newspapers from 1875* (Toronto: Bright Press, 1968), pp. 69–79.

71. *Toronto Daily Mail*, 13 August 1892; *Thunder Bay Weekly Herald*, 22 September 1893.

72. *Toronto Daily Mail*, 13 August 1892.

73. *Thunder Bay Sentinal*, 15 June 1894.

74. Department of Temperance and Moral Reform of the Methodist Church, and the Board of Social Service and Evangelism of the Presbyterian Church, *Report of a Preliminary and General Social Survey of Port Arthur*, March 1913, p. 6.

75. *Fort William Times Journal*, 16 February 1938. See also Ray's reminiscences of the early days in Port Arthur, in *Fort William Times Journal*, 27 May 1962.

76. *Fort William Times Journal*, 18 April 1910.

77. On the social purity and social gospel movements in Canada, see J. S. Woodsworth, *My Neighbour* (reprint, Toronto: University of Toronto Press, 1972); Richard Allen, *The Social Passion: Religion and Social Reform in Canada, 1914–1928* (Toronto: University of Toronto Press, 1971); Richard Allen, ed., *The Social Gospel in Canada*, Mercury Series No. 9 (Ottawa: National Museum of Man, National Mu-

seums of Canada, 1975); Joan Sangster, "The Making of a Socialist-Feminist: The Early Career of Beatrice Bridgen, 1888–1941," *Atlantis* 13, no. 1 (Fall 1987): 13–28. On the racial fears of the labor movement, see Donald Avery, *Dangerous Foreigners: European Immigrant Workers and Labour Radicalism in Canada, 1896–1932* (Toronto: McClelland and Stewart, 1979). On race and the women's movement, see Howard Palmer, *Patterns of Prejudice: A History of Nativism in Alberta* (Toronto: McClelland and Stewart, 1982), pp. 39–40 and 80–82; Carol Lee Bacchi, *Liberation Deferred?* (Toronto: University of Toronto Press, 1983), pp. 50–55 and 104–16; Mariana Valverde, *The Age of Soap, Light and Water* (Toronto: McClelland and Stewart, 1991); idem, "When the Mother of the Race Is Free: Race, Reproduction and Sexuality in First-Wave Feminism," and Ruth Frager, "Competing Claims of Class, Ethnicity and Gender in the Eaton Strikes of 1912 and 1934," both in Franca Iacovetta and Mariana Valverde, eds., *Gender Conflicts: Essays in Women's History* (Toronto: University of Toronto Press, 1992). On Canadian government policy toward deportation of the morally and politically undesirable, see Barbara Roberts, *Whence They Came: Deportation from Canada, 1900–1935* (Ottawa: University of Ottawa Press, 1988), pp. 11–36 and 71–98.

78. *Fort William Daily Times*, 21 August 1909.

79. Marvin MacDonald, "Protestant Reaction to Non-English Immigration in Port Arthur and Fort William, 1903–1914," M.A. thesis, Lakehead University, 1976, pp. 91–125. On city missions in Canada, see also Paul Rutherford, ed., *Saving the Canadian City* (Toronto: University of Toronto Press, 1974), pp. 155–64; and Judith Fingard, *Dark Side*, pp. 117–34. On the coal dock strike in Fort William, see Jean Morrison, "Ethnicity and Violence: The Lakehead Freight Handlers before World War I," in Gregory S. Kealey and Peter Warrian, eds., *Essays in Canadian Working Class History* (Toronto: McClelland and Stewart, 1976), pp. 143–60.

80. *Sarnia Observer*, 28 July 1882. On early perceptions of native sexuality, see Sylvia Van Kirk, *Many Tender Ties: Women in Fur-Trade Society, 1670–1870* (Winnipeg: Watson and Dwyer, 1980), pp. 25–27.

81. *Sudbury Star*, 6 October 1926. Saskatchewan was the first jurisdiction to forbid white women from working in Asian establishments, in 1912. See Ken Adachi, *The Enemy That Never Was: A History of the Japanese Canadians* (Toronto: McClelland and Stewart, 1976), p. 94. On immigration policy and social opinions about Chinese immigration, see Peter Ward, *White Canada Forever: Popular Attitudes and Public Policy Towards Orientals in British Columbia* (Montreal: McGill-Queen's University Press, 1978); and Dora Nipp, "But Women Did Come: Working Chinese Women in the Interwar Years," in Jean Burnet, ed., *Looking into My Sister's Eyes: An Exploration in Women's History* (Toronto: Multicultural History Society of Ontario, 1986), pp. 179–94.

82. MacDonald, "Protestant Reaction," p. 19. The link between race and crime was also featured prominently in the ideas put forth by the early twentieth-century eugenics movement. See A. McLaren, *Our Own Master Race*, p. 52.

83. On the way newspapers helped create in their readers' minds the association between immigrants and crime, see John R. Abbott, "Ethnicity as a Dynamic Factor in the Education of an Industrializing Town: The Case of Sault Ste. Marie, 1895–1914," *Ontario History* 79, no. 4 (December 1987): 327–52. For an earlier period, see

James Reaney, "Myths in Some Nineteenth-Century Ontario Newspapers," in Frederick H. Armstrong, Hugh A. Stevenson, and J. Donald Wilson, eds., *Aspects of Nineteenth-Century Ontario: Essays Presented to James J. Talman* (Toronto: University of Toronto Press, 1974), pp. 253–66.

84. *Cobalt Nugget*, 21 May 1914; Egerton Ryerson Young, *Stories from Indian Wigwans and Northern Campfires* (London: Charles Kelly, 1893; reprint, Toronto: Coles, 1970), pp. 145–49.

85. G. Geller, "The Wartime Elections Act of 1917 and the Canadian Women's Movement," *Atlantis* 2, no. 1 (Autumn 1976): 88–106. On Denison, see Deborah Gorham, "Flora MacDonald Denison: Canadian Feminist," in Linda Kealey, ed., *A Not Unreasonable Claim: Women and Reform in Canada, 1880s–1920s* (Toronto: Women's Press, 1979), pp. 47–70.

86. Alice Chown, *The Stairway* (Boston: Cornhill Co., 1921; reprint, Toronto: University of Toronto Press, 1988), pp. 249–50.

87. Frances Swyirpa, "Outside the Block Settlement: Ukrainian Women in Ontario during the Formative Years of Community Consciousness," in Jean Burnet, *Looking into My Sister's Eyes*.

88. Lindstrom-Best, *Defiant Sisters*, pp. 74–77. On the sexual radicalism of the Finns in Canada, see also Janice Newton, "Enough of Exclusive Masculine Thinking: The Feminist Challenge to the Early Canadian Left, 1900–1918," Ph.D. diss., York University, 1987, pp. 246–310.

89. Jennifer Terry, "Theorizing Deviant History," *differences* 3, no. 1 (Summer 1991): 55–74.

90. Ann duCille, "'Othered' Matters: Reconceptualizing Dominance and Difference in the History of Sexuality in America," *Journal of the History of Sexuality* 1, no. 1 (July 1990): p. 104. See also the response by D'Emilio and Freedman in the same issue, pp. 128–130.

CHAPTER SIX

1. *Toronto Globe and Mail*, 21 December 1989; and *Toronto Star*, 24 June 1990. Bourassa was exonerated by the inquiry, and *Toronto Globe and Mail* columnist Michael Valpy has suggested that Bourassa was, in his words, "juiced" by the media. *Toronto Globe and Mail*, 17 December 1990.

2. On the turn-of-the-century rural problem, see Malcolm Graham Decarie, "The Prohibition Movement in Ontario, 1894–1916," Ph.D. diss., Queen's University, 1972; F. J. K. Griezec, "Power to the People: The Beginning of Agrarian Revolt in Ontario, the Maintoulin By-Election, October, 1924, 1918," *Ontario History* 56, no. 1 (March 1977): 33–54; William Irvine, *The Farmer in Politics* (Toronto: McClelland and Stewart, 1920; reprint, Toronto: McClelland and Stewart, 1976); John MacDougall, *Rural Life in Canada: Its Trends and Tasks* (Toronto: Westminister Co., 1913; reprint, Toronto: University of Toronto Press, 1973); and W. R. Young, "Conscription, Rural Depopulation and the Farmers of Ontario," *Canadian Historical Review* 53, no. 3 (1972): 289–320.

3. H. V. Nelles, *The Politics of Development* (Toronto: Macmillan, 1974), p. 55. Other studies of aspects of the economic and social history of northern Ontario are: Cynthia Abelle, "The Mothers of the Land Must Suffer: Child and Maternal Wel-

fare in Rural and Outpost Ontario, 1918–1940," *Ontario History* 80, no. 3 (September 1988): 183–205; John Abbott, "Ethnicity as a Dynamic Factor in the Education of an Industrializing Town: The Case of Sault Ste. Marie, 1895–1914," *Ontario History* 79, no. 4 (December 1987): pp. 327–52; Elizabeth Arthur, ed., *The Thunder Bay District, 1821–1892* (Toronto: University of Toronto Press, 1971); idem, "Beyond Superior: Ontario's New Found Land," in Roger Hall, William Westfall, and Laurel Sefton MacDowell, eds., *Patterns of the Past: Interpreting Ontario's History* (Toronto: Dundern, 1988), pp. 130–49; Doug Baldwin, "The Life of a Silver Miner in Northern Ontario," *Labour/Le Travailler* 2 (1977): 79–107; Edwin Bradwin, *The Bunkhouse Man: A Study of the Work and Pay in the Camps of Canada, 1903–1914* (New York: Columbia University Press, 1928; reprint, Toronto: University of Toronto Press, 1972); Matt Bray and Ernie Epp, eds., *A Vast and Magnificent Land* (Thunder Bay, Ont.: Lakehead University Press, 1984); Gordon Brock, *The Province of Northern Ontario* (Cobalt, Ont.: Highway Bookshop, 1978); Max Guennel, "Port Arthur Views Progress, 1910–1913," B.A. paper, Lakehead University, 1975; Marvin MacDonald, "Protestant Reaction to Non-English Immigration in Port Arthur and Fort William, 1903–1914," M.A. thesis, Lakehead University, 1976; Antonio Pucci and John Potestio, eds., "Thunder Bay's People," *Polyphony* 9, no. 2 (1987); Ian Radforth, *Bushworkers and Bosses: Logging in Northern Ontario* (Toronto: University of Toronto Press, 1987); Oiva Saarinen, "Sudbury: A Historical Case Study of Multiple Urban-Economic Transformation," *Ontario History* 82, no. 1 (March 1990): 53–81; and Thorold J. Tronrud, "Frontier Social Structure: The Canadian Lakehead, 1871 and 1881," *Ontario History* 79, no. 2 (June 1987): 145–65.

4. On urban development in the North, see Oiva Saarinen, "Cities and Towns," in Bray and Epp, *A Vast and Magnificent Land*, pp. 147–64; idem, "Sudbury"; and Tronrud, "Frontier Social Structure."

5. Barbara Roberts, "Ladies, Women and the State: Managing Female Immigration, 1880–1920," in Roxana Ng, Gillian Walker, and Jacob Muller, eds., *Community Organization and the Canadian State* (Toronto: Garamond, 1990), pp. 108–30. See also Mariana Valverde and Lorna Weir, "The Struggles of the Immoral: Preliminary Remarks on Moral Regulation," *Resources for Feminist Research* 17, no. 3 (September 1988): 31.

6. On how 'immorality' was used as a criterion for deportation historically, see Barbara Roberts, *Whence They Came* (Ottawa: University of Ottawa Press, 1988), pp. 109–23.

7. Carol Smith-Rosenburg, "Davy Crockett as Trickster: Pornography, Liminality and Symbolic Inversion in Victorian America," in *Disorderly Conduct: Visions of Gender in Victorian America* (New York: Oxford University Press, 1985), p. 91.

8. Rob Sheilds, *Places on the Margin* (London: Routledge, 1990), pp. 11, 29.

9. Laura Engelstein, "Morality and the Wooden Spoon: Russian Doctors View Syphilis, Social Class and Sexual Behavior, 1890–1905," in Catherine Gallagher and Thomas Laquer, eds., *The Making of the Modern Body: Sexuality and Society in the Nineteenth Century* (Berkeley: University of California Press, 1987), pp. 169–208.

10. Ibid., pp. 179–85.

11. Smith-Rosenburg, "Davy Crockett," p. 90.

12. Nelles, *Politics of Development*, p. 52.

13. James Doyle, "The Image of Northern Ontario in English Canadian Literature," *Laurentian University Review* 8 (1975): 105. For similar sentiments about the development of western Canada, see Douglas Owram, *The Promise of Eden* (Toronto: University of Toronto Press, 1980).

14. Patricia Jasen, "Wild Men: Voyageurs and the Cult of the Primitive in Nineteenth-Century Tourism," paper presented at the Canadian Historical Association Annual Meeting, June 1991.

15. T. Morris Langstreth, *The Lake Superior Country* (Toronto: McClelland and Stewart, 1924), p. 9.

16. John Foster Fraser, *Canada as It Is* (London: Carswell and Co., 1905), pp. 90–91. I thank Dennis Dubinsky for directing me to this source.

17. Langstreth, *Lake Superior Country*, pp. 25–26.

18. Owen Williamson, *The Northland Ontario* (Toronto: Ryerson Press, 1946), p. 106.

19. Jasen, "Wild Men," p. 21; Wilfred William Campbell, *The Beauty, History, Romance and Mystery of the Canadian Lake Region* (Toronto: Musson, 1910), pp. 26 and 139; Ontario Department of Travel and Publicity, *Beautiful Ontario*, 1932, p. 28; and Williamson, *Northland Ontario*, p. 91. On the construction of the Canadian North as a tourist area, see also Alexander Wilson, *The Culture of Nature: North American Landscape from Disney to the Exxon Valdez* (Toronto: Between the Lines, 1991), pp. 19–51.

20. Carl Berger, "The True North Strong and Free," in J. M. Bumstead, ed., *Interpreting Canada's Past* (Toronto: Oxford University Press, 1986), vol. 2, p. 159; Radforth, *Bushworkers*, p. 9.

21. Temiskaming and Northern Ontario Railway, *A Plain Tale of Plain People: Pioneer Life in New Ontario* (Toronto: William Briggs, 1913), p. 23. See also, for example, Department of Agriculture, *Information for Intending Settlers—Muskoka and Lake Nipissing Districts* (Ottawa, 1880); Ontario Ministry of Agriculture, *The Newer Districts of Ontario: Information for Prospective Settlers* (Toronto: Warwick, 1898); Commissioner of Crown Lands for Ontario, *Northern Districts of Ontario Canada* (Toronto: Warwick, 1899); Ottawa Minister of the Interior, *Canada: The Thunder Bay, Kenora and Rainy River Districts of New Ontario* (1913); Ontario Ministry of Agriculture, *Northern Ontario, Canada: A New Land Nearby* (1916).

22. Temiskaming and Northern Ontario Railway, *Greater Ontario: The Poor Man's Hope* (Toronto: William Briggs, 1916).

23. Langstreth, *Lake Superior Country*, p. 303.

24. Ellen Knox, *The Girl of the New Day* (Toronto: McClelland and Stewart, 1919), p. 68.

25. Aili Schneider, *The Finnish Baker's Daughter* (Toronto: Multicultural History Society of Ontario, 1986), pp. 20–22.

26. National Archives of Canada (hereafter NAC), MG 29, C114, Belle Kettridge diary, January 1892.

27. NAC, MG 31, H7, Elizabeth MacEwan, "Early Days in Cobalt," manuscript, 1955.

28. Ibid.

29. Radforth, *Bushworkers*, p. 102.

30. Schneider, *Finnish Baker's Daughter*, p. 84; MacEwan, "Early Days in Cobalt."

31. Berger, "The Truth North," pp. 162–70.

32. Raymond Williams, *The Country and the City* (London: Chatto and Windus, 1973; reprint, London: Hogarth Press, 1985), pp. 192 and 197.

33. Quoted in David Jones, "There Is Some Power about Land: The Western Canadian Agrarian Press and Country Life Ideology," *Journal of Canadian Studies* 17, no. 3 (1982): 102.

34. Leonore Davidoff, Jean L'Esperance, and Howard Newby, "Landscape with Figures: Home and Community in English Society," in Juliet Mitchell and Ann Oakley, eds., *The Rights and Wrongs of Women* (Harmondsworth, England: Penguin, 1976), pp. 139–75.

35. Ibid., pp. 143, 153.

36. Mary Poovey, *Uneven Developments: The Ideological Work of Gender in Mid-Victorian England* (Chicago: University of Chicago Press, 1988), p. 12. See also Chris Weedon, *Feminist Practice and Poststructuralist Theory* (Oxford: Basil Blackwell, 1987), pp. 12–42 and 126–35; Julie Guard, "Dealing with Difference: Power in the New Feminist Historiography," paper presented at the Canadian Women's Studies Association Annual Meeting, June 1990; and Joan Scott, "Deconstructing Equality-versus-Difference, or, The Uses of Poststructuralist Theory for Feminism," *Feminist Studies* 14, no. 1 (Spring 1988): 33–49.

37. Shields, *Places*, p. 4.

38. MacDougall, *Rural Life*, p. 38.

39. Ibid., p. 47. See also Edward Amey, *Farm Life as It Should Be, and Farm Labourers' and Servant Girls' Grievances* (Toronto: Ellis and Moore, 1885). On rural women's social, political and economic life in this period, see Majorie Cohen, *Women's Work, Markets, and Economic Development in Nineteenth-Century Ontario* (Toronto: University of Toronto Press, 1988); Margaret Kechnie, "The United Farm Women of Ontario: Developing a Political Consciousness," *Ontario History* 77, no. 4 (December 1985): 267–80; Mary Kinnear, "Do You Want Your Daughter to Marry a Farmer? Women's Work on the Farm, 1922," *Papers in Rural History* 6 (1986): 137–53; and Pauline Rankin, "The Politicization of Ontario Farm Women," in Linda Kealey and Joan Sangster, eds., *Beyond the Vote: Canadian Women and Politics* (Toronto: University of Toronto Press, 1989), pp. 309–32.

40. MacDougall, *Rural Life*, pp. 47–48.

41. John Bullen, "Hidden Workers: Child Labour and the Family Economy in Late Nineteenth-Century Urban Ontario," *Labour/Le Travail* 18 (Fall 1986): 179; Andrew Jones and Leonard Rutman, *In the Children's Aid: J. J. Kelso and Child Welfare in Ontario* (Toronto: University of Toronto Press, 1981), p. 108. Judith Fingard notes the same strategy for the rehabilitation of delinquents in Nova Scotia, in *The Dark Side of Life in Victorian Halifax* (Porter's Lake, Nova Scotia: Pottersfield Press, 1989), p. 194. On medical views of regionalism, see Angus McLaren, *Our Own Master Race* (Toronto: McClelland and Stewart, 1990), pp. 54–55.

42. Knox, *Girl of the New Day*, pp. 66–67.

43. MacDougall, *Rural Life*, pp. 123–48.

44. Department of Temperance and Moral Reform of the Methodist Church et al., *Report on a Rural Survey*, December–January 1913–14, pp. 28–29.

45. *Stratford Evening Beacon*, 10 April 1895.

46. Jones, "There Is Some Power," p. 105.

47. *Woodstock Sentinal Review*, 21 October 1881.

48. *Goderich Signal*, 1 March 1894.

49. Department of Temperance and Moral Reform of the Methodist Church et al., *Report on a Rural Survey*, p. 24.

50. Michael Cross, "Violence and Authority: The Case of Bytown," and Terry Chapman, "The Anti-Drug Crusade in Western Canada, 1885–1925," both in D. J. Bercuson and L. A. Knafla, eds., *Law and Society in Canada in Historical Perspective* (Calgary: University of Calgary, 1979), pp. 89, 5.

51. John R. Abbott, "Accomplishing a Man's Task: Rural Women Teachers, Male Culture and the School Inspectorate in Turn-of-the-Century Ontario," *Ontario History* 78, no. 4 (December 1986): 313–30; on logging camps and prostitution, see Decarie, "Prohibition Movement," p. 16; J. G. Shearer, "Canada's War on the White Slave Trade," in Ernest A. Bell, ed., *War on the White Slave Trade* (reprint, Toronto: Coles, 1980), p. 342; Janice Newton, "Enough of Exclusive Masculine Thinking: The Feminist Challenge to the Early Canadian Left, 1900–1918," Ph.D. diss., York University, 1987, p. 252; and NAC, MG 28, vol. 57, file 1, National Council of Women Minutes of Annual Meeting, June 1911.

52. Radforth, *Bushworkers*, p. 116. On the association of the ethnic left with sexual immorality, see also Varpu Lindstrom-Best, *Defiant Sisters: A Social History of Finnish Immigrant Women in Canada* (Toronto: Multicultural History Society of Ontario, 1988), pp. 73–78; and Janice Newton, "The Alchemy of Politicization: Socialist Women and the Early Canadian Left," in Franca Iacovetta and Mariana Valverde, eds. *Gender Conflicts: Essays in Women's History* (Toronto: University of Toronto Press, 1992), pp. 118–48. On labor radicalism in northern Ontario, see Irving Abella, *Nationalism, Communism and Canadian Labour* (Toronto: University of Toronto Press, 1973), pp. 86–100; Laurel Sefton MacDowell, *Remember Kirkland Lake: The Gold Miners' Strike of 1941–42* (Toronto: University of Toronto Press, 1983); Jean Morrison, "Ethnicity and Violence: The Lakehead Freight Handlers before World War I," in Gregory S. Kealey and Peter Warrian, eds., *Essays in Canadian Working Class History* (Toronto: McClelland and Stewart, 1976), pp. 143–60; idem, "Ethnicity and Violence: Southern Europeans in Strikes on Thunder Bay's Waterfront before World War I," in John Potestio and Antonio Pucci, eds., *The Italian Immigrant Experience* (Thunder Bay, Ont.: Canadian Italian History Association, 1988), pp. 103–18; Marc Metsaranta, ed., *Project Bay Street: Activities of Finnish-Canadians in Thunder Bay before 1915* (Thunder Bay: Finnish Canadian Historical Society, 1989); Antonio Pucci, "Thunder Bay's Italian Community, 1880s–1940s," in Potestio and Pucci, *Italian Immigrant Experience*, pp. 79–101; idem, "Canadian Industrialization versus the Italian Contadini in a Decade of Brutality, 1902–1912," in Robert Harney and J. Vincenza Scarpaci, eds., *Little Italies in North America* (Toronto: Multicultural History Society of Ontario, 1981), pp. 181–207; and Satu Repo, "Rosvall and Voutilainen: Two Union Men Who Never Died," *Labour/Le Travailleur* 8–9 (Autumn 1981–Spring 1982): 79–102.

53. James Lawler, *The Temiskaming Country: Articles Written by Staff Correspondent of the Mail and Empire*, June 1901.

54. *New Ontario: Excursion of the Canadian Press Association* (Welland: Sears and

Sawle, 1903); *The Thunder Bay, Kenora and Rainy River Districts of New Ontario* (Ottawa: Ministery of the Interior, 1913).

55. Matt Bray, "The Place and the People," in Bray and Epp, *A Vast and Magnificant Land*, p. 12.

56. Department of Temperance and Moral Reform of the Methodist Church et al., *Report of a Preliminary and General Social Survey of Port Arthur*, March 1913, p. 23.

57. John McLaren, "Chasing the Social Evil: Moral Fervour and the Evolution of Canada's Prostitution Laws, 1867–1917," *Canadian Journal of Law and Society* 1 (1986): 149; and idem, "White Slavers: The Reform of Canada's Prostitution Law and Patterns of Enforcement, 1900–1920," *Criminal Justice History* 8 (1987): 81–82; A. McLaren, *Our Own Master Race*, p. 121.

58. Millie Magwood, *Pine Lake: A Story of Northern Ontario* (Toronto: William Briggs, 1901).

59. *Cobalt Nugget*, 25 April 1914. Several years earlier in Cobalt, the town council took up the problem of profanity on city streets, which some complained was making it difficult for "ladies" to walk without being "insulted." Ibid., 20 October 1910.

60. Ibid., 14 April 1914; *Cobalt Daily Nugget*, 20 October 1910; *Sudbury Journal*, 4 November 1909.

61. Provincial Archives of Ontario, RG 22, Criminal Assize Indictments (hereafter cited as CAI), S., Thunder Bay District, 1914; CAI, L., Algoma District, 1906.

62. District Court Judges' Criminal Court (hereafter cited as DCJCC), E., Algoma District, 1924.

63. *Sault Ste. Marie Star*, 12 April 1919; CAI, B., Algoma District, 1922.

64. *Orangeville Sun*, 31 March 1927; NAC, RG 13, Capital Case File 1502A, CC 124, pts. 1–3, 1919–27.

65. *Toronto World*, 20 October, 1916; *Huntsville Forrester*, 16 November 1916.

66. Angus McLaren and Arlene Tigar McLaren, *The Bedroom and the State* (Toronto: McClelland and Stewart, 1986), pp. 93–99; and A. McLaren, *Our Own Master Race*, pp. 76–77 and 150–51.

67. *Toronto World*, 27 October 1916.

68. *Huntsville Forrester*, 16 and 2 November 1916.

69. Ibid., 23 November 1916; Roy Wolfe, "The Summer Resorts of Ontario in the Nineteenth Century," *Ontario History* 54, no. 3 (1962): 149–61.

70. *Peterborough Examiner*, 26 April 1916. See also Joan Sangster's works on the Peterborough badlands, "Tales from Magistrates Court: Women, Criminality and the Courts in Peterborough County, 1920–1950," paper presented to the Law, State and Society in History Conference, Osgoode Hall, Toronto, 16 May 1992.

71. Engelstein, "Morality," p. 173.

72. Mariana Valverde, *The Age of Light, Soap and Water* (McClelland and Stewart, 1991), p. 32.

73. Paul André Linteau, *The Promoters' City* (Toronto: Lorimer, 1985).

74. Diana Pederson, "'Building today for the Womanhood of Tomorrow': Businessmen, Boosters, and the YWCA, 1890–1930," *Urban History Review* 15, no. 3 (February 1987): 238.

75. George Mosse, *Nationalism and Sexuality: Respectability and Abnormal Sexuality in Modern Europe* (New York: Howard Fertig, 1985), p. 9.

76. *Woodstock Sentinal Review,* 26 October 1909; *Stratford Evening Beacon,* 31 March and 2 April 1894. Peter McGahan also notes a debate which took place in the Moncton press in the 1880s, about whether the city was a particularly "sinful" place. McGahan, *Crime and Policing in Maritime Canada* (Fredericton, New Brunswick: Goose Lane Editions, 1986), p. 35.

CONCLUSION

1. Alice Chown, *The Stairway* (Boston: Cornhill Co., 1921; reprint, Toronto: University of Toronto Press, 1988), p. 108.

2. Unidentified newspaper clipping found in Provincial Archives of Ontario, County Court Judges' Criminal Court, Y., Ontario County, 1910.

3. P.A.O., RG 22, Criminal Assize Indictments, C., Thunder Bay District, 1927.

4. An important contribution to our knowledge of the social life of small-town Ontario, which has added significantly to my understanding of the topic, is Lynne Marks, "Ladies, Loafers, Knights and 'Lasses': The Social Dimensions of Religion and Leisure in Late Nineteenth-Century Small-Town Ontario," Ph.D. diss., York University, 1992.

5. Mariana Valverde, "When the Mother of the Race Is Free: Race, Reproduction and Sexuality in First-Wave Feminism," in Franca Iacovetta and Mariana Valverde, eds., *Gender Conflicts: Essays in Women's History* (Toronto: University of Toronto Press, 1992).

6. Judith Allen, *Sex and Secrets: Crimes Involving Australian Women since 1880* (Melbourne: Oxford University Press, 1990); and Steven Seidman, *Romantic Longings: Love in America, 1830–1980* (New York: Routledge, 1991).

7. Carolyn Strange, "The Perils and Pleasures of the City: Single, Wage-Earning Women in Toronto, 1880–1930," Ph.D. diss., Rutgers University, 1991.

8. Linda Gordon, *Heroes of Their Own Lives: The Politics and History of Family Violence* (New York: Viking, 1988).

BIBLIOGRAPHY

PRIMARY SOURCES

CRIMINAL CASE FILES

Provincial Archives of Ontario, RG 22
a. Criminal assize indictments in the following counties/districts:

Algoma
Carleton
Cochrane
Dufferin
Elgin
Frontenac
Huron
Kenora
Lambton
Leeds and Grenville
Lincoln
Muskoka
Nipissing

Norfolk
Ontario
Oxford
Parry Sound
Perth
Peterborough
Prince Edward
Rainy River
Stormont, Dundas and Glengarry
Sudbury
Temiskaming
Thunder Bay

b. County/district court judges' criminal court indictments in the following
counties/districts:

Algoma
Carleton
Elgin
Huron
Lambton

Leeds and Grenville
Lincoln
Ontario
Perth
Stormont, Dundas and Glengarry

National Archives of Canada, RG 13, Capital Case Files

Chatelle, Amede	Napolitano, Angelina
Jardine, Edward	Robinson, Annie
McCabe, Maria	Thompson, Lovica

Department of Justice, file 63 1894, letters and submissions to the Department of Justice regarding changes to the 1892 criminal code

Newspaper Collections

Brockville Times	*North Bay Nugget*
Brockville Recorder	*Orangeville Sun*
Cobalt Nugget	*Oshawa Daily Times*
Cochrane Claybelt	*Ottawa Citizen*
Cochrane Northland	*Ottawa Journal*
Cornwall Freeholder	*Parry Sound North Star*
Cornwall Standard	*Peterborough Examiner*
Fort William Daily Journal	*Port Arthur Herald*
Fort William Liberator	*St. Thomas Daily Times*
Fort William Times Journal	*Sarnia Observer*
Gananoque Reporter	*Sault Ste. Marie Star*
Goderich Signal	*Simcoe British Canadian*
Goderich Star	*Stratford Evening Beacon*
Hamilton Palladium of Labour	*Stratford Herald*
Hamilton Spectator	*Stratford Times*
Huntsville Forester	*Sudbury Journal*
Kenora Miner and News	*Sudbury Star*
Kingston Daily British Whig	*Thunder Bay Sentinal*
Kirkland Lake Northern News	*Toronto Mail*
Listowel Banner	*Toronto World*
Muskoka Herald	*Whitby Chronicle*
New Liskeard Speaker	*Whitby Gazette and Chronicle*
Norfolk Reformer	*Woodstock Sentinal-Review*

Manuscript Collections

National Archives of Canada, MG 29, 30 and 31

Allen, Lois	MacEwan, Elizabeth
Kettredge, Belle	Mansfield, Lempi

National Archives of Canada, MG 28, I, 129. Papers of the Montreal Society for the Protection of Women and Children

Thomas Fisher Rare Book Room, University of Toronto, John Charlton Collection

United Church Archives, Methodist Church of Canada, Social Survey Reports for Fort William, Port Arthur, Huron County

Bibliography

Government Documents

Canada, House of Commons *Debates*   1886 (April)
1882 (February, March)   1887 (April, May)
1883 (March)   1890 (April)
1885 (February, March, June)

SECONDARY SOURCES

Abbott, John R. "Accomplishing a Man's Task: Rural Women Teachers, Male Culture and the School Inspectorate in Turn-of-the-Century Ontario." *Ontario History* 78, no. 4 (December 1986): 313–30.

———. "Ethnicity as a Dynamic Factor in the Education of an Industrializing Town: The Case of Sault Ste. Marie, 1895–1914." *Ontario History*, 79, no. 4 (December 1987): 327–52.

Abelle, Cynthia. "The Mothers of the Land Must Suffer: Child and Maternal Welfare in Rural and Outpost Ontario, 1918–1940." *Ontario History* 80, no. 3 (September 1988): 183–205.

Acton, Janice, Penny Goldsmith, and Bonnie Shepard, eds. *Women at Work, 1850–1930*. Toronto: Women's Press, 1974.

Allen, Richard. *The Social Passion: Religion and Social Reform in Canada, 1914–1928*. Toronto: University of Toronto Press, 1971.

Amey, Edward. *Farm Life as It Should Be and Farm Labourers' and Servant Girls' Grievances*. Toronto: Ellis and Moore, 1885.

Arnold, Marybeth Hamilton. "The Life of a Citizen in the Hands of a Woman: Sexual Assault in New York City, 1790–1820." In *Passion and Power: Sexuality in History*. Edited by Kathy Peiss and Christina Simmons. Philadelphia: Temple University Press, 1989.

Arthur, Elizabeth. "Beyond Superior: Ontario's New Found Land." In *Patterns of the Past: Interpreting Ontario's History*, 130–49. Edited by Roger Hall, William Westfall, and Laurel Sefton MacDowell. Toronto: Dundern, 1988.

———. *The Thunder Bay District, 1821–1892*. Toronto: University of Toronto Press, 1971.

Ayers, Pat, and Jan Lambertz. "Marriage Relations, Money and Domestic Violence in Working-Class Liverpool, 1919–1939." In *Labour and Love: Women's Experience of Home and Family, 1850–1940*, pp. 195–222. Edited by Jane Lewis. Oxford: Basil Blackwell, 1986.

Bacchi, Carol Lee. *Liberation Deferred? The Ideas of the English-Canadian Suffragists, 1877–1918*. Toronto: University of Toronto Press, 1983.

Backhouse, Constance. "Nineteenth-Century Canadian Rape Law, 1800–1892." In *Essays in the History of Canadian Law*, 2: 200–247. Edited by David Flaherty. Toronto: University of Toronto Press, 1983.

———. "Desperate Women and Compassionate Courts: Infanticide in Nineteenth-Century Canada." *University of Toronto Law Journal* 34 (1984): 447–78.

———. "Nineteenth-Century Canadian Prostitution Law: Reflection of a Discriminating Society." *Histoire Sociale/Social History* 18, no. 36 (November 1985): 387–423.

———. *Petticoats and Prejudice: Women and Law in Nineteenth-Century Canada.* Toronto: Women's Press, 1991.

———. "The Tort of Seduction: Fathers and Daughters in Nineteenth Century Canada." *Dalhousie Law Journal* 10, no. 1 (June 1986): 45–80.

Backhouse, Constance, and Leah Cohen. *The Secret Oppression: Sexual Harassment of Working Women.* Toronto: Macmillan, 1978.

Bailey, Beth. *From Front Porch to Back Seat: Courtship in Twentieth-Century America.* Baltimore: Johns Hopkins University Press, 1988.

Baldwin, Doug. "The Life of a Silver Miner in Northern Ontario." *Labour/Le Travailleur* 2 (1977): 79–107.

Ball, Christine. "Female Sexual Ideologies in Mid to Late Nineteenth-Century Canada." *Canadian Journal of Women and the Law* 1, no. 2 (1983): 324–38.

Banks, Margaret. "The Evolution of the Ontario Courts, 1788–1981." In *Essays in the History of Canadian Law* 2: 418–91. Edited by David Flaherty. Toronto: University of Toronto Press, 1983.

Barker-Benfield, G. J. *The Horrors of the Half-Known Life: Male Attitudes toward Women and Sexuality in Nineteenth-Century America.* New York: Harper and Row, 1976.

Barrett, Michèle, and Mary McIntosh. *The Anti-Social Family.* London: Verso, 1982.

Barrett, Michèle, and Rosalind Coward. "Don't Talk to Strangers." *New Socialist* 32 (November 1985): 21–23.

Bauer, Carol, and Lawrence Ritt. "A Husband Is a Wife-Beating Animal: Francis Power Cobbe Confronts the Wife Abuse Problem in Victorian England." *International Journal of Women's Studies* 6, no. 2 (March–April 1983): 99–118.

Bell, E. A. *Fighting the Traffic in Young Girls.* Chicago: National Bible House, 1911.

Bell, Laurie, ed. *Good Girls/Bad Girls: Sex Trade Workers and Feminists Face to Face.* Toronto: Women's Press, 1987.

Bercuson, David, and L. A. Knafla, eds. *Law and Society in Canada in Historical Perspective.* Calgary: University of Calgary Press, 1979.

Berger, Carl. "The True North Strong and Free." In *Interpreting Canada's Past*, 2: 157–74. Edited by J. M. Bumstead. Toronto: Oxford University Press, 1986.

Bland, Lucy. "Guardians of the Race or Vampires upon the Nation's Health? Female Sexuality and Its Regulation in Early Twentieth-Century Britain." In *The Changing Experience of Women*, 373–88. Edited by Elizabeth Whitelegg et al. Oxford: Basil Blackwell, 1982.

———. "In the Name of Protection: The Policing of Women in the First World War." In *Women-in-Law: Explorations in Law, Family and Sexuality*, 23–49. Edited by Julia Brophy and Carol Smart. London: Routledge and Kegan Paul, 1985.

———. "Marriage Laid Bare: Middle Class Women and Marital Sex, 1880–1914." In *Labour and Love: Women's Experience of Home and Family*, 123–46. Edited by Jane Lewis. Oxford: Basil Blackwell, 1986.

Bliss, Michael. "Pure Books on Avoided Subjects: Pre-Freudian Sexual Ideas in Canada." In *Studies in Canadian Social History*, 326–46. Edited by Michiel Horn and Ronald Sabourin. Toronto: McClelland and Stewart, 1974.

Bock, Gisela. "Women's History and Gender History: Aspects of an International Debate." *Gender and History* 1, no. 1 (Spring 1989): 7–30.

Bogue, Allan. "The Agricultural Press in Ontario in the 1880s." *Ontario History* 38 (1946): 43–49.

Bradwin, Edmund. *The Bunkhouse Man: A Study of the Work and Pay in the Camps of Canada, 1903–1914.* New York: Columbia University Press, 1928; reprint, Toronto: University of Toronto Press, 1972.

Bray, Matt, and Ernie Epp, eds. *A Vast and Magnificent Land.* Thunder Bay, Ont.: Lakehead University Press, 1984.

Breines, Wini, and Linda Gordon. "The New Scholarship on Family Violence." *Signs* 8, no. 3 (Spring 1983): 490–531.

Brock, Gordon. *The Province of Northern Ontario.* Cobalt, Ont.: Highway Bookshop, 1978.

Brooks, Alan A., and Catherine Wilson. "Working Away from the Farm: The Young Women of North Huron, 1910–1930." *Ontario History* 77, no. 4 (December 1985): 281–300.

Brophy, Julia, and Patricia Smart, eds. *Women-in-Law: Explorations in Law, Family and Sexuality.* London: Routledge and Kegan Paul, 1985.

Brownmiller, Susan. *Against Our Will: Men, Women and Rape.* New York: Bantam, 1975.

Buchbinder, Howard, Varda Burstyn, Dinah Forbes, and Mercedes Steedman. *Who's on Top? The Politics of Heterosexuality.* Toronto: Garamond, 1987.

Bularzik, Mary. "Sexual Harassment at the Workplace: Historical Notes." *Radical America* 12, no. 4 (July–August 1978): 25–41.

Bullen, John. "Hidden Workers: Child Labour and the Family Economy in Late Nineteenth-Century Urban Ontario." *Labour/Le Travail* 18 (Fall 1986): 163–88.

Burnet, J. R. "The Urban Community and Changing Moral Standards." In *Studies in Canadian Social History,* 298–325. Edited by Michiel Horn and Ronald Sabourin. Toronto: McClelland and Stewart, 1974.

Burnet, Jean, ed. *Looking into My Sister's Eyes: An Exploration in Women's History.* Toronto: Multicultural History Society of Ontario, 1986.

Burstyn, Varda. "Economy, Sexuality, Politics: Engels and the Sexual Division of Labour." *Socialist Studies: A Canadian Annual* (1983): 19–39.

———, ed. *Women against Censorship.* Toronto: Douglas and McIntyre, 1985.

Burstyn, Varda, and Dorothy Smith. *Women, Class, Family and the State.* Toronto: Garamond, 1985.

Campbell, Majorie Freeman. *A Century of Crime: The Development of Crime Detection Methods in Canada.* Toronto: McClelland and Stewart, 1970.

Cartledge, Sue, and Joanna Ryan. *Sex and Love: New Thoughts on Old Contradictions.* London: Women's Press, 1983.

Chapman, Terry. "The Measurement of Crime in Nineteenth-Century Canada: Some Methodological and Philosophical Problems." In *Crime and Criminal Justice in Europe and Canada,* 147–56. Edited by Louis A. Knafla. Waterloo, Ont.: Wilfrid Laurier University Press, 1981.

————. "An 'Oscar Wilde Type': The Abominable Crime of Buggery in Western Canada, 1890–1920." *Criminal Justice History* 5 (1983): 97–118.

————. "Sex Crimes in Western Canada, 1890–1920." Ph.D. diss., University of Alberta, 1984.

Chown, Alice. *The Stairway.* Boston: Cornhill Co., 1921; reprint, Toronto: University of Toronto Press, 1988.

Clark, Anna. "Whores and Gossips: Sexual Reputation in London, 1770–1825." In *Current Issues in Women's History,* 231–48. Edited by Arina Angerman, Geerte Binnema, Annamiebe Keunen, Vefie Poels, and Jacqueline Zirkzee. London: Routledge and Kegan Paul, 1989.

Clark, Christopher St. George. *Of Toronto the Good.* Montreal: Toronto Publishing, 1898.

Clark, Lorene, and Debra Lewis. *Rape: The Price of Coercive Sexuality.* Toronto: Women's Press, 1977.

Cohen, Majorie. *Women's Work, Markets and Economic Development in Nineteenth-Century Ontario.* Toronto: University of Toronto Press, 1988.

Cole, Susan. "Sexuality and Its Discontents." *Broadside* 6, no. 6 (April 1985): 8–9.

Collette, Christine. "Socialism and Scandal: The Sexual Politics of the Early Labour Movement." *History Workshop Journal* 23 (Spring 1987): 102–11.

Cook, Ramsay. *The Regenerators: Social Criticism in Late Victorian English Canada.* Toronto: University of Toronto Press, 1985.

Coombe, Rosemary J. "'The Most Disgusting, Disgraceful and Inequitous Proceeding in Our Law': The Action for Breach of Promise of Marriage in Nineteenth-Century Ontario." *University of Toronto Law Journal* 38 (1988): 64–108.

Cott, Nancy. "Passionlessness: An Interpretation of Victorian Sexual Ideology, 1790–1850." *Signs* 4 (1978): 219–36.

Coulter, Rebekah. "The Young of Edmonton, 1921–1931." In *Childhood and Family in Canadian History,* 143–59. Edited by Joy Parr. Toronto: McClelland and Stewart, 1982.

Coward, Rosalind. *Female Desires.* New York: Grove Press, 1985.

Craven, Paul. "Law and Ideology: The Toronto Police Court, 1850–1880." In *Essays in the History of Canadian Law,* 2: 248–307. Edited by David Flaherty. Toronto: University of Toronto Press, 1983.

Cumberland, Barlow, ed. *Northern Lakes of Canada.* Toronto: Hunter Rose and Co., 1886.

Curtis, Bruce. "Illicit Sex and Public Education in Ontario, 1840–1907." *Historical Studies in Education* 1, no. 1 (Spring 1989): 73–94.

Davidoff, Leonore, Jean L'Esperance, and Howard Newby. "Landscape with Figures: Home and Community in English Society." In *The Rights and Wrongs of Women,* 139–75. Edited by Juliet Mitchell and Ann Oakley. Harmondsworth, England: Penguin, 1976.

Davis, Angela. *Women, Race and Class.* New York: Random House, 1981.

Decarie, Malcolm Graham. "The Prohibition Movement in Ontario, 1894–1916." Ph.D. diss., Queen's University, 1972.

de la Cour, Lykke. "'Tis Not as It Should Be: The Regulation of Unwed Motherhood in Ontario, 1870s–1920s." Manuscript, York University, January 1990.

D'Emilio, John and Estelle Freedman. *Intimate Matters: A History of Sexuality in America*. New York: Harper and Row, 1988.
———. "A Response to Ann duCille's 'Othered' Matters." *Journal of the History of Sexuality* 1, no. 1 (July 1990): 128–30.
Doyle, James. "The Image of Northern Ontario in English Canadian Literature." *Laurentian University Review* 8 (1975): 103–16.
Dubinsky, Karen. "The Modern Chivalry: Women and the Knights of Labor in Ontario, 1880–1891." M.A. thesis, Carleton University, 1985.
DuCille, Ann. "'Othered' Matters: Reconceptualizing Dominance and Difference in the History of Sexuality in America." *Journal of the History of Sexuality* 1, no. 1 (July 1990): 102–27.
Dumaresq, Delia. "Rape: Sexuality in the Law." *MF* 5 (1981): 41–59.
Eisenstein, Hester. *Contemporary Feminist Thought*. Boston: G. K. Hall, 1983.
Feminist Review Collective. *Sexuality: A Reader*. London: Virago, 1987.
Fingard, Judith. *The Dark Side of Life in Victorian Halifax*. Porter's Lake, Nova Scotia: Pottersfield Press, 1989.
Foucault, Michel. *The History of Sexuality: An Introduction*. New York: Vintage, 1978.
Franklin, Sarah, and Jackie Stacey. "Dyketactics for Difficult Times." *Feminist Review*, no. 29 (Spring 1988): 136–51.
Fraser, John Foster. *Canada as It Is*. London: Carswell Co., 1905.
Freedman, Estelle. "Uncontrolled Desires: The Response to the Sexual Psychopath, 1920–1960." *Journal of American History* 74, no. 1 (June 1987): 83–106.
Gallagher, Catherine, and Thomas Laquer, eds. *The Making of the Modern Body: Sexuality and Society in the Nineteenth Century*. Berkeley: University of California Press, 1987.
Gillis, John. "Servants, Sexual Relations and the Risk of Illegitimacy in London, 1801–1900." In *Sex and Class in Women's History*, 114–45. Edited by Judith L. Newton, Mary P. Ryan, and Judith R. Walkowitz. London: Routledge and Kegan Paul, 1983.
Gordon, Linda. *Heros of Their Own Lives: The Politics and History of Family Violence*. New York: Viking, 1988.
———. "The Politics of Child Sexual Abuse: Notes from American History." *Feminist Review*, no. 28 (January 1988): 88–102.
Gorham, Deborah. "The 'Maiden Tribute of Modern Babylon Re-Examined': Child Prostitution and the Idea of Childhood in Late Victorian England." *Victorian Studies* 21, no. 3 (Spring 1978): 353–79.
Guberman, Connie, and Margie Wolfe, eds. *No Safe Place: Violence against Women and Children*. Toronto: Women's Press, 1985.
Guennel, Max. "Port Arthur Views Progress, 1910–1913." B.A. paper, Lakehead University, 1975.
Hamilton, Roberta. "Walking Warily: Feminism and Postmodernism." Paper presented at the Canadian Association of Sociology and Anthropology Annual Meeting, June 1990.
Harris, Ruth. "Melodrama, Hysteria and Feminine Crimes of Passion in the Fin-de-Siecle." *History Workshop Journal* 25 (Spring 1988): 31–63.

Hartman, Heidi, and Ellen Ross. "Comment on 'On Writing the History of Rape.'" *Signs* 3, no. 4 (1978): 931–35.

Harvey, Katherine. "To Love, Honour and Obey: Wife Battering in Working-Class Montreal, 1869–1879." *Urban History Review* 19, no. 2 (October 1990): 128–40.

Hay, Douglas. "Property, Authority and the Criminal Law." In *Albion's Fatal Tree: Crime and Society in Eighteenth-Century England*, 17–64. Edited by Douglas Hay, Peter Linebaugh, John G. Rule, E.P. Thompson, and Cal Winslow. New York: Pantheon, 1975.

Hollway, Wendy. "I Just Wanted to Kill a Woman: Why? The Ripper and Male Sexuality." In *Sexuality: A Reader*, 123–33. Edited by Feminist Review Collective. London: Virago, 1987.

Houston, Susan. "The 'Waifs' and 'Strays' of a Late Victorian City: Juvenile Delinquents in Toronto." In *Childhood and Family in Canadian History*, 129–42. Edited by Joy Parr. Toronto: McClelland and Stewart, 1982.

Iacovetta, Franca, and Mariana Valverde, eds. *Gender Conflicts: Essays in Women's History*. Toronto: University of Toronto Press, 1992.

Irvine, Janice. *Disorders of Desire: Sex and Gender in Modern American Sexology*. Philadelphia: Temple University Press, 1990.

Jeffreys, Sheila. *The Spinster and Her Enemies: Female Sexuality in Britain, 1880–1930*. London: Pandora Press, 1985.

Jones, Andrew, and Leonard Rutman. *In the Children's Aid: J. J. Kelso and Child Welfare in Ontario*. Toronto: University of Toronto Press, 1981.

Jones, David. "There Is Some Power about Land: The Western Canadian Agrarian Press and Country Life Ideology." *Journal of Canadian Studies* 17, no. 3 (1982): 97–108.

Katz, Jonathan Ned. "The Invention of Heterosexuality." *Socialist Review* 20, no. 1 (March 1990): 7–33.

Kealey, Gregory S., and Bryan Palmer. *Dreaming of What Might Be: The Knights of Labor in Ontario, 1880–1900*. Toronto: New Hogtown Press, 1987.

Kealey, Linda, ed. *A Not Unreasonable Claim: Women and Reform in Canada, 1880s–1920s*. Toronto: Women's Press, 1979.

Kealey, Linda, and Joan Sangster, eds. *Beyond the Vote: Canadian Women and Politics*. Toronto: University of Toronto Press, 1989.

Kechnie, Margaret. "The United Farm Women of Ontario: Developing a Political Consciousness." *Ontario History* 77, no. 4 (December 1985): 267–80.

Kinnear, Mary. "Do You Want Your Daughter to Marry a Farmer? Women's Work on the Farm, 1922." *Papers in Rural History* 6 (1986): 137–53.

Kinsman, Gary. *The Regulation of Desire*. Montreal: Black Rose Press, 1987.

Knafla, Louis. *Crime and Criminal Justice in Europe and North America*. Waterloo, Ont.: Wilfrid Laurier University Press, 1981.

Knox, Ellen. *The Girl of the New Day*. Toronto: McClelland and Stewart, 1919.

Koop, Alvin, and Sheila Koop. "Going to Town." In *The County Town in Rural Ontario's Past*, 80–90. Edited by A. A. Brooks. Guelph, Ont.: University of Guelph Press, 1981.

Lachance, André. "Women and Crime in Canada in the Early Eighteenth Century,

1712–1759." In *Crime and Criminal Justice in Europe and Canada*, 157–68. Edited by Louis Knafla. Waterloo, Ont.: Wilfrid Laurier University Press, 1981.

Laquer, Thomas. *Making Sex: Body and Gender from the Greeks to Freud*. Cambridge: Harvard University Press, 1990.

Lambertz, Jan. "Sexual Harassment in the Nineteenth-Century English Cotton Industry." *History Workshop Journal* 19 (Spring 1985): 29–61.

Langer, William. "Infanticide: A Historical Survey." *History of Childhood Quarterly* 1, no. 3 (Winter 1974): 353–66.

Leach, William. *True Love and Perfect Union: The Feminist Reform of Sex and Society*. New York: Basic Books, 1980.

Lederer, Laura, ed. *Take Back the Night: Women on Pornography*. New York: William Morrow, 1980.

Leidholdt, Dorchen, and Janice G. Raymond. *The Sexual Liberals and the Attack on Feminism*. New York: Pergamon Press, 1990.

Levesque, Andrée. "Deviants Anonymous: Single Mothers at the Hôpital de la Misercorde in Montreal, 1929–1939." *Historical Papers* (1984): 168–83.

Light, Beth, and Joy Parr. *Canadian Women on the Move, 1867–1920*. Toronto: Ontario Institute for Studies in Education Press, 1983.

Lindemann, Barbara. "To Ravish and Carnally Know: Rape in Eighteenth-Century Massachusetts." *Signs* 10, no. 1 (Autumn 1984): 63–82.

Lindstrom-Best, Varpu. *Defiant Sisters: A Social History of Finnish Immigrant Women in Canada*. Toronto: Multicultural History Society of Ontario, 1988.

Little, Margaret. "Mothers First and Foremost: A Socialist Feminist Analysis of Ontario Mothers' Allowance." Paper presented at the Canadian Political Science Association Annual Meeting, June 1990.

London Feminist History Workshop. *The Sexual Dynamics of History*. London: Pluto Press, 1983.

London Rape Crisis Centre. *Sexual Violence: The Reality for Women*. London: Women's Press, 1984.

Longstreth, T. Morris. *The Lake Superior Country*. Toronto: McClelland and Stewart, 1924.

Lunbeck, Elizabeth. "A New Generation of Women: Progressive Psychiatrists and the Hypersexual Female." *Feminist Studies* 13, no. 3 (Fall 1987): 513–43.

McCauley, Beth. "Beyond the Bounds of Respectability." M.A. thesis, University of Toronto, 1986.

MacDonald, Marvin. "Protestant Reaction to Non-English Immigration in Port Arthur and Fort William, 1903–1914." M.A. thesis, Lakehead University, 1976.

MacDougall, John. *Rural Life in Canada: Its Trends and Tasks*. Toronto: Westminister, 1913; reprint, Toronto: University of Toronto Press, 1973.

McGahan, Peter. *Crime and Policing in Maritime Canada: Chapters from the Urban Record*. Fredericton, New Brunswick: Goose Lane Editions, 1988.

McLaren, Angus. *Our Own Master Race: Eugenics in Canada, 1885–1945*. Toronto: McClelland and Stewart, 1990.

McLaren, Angus, and Arlene Tigar McLaren. *The Bedroom and the State*. Toronto: McClelland and Stewart, 1986.

McLaren, John. "Chasing the Social Evil: Moral Fervour and the Evolution of Canada's Prostitution Laws, 1867–1917." *Canadian Journal of Law and Society* 1 (1986): 125–65.

———. "White Slavers: The Reform of Canada's Prostitution Laws and Patterns of Enforcement, 1900–1920." *Criminal Justice History* 8 (1987): 53–119.

MacLeod, Mary, and Ester Saraga. "Challenging the Orthodoxy: Toward a Feminist Theory and Practice." *Feminist Review*, no. 28 (January 1988): 40–65.

Marks, Lynne. "The Knights of Labor and the Salvation Army: Religion and Working-Class Culture in Ontario, 1882–1890." *Labour/Le Travail* 28 (1991): 89–128.

———. "Ladies, Loafers, Knights and 'Lasses': The Social Dimensions of Religion and Leisure in Late Nineteenth-Century Small-Town Ontario." Ph.D. diss., York University, 1992.

Maroney, Heather Jon. *Feminism and Political Economy: Women's Work, Women's Struggles*. Toronto: Metheun, 1987.

Maynard, Steven. "Rough Work and Rugged Men: The Social Construction of Masculinity in Working-Class History." *Labour/Le Travail* 23 (Spring 1989): 159–70.

Meyerowitz, Joanne. *Women Adrift: Independent Wage Earners in Chicago, 1880–1930*. Chicago: University of Chicago Press, 1988.

Mills, Elizabeth. "One Hundred Years of Fear: Rape and the Medical Profession." In *Judge, Lawyer, Victim, Thief: Women, Gender Roles and Criminal Justice*, 29–62. Edited by Nicole Hahn Rafter and Elizabeth Stanko. Boston: Northeastern University Press, 1982.

Mort, Frank. *Dangerous Sexualities: Medico-Moral Politics in England since 1830*. London: Routledge and Kegan Paul, 1987.

Morton, Marian. "Seduced and Abandoned in an American City: Cleveland and Its Fallen Women, 1869–1936." *Journal of Urban History* 11 (August 1985): 443–69.

Murphy, Emily. *The Black Candle*. Toronto: Thomas Allen, 1922.

Nelles, H. V. *The Politics of Development*. Toronto: Macmillan, 1974.

Nestle, Joan. *A Restricted Country*. Ithaca, N.Y.: Firebrand Books, 1987.

Newton, Janice. "Enough of Exclusive Masculine Thinking: The Feminist Challenge to the Early Canadian Left, 1900–1918." Ph.D. diss., York University, 1987.

Odem, Mary. "Single Mothers, Delinquent Daughters, and the Juvenile Court in Early 20th Century Los Angeles." *Journal of Social History* 25, no. 1 (Fall 1991): 27–43.

———. "Statutory Rape Prosecutions in Alameda Couny, California, 1910–1920." Paper presented at the Organization of American Historians Annual Meeting, April 1989.

Olsen, Ruth. "Rape: An 'Un-Victorian' Aspect of Life in Upper Canada." *Ontario History* 68, no. 2 (June 1976): 75–79.

Owram, Douglas. *The Promise of Eden*. Toronto: University of Toronto Press, 1980.

Palmer, Bryan. "Discordant Music: Charivaris and Whitecapping in Nineteenth Century North America." *Labour/Le Travail* 3 (1978): 5–62.

———. "Response to Joan Scott." *International Labor and Working-Class History*, no. 31 (Spring 1987): 14–23.

———. *Working Class Experience: The Rise and Reconstitution of Canadian Labour, 1800–1980.* Toronto: Butterworths, 1983.

Parker, Graham. *An Introduction to Canadian Criminal Law.* Toronto: Metheun, 1983.

———. "Is a Duck an Animal? An Exploration of Bestiality as a Crime." *Criminal Justice History* 7 (1986): 95–109.

———. "The Legal Regulation of Sexual Activity and the Protection of Females." *Osgoode Hall Law Journal* 21, no. 2 (June 1983): 187–244.

———. "The Origins of the Canadian Criminal Code." In *Essays in the History of Canadian Law,* 1: 249–81. Edited by David Flaherty. Toronto: University of Toronto Press, 1981.

Parr, Joy. *The Gender of Breadwinners.* Toronto: University of Toronto Press, 1990.

Pederson, Diana. "'Building Today for the Womanhood of Tomorrow': Businessmen, Boosters and the YWCA, 1890–1930." *Urban History Review* 15, no. 3 (February 1987): 225–40.

———. "Keeping Our Good Girls Good: The YWCA and the 'Girl Problem,' 1870–1930." *Canadian Women's Studies* 7, no. 4 (Winter 1986): 20–24.

Peiss, Kathy. *Cheap Amusements: Working Women and Leisure in Turn-of-the-Century New York.* Philadelphia: Temple University Press, 1986.

Peiss, Kathy, and Christina Simmons, eds. *Passion and Power: Sexuality in History.* Philadelphia: Temple University Press, 1989.

Pistono, Steven. "Susan Brownmiller and the History of Rape." *Women's Studies* 14 (1988): 265–76.

Pitsula, James. "The Treatment of Tramps in Late Nineteenth-Century Toronto." *Historical Papers* (1980): 116–32.

Pleck, Elizabeth. *Domestic Tyranny: The Making of American Social Policy against Family Violence from Colonial Times to the Present.* New York: Oxford University Press, 1987.

———. "Feminist Responses to 'Crime against Women,' 1868–1896." *Signs* 8, no. 3 (Spring 1983): 451–70.

———. "Wife Beating in Nineteenth-Century America." *Victimology* 4, no. 1 (Fall 1979): 60–74.

Poovey, Mary. "Feminism and Deconstruction." *Feminist Studies* 14, no. 1 (Spring 1988): 51–65.

———. *Uneven Developments: The Ideological Work of Gender in Mid-Victorian England.* Chicago: University of Chicago Press, 1988.

Prentice, Alison, Paula Bourne, Gail Cuthbert Brandt, Beth Light, Wendy Mitchinson, and Naomi Black. *Canadian Women: A History.* Toronto: Harcourt Brace Jovanovich, 1988.

Pucci, Antonio. "Thunder Bay's Italian Community, 1880s–1940s." In *The Italian Immigrant Experience,* 79–102. Edited by John Potestio and Antonio Pucci. Thunder Bay, Ont.: Canadian Italian Historical Association, 1988.

Radforth, Ian. *Bushworkers and Bosses: Logging in Northern Ontario.* Toronto: University of Toronto Press, 1987.

Riley, Denise. *Am I That Name? Feminism and the Category of 'Women' in History.* Minneapolis: University of Minnesota Press, 1988.

Roper, Lyndal. "Will and Honor: Sex, Words and Power in Augsburg Criminal Trials." *Radical History Review* 43 (Winter 1989): 45–71.

Rosenzweig, Roy. *Eight Hours for What We Will: Workers and Leisure in an Industrial City, 1870–1920.* Cambridge: Cambridge University Press, 1983.

Ross, Becki. "The House That Jill Built: Reconstructing the Lesbian Organization of Toronto, 1976–1980." Ph.D. diss., University of Toronto, 1992.

Ross, Ellen. "Fierce Questions and Taunts: Married Life in Working-Class London, 1870–1914." *Feminist Studies* 8 (Fall 1982): 575–602.

———. "Not the Sort That Would Sit on the Doorstep: Respectability in Pre–World War One London Neighbourhoods." *International Labour and Working-Class History* 27 (Spring 1985): 39–59.

Rothman, Ellen. *Hands and Hearts: A History of Courtship in America.* New York: Basic Books, 1984.

Ruggiero, Guido. *The Boundaries of Eros: Sex Crime and Sexuality in Renaissance Venice.* New York: Oxford University Press, 1985.

Rule, Jane. "Teaching Sexuality." In *Flaunting It!* 162–65. Edited by Ed Jackson and Stan Persky. Vancouver: New Star, 1985.

Sangster, Joan. *Dreams of Equality: Women on the Canadian Left, 1920–1950.* Toronto: McClelland and Stewart, 1989.

Schechter, Susan. *Women and Male Violence: The Visions and Struggles of the Battered Women's Movement.* Boston: South End Press, 1982.

Schneider, Aili. *The Finnish Baker's Daughter.* Toronto: Multicultural History Society of Ontario, 1986.

Schwendinger, Julia, and Herman Schwendinger. *Rape and Inequality.* Beverly Hills, Calif.: Sage, 1983.

Scott, Joan. "Deconstructing Equality-versus-Difference; or, The Uses of Poststructuralist Theory For Feminism." *Feminist Studies* 14, no. 1 (Spring 1988): 33–49.

———. *Gender and the Politics of History.* New York: Columbia University Press, 1988.

———. "On Language, Gender and Working-Class History." *International Labor and Working-Class History*, no. 31 (Spring 1987): 1–13.

Segal, Lynne. *Is the Future Female? Troubled Thoughts on Contemporary Feminism.* London: Virago, 1987.

———. *Slow Motion: Changing Masculinities, Changing Men.* London: Virago, 1990.

Shorter, Edward. "On Writing the History of Rape." *Signs* 3, no. 2 (1977): 471–82.

Simmons, Christina. "Modern Sexuality and the Myth of Victorian Repression." In *Passion and Power: Sexuality in History*, 157–77. Edited by Kathy Peiss and Christina Simmons. Philadelphia: Temple University Press, 1989.

Smart, Carol, and Barry Smart. "Accounting for Rape: Reality and Myth in Press Reporting." In *Women, Sexuality and Social Control*, 87–103. Edited by Carol Smart and Barry Smart. London: Routledge and Kegan Paul, 1978.

Smith-Rosenburg, Carol. *Disorderly Conduct: Visions of Gender in Victorian America.* New York: Oxford University Press, 1985.

Snell, James. "The 'White Life for Two': The Defence of Marriage and Sexual Morality in Canada, 1890–1914." *Histoire Sociale/Social History* 16, no. 31 (May 1983): 111–28.

Bibliography

Snell, James, and Cynthia Abelle. "Regulating Nuptuality: Restricting Access to Marriage in Early Twentieth-Century English-Speaking Canada." *Canadian Historical Review* 69, no. 4 (December 1988): 466–89.

Snitow, Ann, Christine Stansell, and Sharon Thompson, eds. *Powers of Desire: The Politics of Sexuality*. New York: Monthly Review Press, 1983.

Soman, Alfred. "Deviance and Criminal Justice in Western Europe, 1300–1800: An Essay in Structure." *Criminal Justice History* 1 (1980): 1–28.

Stanko, Elizabeth. *Intimate Intrusions*. London: Routledge and Kegan Paul, 1985.

Stansell, Christine. *City of Women: Sex and Class in New York, 1789–1860*. New York: Alfred A. Knopf, 1986.

———. "A Response to Joan Scott." *International Labor and Working-Class History*, no. 31 (Spring 1987): 24–29.

Stimpson, Catherine, and Ethel Spector Person, eds. *Women: Sex and Sexuality*. Chicago: University of Chicago Press, 1980.

Strange, Carolyn. "The Criminal and Fallen of Their Sex: The Establishment of Canada's First Women's Prison, 1874–1901." *Canadian Journal of Women and the Law* 1, no. 1 (1985): 79–92.

———. "The Perils and Pleasures of the City: Single, Wage-Earning Women in Toronto, 1880–1930." Ph.D. diss., Rutgers University, 1991.

Strong-Boag, Veronica. *The New Day Recalled. Lives of Girls and Women in English Canada, 1919–1939*. Toronto: Copp-Clark Pitman, 1988.

———. *The Parliament of Women: The National Council of Women of Canada, 1893–1929*. Ottawa: National Museums of Canada, 1976.

Sutherland, Neil. *Children in English Canadian Society: Framing the Nineteenth-Century Consensus*. Toronto: University of Toronto Press, 1976.

Swainson, Donald. "Schuyler Shibley and the Underside of Victorian Ontario." *Ontario History* 65, no. 1 (March 1973): 51–60.

Taylor, Barbara. *Eve and the New Jerusalem: Socialism and Feminism in the Nineteenth Century*. London: Virago, 1983.

Teatero, William. "A Dead and Alive Way Never Does: The Pre-Political Professional World of John A. MacDonald." M.A. thesis, Queen's University, 1978.

Terry, Jennifer. "Theorizing Deviant Historiography." *differences* 3, no. 1 (Summer 1991): 55–74.

Tomaselli, Sylvana, and Roy Porter, eds. *Rape: An Historical and Social Enquiry*. London: Basil Blackwell, 1986.

Tomes, Nancy. "A 'Torrent of Abuse': Crimes of Violence between Working Class Men and Women in London, 1840–1875." *Journal of Social History* 11, no. 3 (Spring 1978): 329–45.

Trembley, David. "Dimensions of Crime and Punishment at the Lakehead, 1873–1903." M.A. thesis, Lakehead University, 1983.

———. "Dimensions of Crime at the Lakehead, 1873–1903." Thunder Bay Historical Museum Society *Papers and Records* 10 (1982): 28–35.

Tronrud, Thorold J. "Frontier Social Structure: The Canadian Lakehead, 1871 and 1881." *Ontario History* 79, no. 2 (June 1987): 145–165.

Valverde, Mariana. *The Age of Light, Soap and Water: Moral Reform in English Canada, 1885–1925*. Toronto: McClelland and Stewart, 1991.

————. "The Love of Finery: Fashion and the Fallen Women in Nineteenth-Century Social Discourse." *Victorian Studies* 32, no. 2 (Winter 1989): 169–88.

————. "The Rhetoric of Reform: Tropes and the Moral Subject." *International Journal of the Sociology of the Law* 18, no. 1 (1990): 61–72.

————. *Sex, Power and Pleasure*. Toronto: Women's Press, 1987.

Valverde, Mariana, and Lorna Weir. "The Struggles of the Immoral: Preliminary Remarks on Moral Regulation." *Resources for Feminist Research* 17, no. 3 (September 1988): 31–34.

Vance, Carol, ed. *Pleasure and Danger: Exploring Female Sexuality*. Boston: Routledge and Kegan Paul, 1984.

Vicinus, Martha. "Sexuality and Power: A Review of Current Work on the History of Sexuality." *Feminist Studies* 8, no. 1 (Spring 1982): 133–56.

Walkowitz, Judith. "Jack the Ripper and the Myth of Male Violence." *Feminist Studies* 8, no. 3 (1982): 542–72.

————. *Prostitution and Victorian Society: Women, Class and the State*. Cambridge: Cambridge University Press, 1980.

Ward, Peter. "Courtship and Social Space in Nineteenth-Century English Canada." *Canadian Historical Review* 68, no. 1 (1987): 35–62.

————. *Courtship, Love and Marriage in Nineteenth-Century English Canada*. Montreal: McGill-Queen's University Press, 1990.

————. "Unwed Motherhood in Nineteenth-Century English Canada." *Historical Papers* (1981): 34–56.

Watney, Simon. "The Spectacle of AIDS." In *AIDS: Cultural Analysis, Cultural Activism*, 71–88. Edited by Douglas Crimp. Cambridge: MIT Press, 1988.

Watt, D. A. *Moral Legislation*. Montreal: Gazette Printing, 1890.

Weedon, Chris. *Feminist Practice and Poststructuralist Theory*. Oxford: Basil Blackwell, 1987.

Weeks, Jeffrey. *Sex, Politics and Society: The Regulation of Sexuality since 1800*. London: Longmans, 1981.

————. *Sexuality*. Sussex, England: Ellis Horwood, 1986.

————. *Sexuality and Its Discontents: Meanings, Myths and Modern Sexualities*. Boston: Routledge and Kegan Paul, 1985.

Williams, David R. "Mining Camps and Frontier Communities of British Columbia." In *Law and Justice in a New Land*, 215–33. Edited by Louis Knafla. Toronto: Carswell, 1986.

Williams, Raymond. *The Country and the City*. London: Chatto and Windus, 1973; reprint, London: Hogarth Press, 1985.

Williamson, Owen. *The Northland Ontario*. Toronto: Ryerson Press, 1946.

Wohl, Anthony. "Sex and the Single Room: Incest among the Victorian Working Class." In *The Victorian Family: Structure and Stress*, 197–216. Edited by Anthony Wohl. New York: St. Martin's Press, 1978.

Wolfe, Roy. "The Summer Resorts of Ontario in the Late Nineteenth Century." *Ontario History* 54, no. 3 (1962): 149–61.

Wood-Allen, Mary. *What a Young Woman Ought to Know*. Philadelphia: Vir Publishing, 1889.

INDEX

9848